Collins *practical gardener*

TREES & SHRUBS

KEITH RUSHFORTH

Collins Lifestyle
An Imprint of Harper*Collins**Publishers*

First published in Great Britain in 2005 by
HarperCollins*Publishers* Ltd.

Photography by Tim Sandall and Keith Rushforth. For a detailed breakdown, see page 160.

Photographic props: Coolings Nurseries, Rushmore Hill, Knockholt, Kent, TN14 7NN, UK, www.coolings.co.uk

Design and Editorial: Focus Publishing, Sevenoaks, Kent, UK.

Project Editor: Guy Croton

Editor: Vanessa Townsend

Project Coordinator: Caroline Watson

Designer: Philip Clucas MSIAD

Illustration: David Etherington and David Graham

For HarperCollins*Publishers*:

Managing Editor: Angela Newton

Art Direction: Luke Griffin

Editor: Alastair Laing

Production: Chris Gurney

ISBN 0-06-078633-7

Color reproduction by Colourscan

Printed and bound by Printing Express, Hong Kong

Contents

Introduction

The main reason for having trees and larger shrubs in the garden is for their display of foliage which, after all, is present for at least half the year, or permanently in the case of evergreens. Foliage can take on a bewildering array of shapes and sizes, ranging from the large floppy leaves of Paulownia and Catalpa, through the small leaves of Betula, which cast only a dappled shade and are therefore excellent for seating areas, to the green twigginess of *Genista aetnensis*, a tree form of broom. Another aspect of foliage is fall color, which is unsurpassed in trees like *Nyssa sylvatica* and *Acer griseum*, or the color of new growth in spring.

Although the main feature of trees and shrubs tends to be their foliage, the flowers, fruit, and bark may also provide startling color and interest throughout the year. The flowering season can start early, in the middle of winter for trees such as *Acacia dealbata*, *Cornus mas*, and *Hamamelis mollis*, continuing throughout spring and summer, and on into early fall for Oxydendrum and *Prunus subhirtella* 'Autumnalis'. Fall is also often the season when some trees and shrubs produce wonderful displays of brightly colored fruit, in particular many Sorbus varieties. And for the winter season, the bark of many Betula, Eucalyptus, and Acer can be a major feature. A few trees and shrubs are even grown for their exquisite scent, which can fill an entire garden with a pleasing aroma, such as Tilia and Idesia.

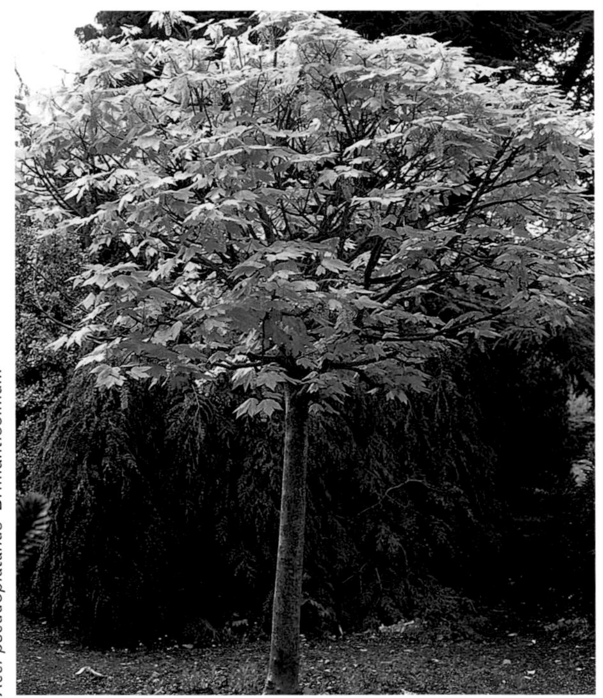

Acer pseudoplatanus 'Brilliantissimum'

Given their size and permanence, trees and shrubs will often provide the key notes of form and structure in a garden, whether they are used to mark boundaries between different areas, to create height and a background for borders, or planted on their own for special interest. For this reason the shape or habit of a tree is perhaps just as important as its foliage and flowers when deciding what to plant. From the upright columns of many conifers such as Abies, Picea, Chamaecyparis, and Juniperus, through the broad spread of trees such as Aesculus and *Quercus robur*, almost any architectural effect can be achieved. Other ideas for the garden include the compact growth of Fagus or Taxus trained as hedging, or the arching habit of *Acer forrestii* and *Cornus kousa*, as well as the clump effect of the numerous spaced stems in Phyllostachys bamboos.

There is no reason why you cannot have a planting scheme comprised entirely of shrubs and trees. They are very low-maintenance plants, so if you have limited time to spend in the garden, this represents a sensible choice. Once established, they require very little effort compared to lawns, herbaceous plants, and summer bedding, yet they can be just as colorful and interesting.

There is no formal definition of what constitutes a tree and what a shrub, except that they both need to be woody in some way. Yet woody plants show a continuous range from subshrubs that are only woody at the base, through to enormous trees, with shrubs somewhere in the middle. Included in this volume are the larger-growing woody plants, cultivated primarily for shelter and screening and to define the shape and use of the garden. They are often expected to grow quickly to more than 6ft (1.8m) in height—and some to much more!

Most of this book is devoted to broad-leaved woody plants and to the taller-growing conifers. However, you will also find a section on bamboos and a page on palms and tree ferns—as an introduction to some of the more exotic trees and shrubs that it is possible to grow. For more planting options in this exciting area of gardening, see the companion volume *Architectural Plants*.

How to Use This Book

This book is divided into three main parts. The opening chapters guide you through all areas of garden practice, from assessing your site, through planting and general care, to propagation techniques. A comprehensive plant directory follows, with individual entries on over 150 of the most commonly available trees and larger shrubs, listed in alphabetical order. All the most popular trees and larger shrubs are included, covering many different styles of gardening and uses. This section is followed by pages devoted to bamboos, tree ferns and palms, and conifers. The final section of the book covers plant problems. Troubleshooting pages allow you to diagnose the likely cause of any problems, and a directory of pests and diseases offers advice on how to solve them.

latin name of the plant genus, followed by its **common name**

detailed descriptions give specific advice on care for each plant, including planting and pests and diseases

alphabetical tabs on the side of the page, colour-coded to help you quickly find the plant you want

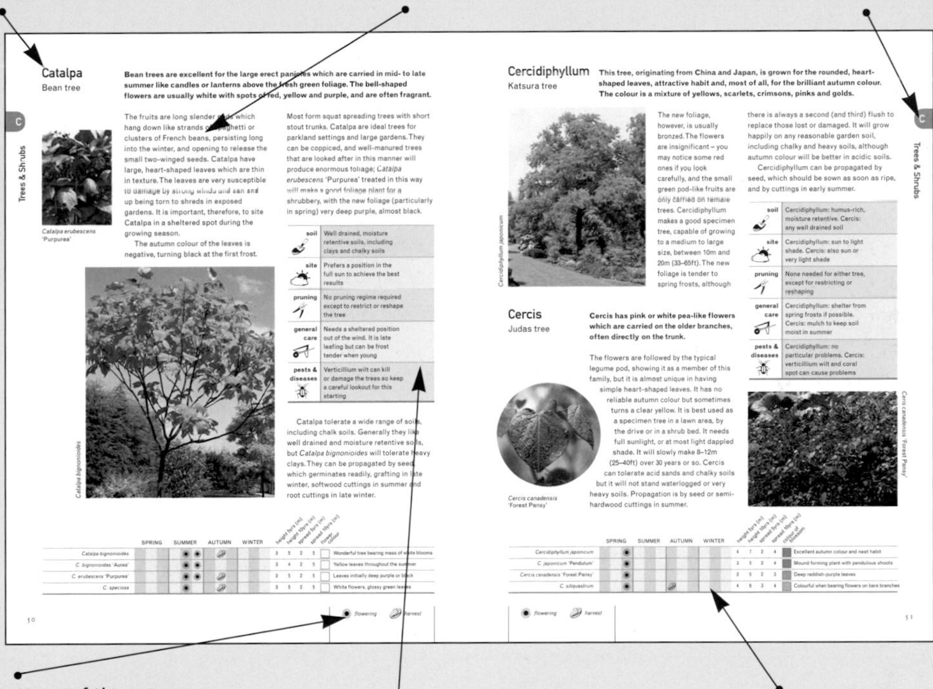

Catalpa
Bean tree

Bean trees are excellent for the large erect panicles which are carried in mid- to late summer like candles or lanterns above the fresh green foliage. The bell-shaped flowers are usually white with spots of red, yellow and purple, and are often fragrant.

C

Trees & Shrubs

Catalpa erubescens 'Purpurea'

The fruits are long slender pods which hang down like strands of spaghetti or clusters of French beans, persisting long into the winter, and opening to release the small two-winged seeds. Catalpa have large, heart-shaped leaves which are thin in texture. The leaves are very susceptible to damage by strong winds and can end up being torn to shreds in exposed gardens. It is important, therefore, to site Catalpa in a sheltered spot during the growing season.

The autumn colour of the leaves is negative, turning black at the first frost.

Most form squat spreading trees with short stout trunks. Catalpa are ideal trees for parkland settings and large gardens. They can be coppiced, and well-manured trees that are looked after in this manner will produce enormous foliage; *Catalpa erubescens* 'Purpurea' treated in this way will make a good foliage plant for a shrubbery, with the new foliage (particularly in spring) very deep purple, almost black.

soil	Well drained, moisture retentive soils, including clays and chalky soils
site	Prefers a position in the full sun to achieve the best results
pruning	No pruning regime required except to restrict or reshape the tree
general care	Needs a sheltered position out of the wind. It is late leafing but can be frost tender when young
pests & diseases	Verticillium wilt can kill or damage the trees so keep a careful lookout for this starting

Catalpa bignonioides

Catalpa tolerate a wide range of soils, including chalk soils. Generally they like well drained and moisture retentive soils, but *Catalpa bignonioides* will tolerate heavy clays. They can be propagated by seed, which germinates readily, grafting in late winter, softwood cuttings in summer and root cuttings in late winter.

	SPRING	SUMMER	AUTUMN	WINTER	height 5yrs (m)	height 10yrs (m)	spread 5yrs (m)	spread 10yrs (m)	flower colour	
Catalpa bignonioides		flowering	harvest		3	5	2	5		Wonderful tree bearing mass of white blooms
C. bignonioides 'Aurea'		flowering			3	4	2	5		Yellow leaves throughout the summer
C. erubescens 'Purpurea'		flowering	harvest		3	5	2	5		Leaves initially deep purple or black
C. speciosa		flowering	harvest		3	5	2	5		White flowers, glossy green leaves

50

flowering harvest

Cercidiphyllum
Katsura tree

This tree, originating from China and Japan, is grown for the rounded, heart-shaped leaves, attractive habit and, most of all, for the brilliant autumn colour. The colour is a mixture of yellows, scarlets, crimsons, pinks and golds.

Cercidiphyllum japonicum

The new foliage, however, is usually bronzed. The flowers are insignificant – you may notice some red ones if you look carefully, and the small green pod-like fruits are only carried on female trees. Cercidiphyllum makes a good specimen tree, capable of growing to a medium to large size, between 10m and 20m (33–65ft). The new foliage is tender to spring frosts, although there is always a second (and third) flush to replace those lost or damaged. It will grow happily on any reasonable garden soil, including chalky and heavy soils, although autumn colour will be better in acidic soils.

Cercidiphyllum can be propagated by seed, which should be sown as soon as ripe, and by cuttings in early summer.

C

Trees & Shrubs

soil	Cercidiphyllum: humus-rich, moisture retentive. Cercis: any well drained soil
site	Cercidiphyllum: sun to light shade. Cercis: also sun or very light shade
pruning	None needed for either tree, except for restricting or reshaping
general care	Cercidiphyllum: shelter from spring frosts if possible. Cercis: mulch to keep soil moist in summer
pests & diseases	Cercidiphyllum: no particular problems. Cercis: verticillium wilt and coral spot can cause problems

Cercis
Judas tree

Cercis has pink or white pea-like flowers which are carried on the older branches, often directly on the trunk.

The flowers are followed by the typical legume pod, showing it as a member of this family, but it is almost unique in having simple heart-shaped leaves. It has no reliable autumn colour but sometimes turns a clear yellow. It is best used as a specimen tree in a lawn area, by the drive or in a shrub bed. It needs full sunlight, or at most light dappled shade. It will slowly make 8–12m (25–40ft) over 30 years or so. Cercis can tolerate acid sands and chalky soils but it will not stand waterlogged or very heavy soils. Propagation is by seed or semi-hardwood cuttings in summer.

Cercis canadensis 'Forest Pansy'

Cercis canadensis 'Forest Pansy'

	SPRING	SUMMER	AUTUMN	WINTER	height 5yrs (m)	height 10yrs (m)	spread 5yrs (m)	spread 10yrs (m)	colour of blossom	
Cercidiphyllum japonicum	flowering				4	7	2	4		Excellent autumn colour and neat habit
C. japonicum 'Pendulum'	flowering				3	5	2	4		Mound forming plant with pendulous shoots
Cercis canadensis 'Forest Pansy'	flowering				3	5	2	3		Deep reddish-purple leaves
C. siliquastrum	flowering		harvest		4	6	3	4		Colourful when bearing flowers on bare branches

flowering harvest

51

a key at the bottom of the page explains what each symbol means

care tables give advice on essential care and maintenance for each tree or shrub including:

- the type and condition of soil
- the best site to position the plant
- any pruning requirements
- general care hints
- any particular problems with pests and diseases

Some tables include more than one genera, if they are listed on the same page

variety charts list recommended varieties for most genera of trees and shrubs, or the best individual species. These display key information to help you choose your ideal plant, showing:

- when the plant is in blossom/flower during the year
- the time when fruits, berries or nuts will appear
- the height and width, given optimum conditions
- the colour of the blossom or flower
- additional comments from the author

Some variety charts show more than one genera, if they are listed on the same page

Assessing Your Garden

Existing features

Your garden will be unique in the opportunities it has to offer and the constraints it might impose. So the first task is to assess what features are already there and how they might affect your plans.

Unless you have a newly-built house, you are likely to find some existing plants in the garden. Using a tape measure and some graph paper, draw a plan of the garden showing all established plants, paths, and other features. The other features will include "good" ones, such as pleasant views, and "bad" ones, like the street light that needs concealing. You should also note down any physical features, such as sloping ground, manhole covers, drain runs, a patio, and a driveway.

Next, consider whether you want to keep any of the existing plants. Especially important is to consider whether the existing plants block out any eyesores. Similarly, do you want to keep any of the other structural features of the existing garden design, such as paths and ponds?

Other factors to consider are the physical constraints of aspect, exposure, and the characteristics of your garden's soil.

Aspect

The major issue with aspect is whether your garden faces north, south, east, or west—that is to say, which parts of your garden will get the most, or least, sun (see opposite page). Each of these orientations will have a different impact upon the climate of the garden, thereby determining which plants will thrive and which will struggle.

However, aspect is also determined by geographical and structural features. These may affect the amount of sun a garden receives as much as, if not more than, its orientation. These features include the proximity of neighboring buildings and large trees, and whether your house is situated on a hill.

Exposure

The degree of exposure to the elements that your garden experiences is another determining factor in what plants will grow. We normally think of this in terms of whether the garden is exposed and therefore colder and requiring hardy plants, as opposed to a sheltered garden where more tender plants can be grown. Life is not quite as simple as this, however, as the factor of increased wind in an exposed site complicates matters. For example,

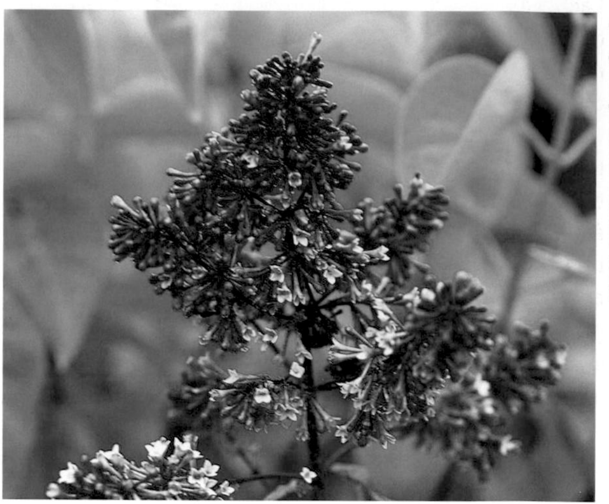

Syringa vulgaris like alkaline soils.

some plants that are perfectly hardy, such as *Catalpa bignonioides* 'Aurea', are ill suited to windy conditions because the large leaves are simply blown to shreds. However, a windy site can give some protection to a plant susceptible to late spring frosts since these usually occur only in still air conditions.

Soil

The next stage is to work out what kind of soil you have, since each type of soil can vary greatly in drainage capacity, fertility, and chemical composition.

The acidity or pH of the soil can have a marked effect upon what it is possible to grow or how the plants will grow. Soils derived from chalk and limestone rocks will be alkaline. These soils are often well drained, with good nutrient-holding capacity, and are excellent for certain shrubs, but rhododendrons will not grow on them because they like only acid soils.

Soils derived from sandstone or from sands and gravels are usually acidic in nature. They will grow a wider range of plants because most plants that tolerate alkaline conditions will also thrive on them. However, sandy soils are often too freely drained and dry out easily, and they do not tend to hold nutrients well.

Soils derived from clays can be either acidic, alkaline, or neutral. However, they are usually poorly drained, and therefore wet and heavy over winter. They are also slow to warm up in the spring, although they have a high nutrient-holding capacity. Each of these soils can be improved by the addition of organic matter.

Specific Conditions

Each garden is different, with its own specific, prevailing conditions to take into account. The illustration below is a representation of a "typical" garden, comprising a number of different elements that usually feature in most gardens.

Of course, your own garden may look very different than the one illustrated here, but you will almost certainly need to take the same factors into account when assessing the suitability of your garden for the cultivation of shrubs and trees. Remember that it is always easier to work with conditions as you find them. Don't try too hard to fight Nature, because Nature usually wins in the end. That said, with a few slight changes to your garden, you can improve your plants' chances of growing considerably, without too much effort and expense.

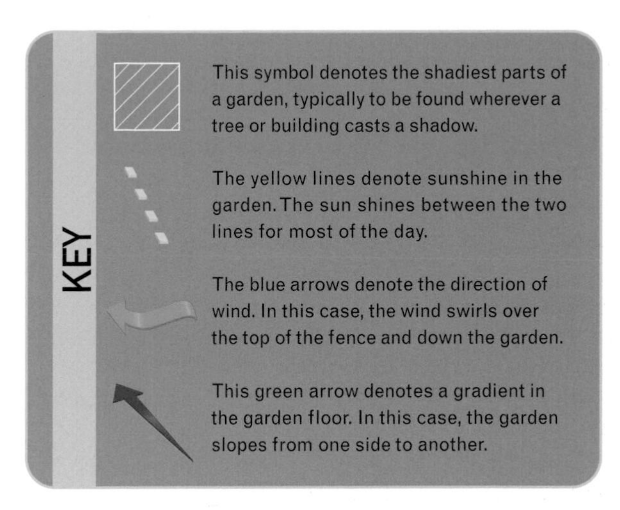

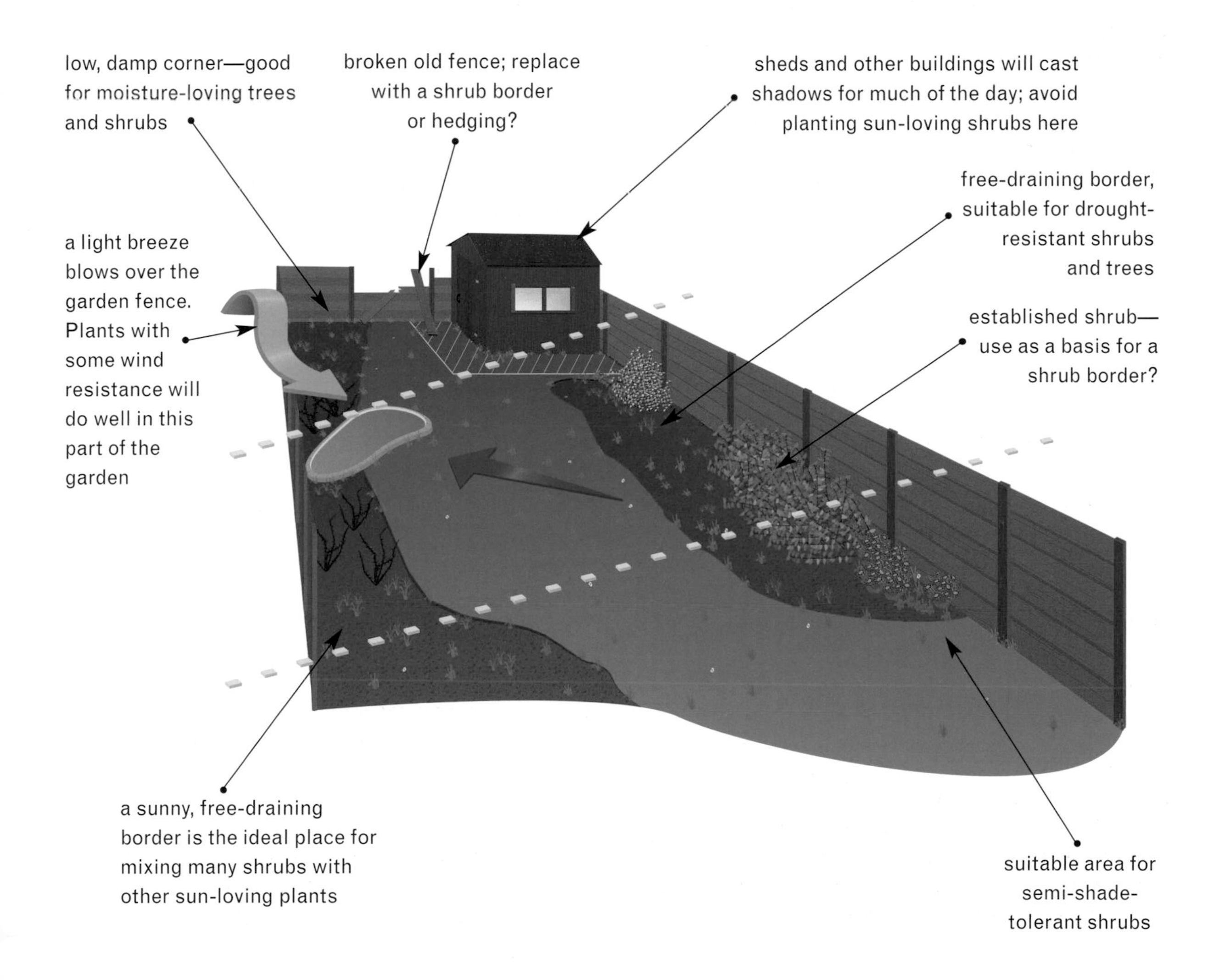

Choosing & Buying Plants

Trees and shrubs come in a wide range of shapes and sizes. Creating the effect you want in the garden requires careful consideration and selection.

Selecting your plants

Trees and large shrubs are used mainly for the contribution they make to the garden through their form, shape, and foliage, and by the decorative features they exhibit, such as flowers, fruits, and bark.

Although a garden is enjoyed most of all when the weather is fine and you can sit and walk around it, you will still be seeing it every day for the rest of the year and you will want it to look good. Few trees and shrubs are in flower or fruit for more than a few weeks so, unless you are interested in only a specific short period, you will need to consider how the plant looks when not making its best display of flower or fruit. Hence the form of the tree, and the eventual height and spread it will achieve when mature, are equally important.

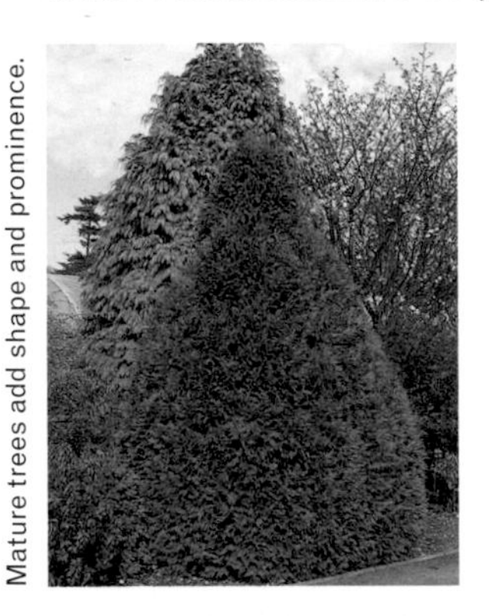

Mature trees add shape and prominence.

Form Form or shape is one of the most important aspects of trees and shrubs. Unless you want to be forever trimming, consider what would be the best shape of tree for the intended spot, the space available, and how you want it to relate to the other planting.

Form, color, and texture should all be considered.

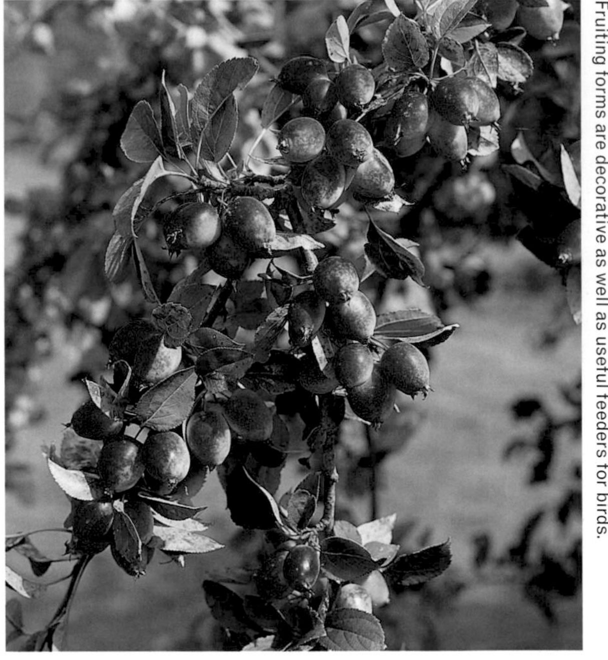

Fruiting forms are decorative as well as useful feeders for birds.

When you come to buy trees and larger shrubs, you will notice that most young plants start with upright and narrow crowns (the upper part). They only make domed or rounded crowns as they mature, with the branches arching out from the main stem. Some of the selected varieties, such as *Eucryphia nymansensis* and *Populus nigra* 'Italica', retain narrow upright crowns; others, such as *Prunus* 'Amanogawa' and *Quercus robur* 'Fastigiata', begin this way but then the erect branches splay out as the plant grows.

There are two main forms of weeping plant: those where the branches are all pendulous, so that the tree will only grow to some height if it is trained or has a tall rootstock, such as *Betula pendula* 'Youngii' and *Fraxinus excelsior* 'Pendula'; and those where only the side branches are pendulous and the tree can grow to a good height thanks to ascending main shoots, for example *Salix sepulcralis* 'Chrysocoma'. Conifers generally have narrow upright crowns, but contain many exceptions, while the whole character of bamboos provides another range of forms.

Foliage The texture of a tree or shrub will depend upon the size and shape of its leaves and whether the plant is deciduous or evergreen. Generally, larger leaves cast a denser shade than small leaves or "pinnate" leaves with opposing leaflets on the leaf stem. However, the very largest leaves, such as those of Catalpa and Paulownia, are thin and therefore let light through, whereas the thick leathery leaves of many evergreens cast a heavy shade.

Foliage color should be mainly green. Green is the most restful color to the eye and there are an infinite number of shades, from the dark glossy green of Ilex to the light yellow-green of *Gleditsia triacanthos* 'Sunburst' and *Acer cappodocicum* 'Aureum' or the blue-greens of many conifers. Strong variegated colors, such as *Populus jackii* 'Aurora', and the deep purples of *Fagus sylvatica* var. *purpurea* (copper beech) and *Cercis canadensis* 'Forest Pansy' can look very attractive, but beware of planting too many of these varieties as they tend to overwhelm the eye.

Fall color, as the leaves assume rich hues of yellow, russet, or red, can give a stunning display. The colors are no less exotic than the purples of a copper beech, but the latter seem to lack their naturalness. Rarely do fall colors clash badly.

Other features Flowers on trees and shrubs should be seen as a bonus, but what a bonus! The range available includes the flamboyance of *Cornus kousa*, Prunus, and Rhododendron, to the discrete loveliness of the blooms of *Pittosporum tenuifolium*. Catkins are also considered to be flowers and have their own subtle beauty, including the pendent catkins of Alnus, Betula, Corylus, and Garrya, which open in early spring, as well as the white erect catkins of Castanea in mid-summer.

Both leaves and flowers can be fragrant. The best leaf aromas are given by the balsam poplars *Populus* 'Balsam Spire' and *Populus jackii* 'Aurora'. The leaves of *Nothofagus antarctica* also emit a similar fragrance.

Fruit effect is primarily a fall to winter characteristic of trees and shrubs. Most of the showy fruits are the fleshy ones, whether the berries of Cotoneaster, Ilex, and Sorbus, or the curious pods of *Decaisnea fargesii*. The capsules of Koelreuteria are also impressive, as are many conifer fruits.

Bark effect is usually a winter phenomenon, in some cases not developed until the wood has fully ripened, and in most cases it is hidden by the leaves before then. Bark effect can either be produced by the quality of the bark on the trunk and main stems, for example Acer, Betula and Eucalyptus, or by the bright color of newly grown twigs, as with *Salix alba* ssp. *vitellina* 'Britzensis', or even by both in the case of *Acer pensylvancum* 'Erythrocladum'.

Designing with trees and shrubs

Once you've decided which characteristics of form, foliage, and decorative features you prefer, the next stage is to draw up some design ideas for how to incorporate trees and shrubs in an overall planting scheme.

Apart from their decorative features, trees can be planted as hedging or screening, to mark out different areas of the garden, to give shade and shelter, as individual landmarks, and to provide a sense of scale. Larger shrubs can be used to create similar effects as trees—bamboos make particularly effective screens—but they can also be combined with other smaller shrubs. They are also effective planted in a mixed bed along with perennials and annuals where they will provide some permanent structure to the planting scheme.

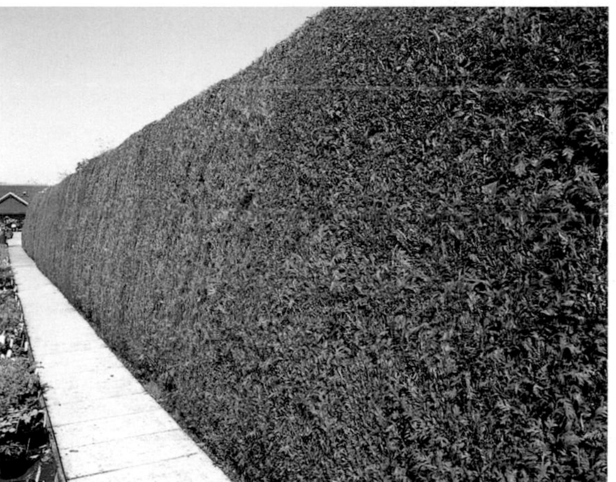

Cupressus leylandii makes fast-growing hedging.

If a shrub has a particularly impressive form or feature, it can be treated as a specimen plant, planted singly or in small groups in a prominent position in the garden where it will act as a focal point. Quite often you will find the overriding reason for planting a tree or shrub is simply to fill unwanted space, but there is no reason why you cannot be creative—even if the original reason is uninspiring!

Buying trees and shrubs

Trees and shrubs can be bought from a variety of sources—garden centers, general and local nurseries, and specialist nurseries.

Garden centers vs. nurseries The main advantage of garden centers is that you will almost always find one in your local area. Garden centers are retail units, selling on plants that are grown elsewhere, and so are likely to stock a uniform quality of product but possibly a limited range. If nothing else, they are bound to stock a full range of accessories and the latest gadgets. However, they are unlikely to offer larger trees, because they are geared to selling what can be fitted in the car and taken home.

Generally, nurseries are likely to have grown the plants sold in the garden centers, so you may find better stock and a wider range, but you will probably need to travel further to find one. They will usually offer a range of larger sizes and hedging plants.

Specialist and "niche" nurseries are well worth considering if you are looking for a very particular type of tree or shrub, or something out of the ordinary, and they are the best option for really large trees. Horticultural societies can help you hunt out specialist nurseries and will often provide comprehensive directories.

HEDGING

Trees and shrubs used for hedges and screens need to have either fairly compact crowns or must tolerate clipping, such as *Buxus sempervirens* (below). Most will allow you to clip them, but for some it is important to get the method and timing right. Plants with large and long-lived leaves will not look good after clipping, as any damaged leaves will remain on the plant for a couple of years. Conifers, with the noticeable exception of Taxus, will only make new growth from existing green foliage and so cannot be reshaped by hard clipping that removes all foliage.

Conifers frequently planted as hedging include Taxus, Chamaecyparis, Cupressus, and Thuja, which all respond well to clipping. Of these, Taxus is undoubtedly the best, though there are others and Tsuga produces a very neat hedge.

The most common broadleaves for hedging are Carpinus, Fagus, and Ligustrum, but almost all those featured in the book can be used. Bamboos make very effective "living" walls, especially the very erect-growing *Semiarundinaria fastuosa*.

TIP

Size matters Avoid buying trees and shrubs that have nearly attained their full size, because they are less likely to thrive than ones bought at no more than a third to a half of their full size. Equally, if the plant is too small, it will be vulnerable to damage and slow to grow. Try to buy plants that are between a quarter and a half of the intended full size if the size is up to 6ft (2m); and aim for a minimum of 1½ft (0.5m) for taller-growing plants. Trees can be moved at sizes up to 40ft (12m), but this requires specialist lifting gear.

Container-grown plants Each supplier will sell trees and shrubs either as container-grown, bare-root, or balled-and-burlapped. The great advantage of buying plants grown in containers is that you will be transporting them home with their root system intact, and as such they are much more likely to thrive when planted out. Container plants can be planted throughout the year, not just in the dormant planting season—mid-fall to the beginning of spring. However, they will need regular watering if planted during the summer months until they have established roots into the soil. In particular, container-grown stock is excellent for evergreens, which can dry out and die if they are planted bare-root and not adequately watered.

The main drawback is that container-grown trees and shrubs can become "potbound" if left for too long. Trees and shrubs should not spend more than two years—preferably only 18 months—in a container before being repotted or planted out. With potbound plants you will often find the roots have filled the container and started to circle around in an effort to find a way out; such plants are unlikely to establish a new root system in the soil when you plant them in your garden. Sometimes the roots escape through the bottom of the container and grow into the sand or soil beneath, and most of these roots will be lost on planting. Potbound plants often show

A healthy container-grown tree.

Potting mix should be near the rim.

Avoid pots with weeds on top.

TIP

Containerized plants Sometimes garden centers containerize shrubs, such as hedging plants, that have been supplied to them as bare-root. There are two ways to tell if a plant has been containerized. First, check the surface of the potting mix; if it is rough, then the plant has probably been newly potted, as a month or two of rain and watering would have smoothed the surface down. Then try lifting up the plant by the stem; if it feels loose and starts to come away in your hand, this means the tree or shrub has been in the container for less than two months. Come back later to buy or go elsewhere—if such a plant is planted out too soon, the potting mix will fall away, damaging the soft new roots.

poor growth because they have exhausted the nutrients in the potting mix.

When buying container plants:

- check that the roots are not spiraling around inside the pot
- look out for too many roots escaping through the drainage holes
- ensure the top growth is healthy and the soil around the plant is not overgrown with weeds
- check to see whether the level of the potting mix has dropped below the rim of the pot (½in/1–2cm below the top)—all container mixes break down over time, so if the level has dropped, this is a sure sign the plant has been in there too long

Bare-root plants Bare-root trees and shrubs weigh much less than container plants and are therefore easier to transport. The main drawback is that much of the root system is left in the nursery soil, which means they can be slow to establish in their new home. However, they can have a more extensive root system than container-grown plants, as in the nursery they will have spread into a much larger volume of soil than a similar-sized container-grown shrub.

When buying bare-root trees or shrubs:

- look for healthy root systems, avoiding plants with damaged, broken or dry roots
- take extra care to prevent the roots from drying out or becoming overheated—in particular, keep them out of strong sunlight

Balled-and-burlapped plants Balled-and-burlapped trees and shrubs are nursery-grown plants that have been lifted with the soil still attached to the roots. To stop the soil falling off the roots and causing them to dry out, the ball of soil is wrapped in burlap or a coarse cloth. Balled-and-burlapped plants weigh more than a similar-sized container-grown plant because soil is heavier than potting mix.

For some items, buying a balled-and-burlapped tree or shrub represents a reasonable compromise between the relative cheapness of bare-root stock—with its increased risk of failure—and the expense of container-grown stock.

With some evergreens, such as field-grown conifers, the rootball should be handled with special care, as the more soil that is knocked off, the greater the risk of failure. Plants that make dense fibrous root systems, such as Rhododendron, are very resilient, and the technique of rootballing is excellent for these.

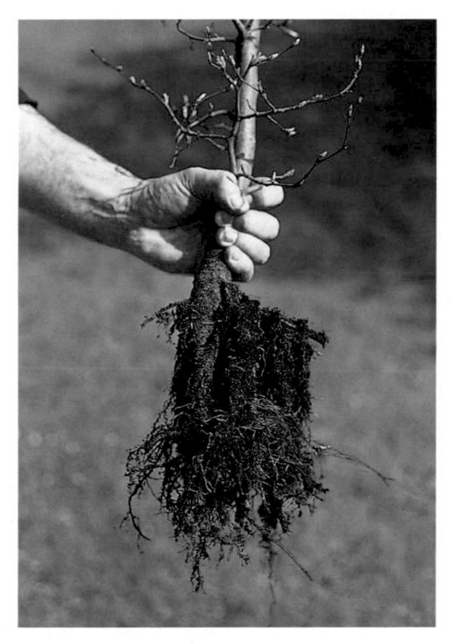

Bare-root plants are easier to transport.

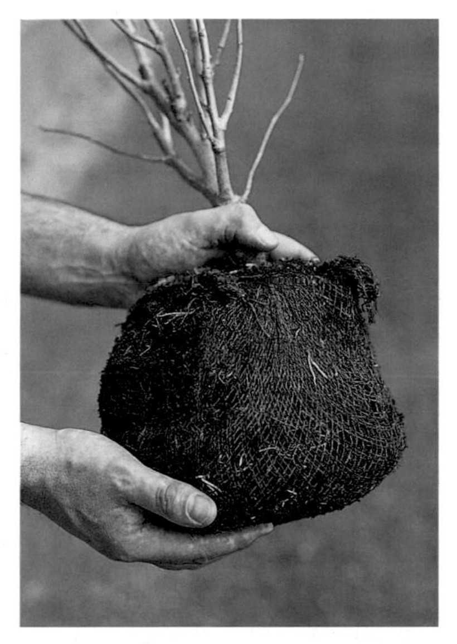

A protected balled-and-burlapped plant.

Planting

Now that you have spent time—and money—buying your carefully chosen trees or shrubs, it is important to give them as good a start as possible.

Preparing the site

Preparation is half the battle when it comes to planting trees and shrubs. Before planting, the site should be in as good a condition as possible, and you need to know where you are going to place each plant. At this stage, the condition of the soil should be your main concern, namely compaction, waterlogging, and weeds.

Compacted soil Trees and shrubs cannot grow in compacted soil for several reasons. Without an adequately porous structure to the soil, water will not be able to drain away, leading to waterlogging (see below). Also air cannot percolate, which means the plant's roots will be unable to obtain oxygen for respiration. Perhaps most importantly, newly planted shrubs will find it difficult or impossible to take hold because the roots will be unable to penetrate the density of the compacted soil.

Compaction is unlikely to be a serious problem if you have an old house, but almost all new houses will have compacted soil in the garden caused by builders' heavy machinery. A lot of hard work is the only solution! You will first need to remove about two digging fork depths of soil, then break up the subsoil underneath with a pickax and replace the topsoil. Rototillers are not useful for this, unfortunately, as they only scratch the surface.

TIP

Roots cannot grow across or into dry soil. However, once established the roots can actually tolerate being dried out, provided the root tips themselves are in moist soil.

Waterlogging Waterlogged soil can kill a plant by drowning the roots. Very few trees and shrubs can actually grow with their roots under water (examples of those that can include Alnus, Metasequoia, Salix, and Taxodium, but all of these will grow much better in well-drained soils). However, many will tolerate short periods of waterlogging during the dormant season. This is because the fine roots that absorb the water, air, and nutrients from the soil, and which are susceptible to being drowned, are not produced during the dormant season. Instead, the plant relies upon the older roots.

Waterlogging is often caused by compaction, although it can also be caused by poorly draining soils, such as clay soils. With these heavy soils, digging in organic matter and applying a layer of organic mulch will help to improve drainage, and has the added benefit of increasing soil fertility. If the soil is persistently waterlogged, short of introducing complicated drainage systems, another method is to make a series of mounds and plant the trees or shrubs into the mounds—but you will still need shrubs tolerant of damp conditions for this to be effective.

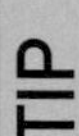

TIP

If you want to plant in a grassy area, then you will obviously need to remove the turf. Place this at the bottom of the planting hole because the turf will compost down and provide added nutrients for the roots. You will have to dig a bigger hole, however! Never, ever place the turf around the tree or shrub, as the grass will grow vigorously to the detriment of the plant, even if you turn the turf upside down.

Weeds Weed control is well worth achieving before anything is planted, to ensure new plants are not competing with weeds for nutrients—and because weeding is more difficult with the plant in place.

Larger weeds can be removed by hand or by digging over the soil with a digging fork. Perennial weeds, such as couch grass, are the biggest problem—even if their upper

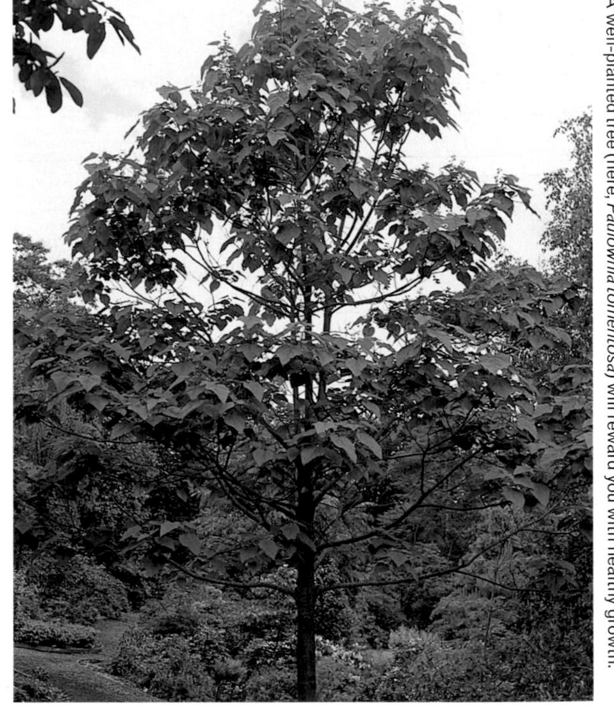

A well-planted tree (here, *Paulownia tomentosa*) will reward you with healthy growth.

foliage is killed, they survive through their underground food stores and return each year. To remove perennial weeds effectively you need to kill them off at the roots. For this it is best to use translocated chemical weed-killers, which are applied to the foliage and then travel down through the plant to attack the roots. However, translocated weed-killers tend not to be selective and will attack weeds and garden plants alike—another reason why it is better to achieve a weed-free soil before planting. Most weed-killers require at least several days to take effect, and often as long as several weeks, before any planting can occur, so always read the label.

TIP

If you dislike using herbicides, try laying sheet mulches (of woven polypropylene and black polyethylene) for several weeks or months before planting to kill off the weeds. If you plant through holes in the sheets, this will help stop weeds coming up after planting. An organic mulch is another option, provided you apply a layer at least 2in (5cm) thick, and has the added benefit of enriching the soil.

Planting the tree or shrub

No tree or shrub likes to be planted deeper than it has been growing. Always plant at the soil mark on the stem made by the nursery soil or at the level of the container. If in doubt, plant on the shallow side.

If you have already dealt with any compaction by digging over the soil, then simply dig a hole sufficient to accommodate the root system.

Another technique is to employ the "two holes" method to give your tree or shrub the best possible start. First, dig a hole at least 6in (15cm) larger than is required. Backfill the hole completely but do not plant. Then dig another hole of the correct proportions from the hole just filled in. This may sound like unnecessary extra work, but digging two holes will ensure the soil around the newly planted tree or shrub is completely broken up so that the roots can extend out freely.

Container plants Before planting container- or pot-grown plants, trim back any damaged top portions to good shoots and check to see if the potting mix has dried out. If it has, it is unlikely to rewet when planted in the ground and you should leave it to soak in a bucket of water for an hour or two. Do not leave it soaking too long or you will kill all the fine roots.

Container-grown stock can be planted at any time of the year, but if this is done during the summer months, plants will require regular watering.

PLANTING A HEDGE

Spacing of hedging plants will depend upon how long you are prepared to wait for the hedge to thicken and what its purpose is—a hedge intended to keep animals in (or out) will need stems closer together than a visual hedge, where the important feature is the wall of foliage. Generally, spacings of between 18in (0.5m) and 3ft (1m) are suitable. For a thicker hedge, double-plant with two alternating rows.

To plant a container-grown tree or shrub:
Dig a hole of the correct depth but ensure it is at least 2in (5cm) wider than the container. Remove the tree or shrub from its pot. If the roots have formed a circular mass in the bottom of the pot, tease them out so they spread as widely as possible. If there are woody circling roots that cannot be teased out, cut them with pruners at three points equally spaced around the circle to allow new roots to form. This will prevent the roots growing in a circling manner, since trees and shrubs with such roots usually end up blowing over. Replace the soil in layers no more than 4–6in (10–15cm) thick. Firm each layer with the ball of your foot or your toes, but avoid firming with the heel, which will almost certainly cause compaction of the soil.

Bare-root plants Bare-root shrubs should only be planted when the plant is dormant, between late fall and early spring. If in leaf, the plant will not be able to absorb enough water to compensate for the loss of roots.

If the roots are dry, soak them in a bucket of water for up to 12 hours. If some are broken or damaged, cut them back using a sharp knife or pruners.

Balled-and-burlapped plants

Balled-and-burlapped trees and shrubs can be planted over a longer period than bare-root ones, but avoid the late spring to early fall period.

Check the condition of the soil. Fibrous-rooted plants such as Rhododendron can safely be soaked if dry, but most balled-and-burlapped shrubs have coarser root systems that will fall apart if wetted. These are best watered in thoroughly after planting. Any damaged top portions should also be trimmed back to good shoots.

A

B

C

D

To plant a bare-root tree or shrub:

Dig the hole to the correct dimensions to hold the roots. Make sure that the hole is even and dug to the correct depth—that is, dig no deeper than the level at which it was planted in the nursery [A].

If any roots are bent so that they are growing into the center of the shrub, bend them back outward. If this cannot be done, prune them off, otherwise you risk the bent roots girdling the other roots and causing the tree or shrub to blow over in the future. Backfill around the roots [B], firming as you go but without compacting the soil [C]. Tie up to a stake, if necessary [D] (see opposite page).

To plant a balled-and-burlapped tree or shrub:

Dig a hole to the same depth as the rootball, but at least 2in (5cm) wider to allow for the roots.

Place the plant in the center of the hole and untie or cut the material used to make the ball (right). Do not try to remove this but simply spread it out in the bottom of the planting pit, where it can be safely left to rot down. Tease out any roots that are free from the soil of the rootball, and bend back or cut off any girdling or circling roots.

Backfill with soil in layers of 4–6in (10–15cm) thick, firming as you go but ensuring the soil does not get compacted. Stake the tree, if necessary.

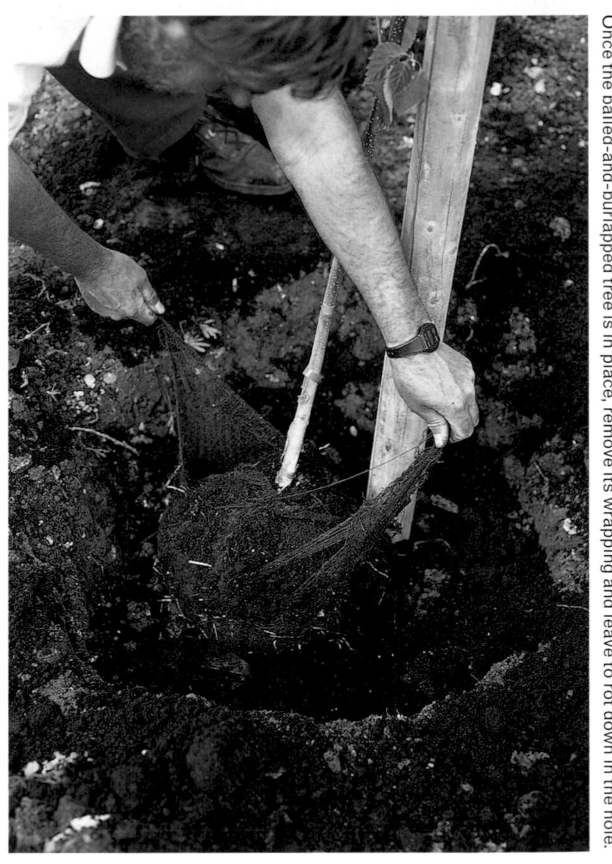

Once the balled-and-burlapped tree is in place, remove its wrapping and leave to rot down in the hole.

Staking

Newly planted trees and shrubs often need staking to help them get established. The purpose of a stake is to hold the roots firm so that the brittle feeder roots are not damaged by the plant rocking in the wind—it is not meant to hold the stem rigid. There should be no more than 2in (5cm) of stake above the tie, as otherwise in windy weather the stem of the tree will flex and rub against the stake, causing damage to the tree.

Once the fine roots have become woody (lignified), the tree or shrub should not need further staking. Stems of trees and shrubs are designed to flex in the wind to dissipate the wind's energy. Holding the stem rigid confuses the plant, as it uses the flexing of the stem to determine how much wood it needs to make. Thus rigidly staked trees—particularly those staked too high—can be thicker at the top and thinner near the stake.

Staked too high.

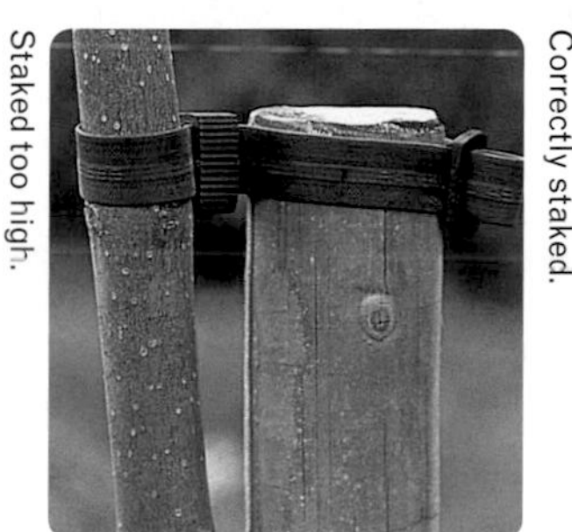

Correctly staked.

You could also use a thin batten, which would allow for more flexibility. For smaller plants, a bamboo cane will usually suffice, giving adequate protection against wind rock but still allowing the stem to flex. Tie in the cane using tape, rather than wire or twine which will cut into the stem. Normally a shrub should not need staking for longer than a year—often only a few months will do—and a larger tree for up to two years. After this time, if it still needs staking, it has probably been planted too deep, in which case you should trim it back and allow it to firm itself rather than continue staking.

Transplanting

Moving established plants can be an alternative to digging up unwanted plants or those that do not fit in their existing position in the new design. Before moving an established plant, consider whether it is worth the effort. Often it would be better to buy a young plant, which may be nearly as large after two or three years.

Small plants less than half their likely mature size, or less than 3ft (1m), can be dug with a spade and moved bare-root, because they will not make adequate rootballs. Small plants can be lifted with all, or nearly all, their roots. Larger plants that have reached almost full size and spread, or at least 6ft (1.8m) in height, can be moved with a rootball.

It is generally best to transplant during the dormant season, from late fall to early spring, although evergreens such as Ilex are better moved when the soil is still warm in early fall, with a thorough watering in.

Another staking method is to place the stake diagonally to the tree.

Transplanting a mature tree or shrub requires care in digging out the rootball. First, make a guideline around the plant, digging a vertical slit a minimum of 12in (30cm) from the stem (or 20–24in/50–60cm for trees and shrubs that are 10–13ft/3–4m high). Remove a spadeful of soil from outside the guideline, working around the plant to dig a trench between 12–20in (30–50cm) deep. You may need to dig down deeper on good soils, but on poorer soils most of the roots will be in the top 12–16in (30–40cm).

Next, use the spade to cut horizontally across from the base of the trench, freeing the tree or shrub from the soil. Gently rock it to one side and slip a folded sheet of polyethylene or similar beneath the rootball. Rock the plant to pull the sheet out at the far side. Then either lift the plant or dig a ramp on one side and drag it to its new position. Replant as for a new balled-and-burlapped plant. The replanted tree or shrub should not need staking if the rootball has remained intact.

Care & Maintenance

Once your new trees or shrubs are planted and in their proper place, the real work begins in looking after them and taking care to bring them on to full maturity.

Mulching

Mulching is a highly effective labor-saving technique and greatly benefits trees and shrubs. A mulch is a layer of material applied to the ground around plants. It restricts the evaporation of water from the soil surface, protects tender roots by maintaining an even soil temperature, helps to keep down weeds, and, if the mulch is organic, feeds the soil with nutrients as it decomposes. As the organic mulch is broken down and incorporated into the soil, this also improves the soil texture so that lighter soils are more able to retain water, and heavy soils are made lighter so they drain more easily.

Organic mulches Bark is an excellent organic mulch material because it is long-lasting, looks good, and is a by-product of timber production. Woodchips are an alternative, though they are better suited to making paths rather than as mulches. Neither of these wood-based mulches, however, will provide significant levels of nutrients.

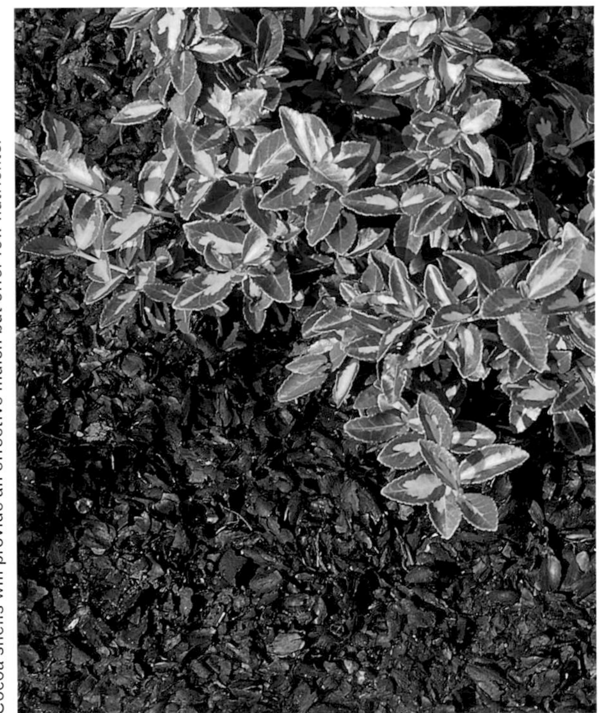

Cocoa shells will provide an effective mulch but offer few nutrients.

Organic mulches with a high nutrient content include peat, peat-substitutes, leaf mold, and manure. Peat tends to break down quickly and is suitable for plants that require organic matter-content in the soil, such as Rhododendron. To stay environmentally friendly, however, choose a peat-substitute instead, since the manufacture of peat soil mixes has resulted in the large-scale destruction of some wetland areas. Leaf mold is formed from composted leaves—much better than burning or bagging them—and will greatly improve the soil. A thick layer of manure can also be used as a mulch with great nutritional benefits, but here, as with leaf mold, the difference between mulching and feeding begins to blur. With manure, ensure that it has been well composted or you may get more weeds than other benefits.

If you are using an organic mulch, spread a layer at least 2in (5cm) but no greater than 3–4in (10cm) thick. Any thinner and the mulch will not work, and birds and animals are likely to create bare patches. Any deeper and you may swamp the plants, causing the mulch to overheat as it breaks down, and this can scorch the stems of your plants.

Inert mulches The two main types of inert mulch are pea gravel and synthetic sheeting (woven polypropylene or polyethylene). Although highly effective at controlling weeds, neither offers any nutritional benefit. The open nature of pea gravel prevents weed growth while providing a surface that can be walked on, and it sets off beautifully small shrubs, such as dwarf conifers. As with organic mulches, pea gravel should generally be laid 2–4in (5–10cm) thick. However, if you need to raise the soil surface for any reason, a layer of pea gravel 12in (30cm) thick will not harm plants, provided they are, of course, taller than 12in (30cm).

Sheet mulches work by allowing rain and water to percolate through the sheet while greatly reducing evaporation from the surface. At the same time, established weeds and those that germinate beneath the mulch are starved of light and eventually die. Similarly, weeds that have managed to germinate on the top of the mulch are unable to root through the sheet and spread. Woven polypropylene is the best material, but black polyethylene sheeting of a minimum 500 gauge or old polyethylene bags, such as potting mix bags, can also be used. These do not allow water to percolate, but provided they are laid around plants in squares of no larger than 3ft (1m), the water will run in from the sides.

Lay the mulching sheet down and cut a cross in it for each plant.

Laying sheet mulches A full sheet is best for covering an entire bed. Lay it over the ground before planting but after initial preparation of the soil. Mark out the positions of the trees or shrubs on the sheet and cut a cross for each one. The size of the cuts will obviously depend upon the size of the plant and its root system. Fold back the four flaps and plant through the center, laying the flaps back around the stem afterward.

For trees and shrubs scattered around the garden, laying individual squares of sheeting around the base of the plant is more practical. Cut a cross-shaped notch if the plant is small enough to fit through the hole. For larger trees and shrubs, cut a slit from one side into the middle of the square, then place it around the shrub and overlap the sheeting to close the slit. Squares should be a minimum of 20sq in (50sq cm), but 1¼sq yd (1sq m) is preferable. Squares are held down either by making slits in the turf just in from each edge with a spade and forcing the sides into the slit, or by holding down the corners with turf or stones.

Feeding

Trees and shrubs generally do not require much additional feeding unless the soil is poor. You can test the amount of nutrients in your garden soil by using kits available at garden centers.

On poor soils, the best solution is to apply a mulch of well-rotted manure or leaf mold at the rate of a wheelbarrow load for every 3¼sq yd (3sq m). Dried manures, such as poultry dung, should be applied at the lower end of the recommended dosage.

Inorganic chemical fertilizers can also be applied, but be wary of the recommended dosage values, which tend to be on the generous side. Too much added nutrients will only result in lush growth at the expense of flowers. This is especially the case if there is an excess of nitrogen in the fertilizer. Unless your plants are showing signs of deficiency in a particular mineral (see pages 154–157), apply a balanced general fertilizer at a rate of 2oz (60g) per 1yd sq (1m sq), feeding once a year, preferably in spring. Soluble fertilizers can be applied using a watering can or by hose attachment, and are particularly effective on light, sandy soils.

Weeding

Weeds take water and nutrients intended for the trees and shrubs, they can smother small plants, and they look untidy—which are all very good reasons for trying to control them. Sheet mulches are particularly effective when applied to new plantings but are less convenient for established beds. Organic mulches will control germinating weeds but are less satisfactory where there are established weeds.

The second method of controlling weeds is to pull them out by hand or with the aid of a hoe or trowel. Take care when hoeing as even shallow hoeing can damage the root systems of trees and shrubs. Hoeing is most effective when the weeds are young and the weather hot and dry, so that the uprooted weeds quickly wither.

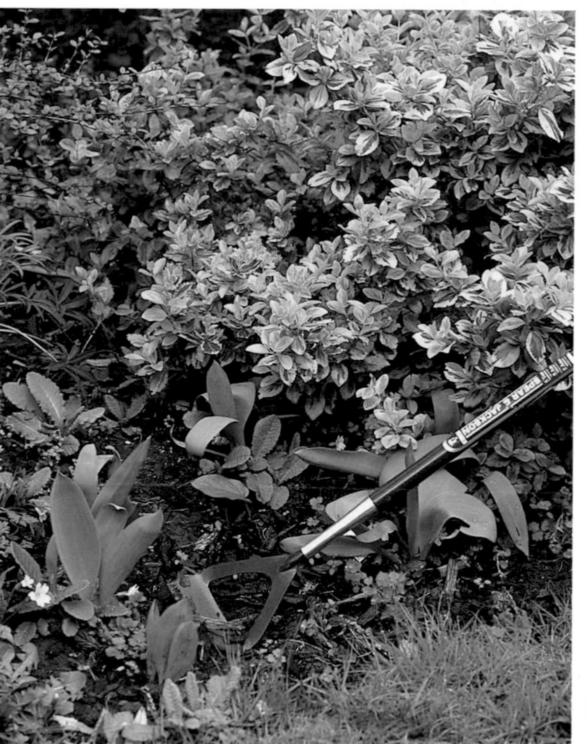

Remove weeds from around shrubs to reduce competition for the nutrients in the soil.

If the weather is wet, many will simply root into the soil again. Pull up large weeds by hand.

If pulling out weeds by hand, hoeing, and mulching does not solve your weed problem, you may choose to use chemical weed-killers, or herbicides. Admittedly, they require the least effort of all the methods of weed control, but you do run the risk of harming your trees or shrubs, especially if you overuse them. Herbicides must be handled with care and, as with all chemicals, strictly in accordance with the manufacturer's recommendations. Herbicides containing glyphosate will kill most weeds. The herbicide is sprayed over the foliage of the weeds and kills by disrupting respiration. Do not spray it onto the foliage of trees and shrubs. (Note: Some members of the rose family can be damaged by soil uptake.)

TIP Weeds respond to feeding far more quickly than trees and shrubs. There is no point applying fertilizer if you have not got the weeds under control—all you will do is increase the competition from weeds to the detriment of your plants.

Watering

For trees and shrubs to grow, water is an essential requirement but it is important to ensure they receive the right amount and do not end up swimming, which can drown them. Also, if they are kept too moist, some shrubs will grow well but fail to flower. So, before using the hose, work out how much water each plant needs.

Working out quantities Specific moisture requirements for particular species or varieties will be covered in the individual plant entries, but generally most trees and shrubs require regular watering during the growing season in the first year after planting. This helps the plant quickly establish itself—then, in later years, less regular watering will be required during periods of drought to promote healthy balanced growth.

Regular liquid feeds will help your trees and shrubs, especially when they are newly planted.

Little water is needed during the winter months. However, newly planted evergreens may need help if there are prolonged dry periods just after planting, particularly in early spring or late fall. The amount of water needed during the summer increases with the strength of the sun. In average temperate climates, the strength of the sun in mid-spring and early fall is sufficient to evaporate roughly ½in (1cm) of water per week; in late spring and late summer, this increases to ¾in (2cm) per week, and in high summer reaches 1in (2.5cm) per week. To work out exactly how much you need to water, measure with a rain gauge the amount of rainfall during the past week, then apply the above amounts minus the rainfall.

You will also need to take into consideration the water-holding capacity of the soil. Well-drained fertile soils, such as loams, will hold almost three times as much water as sandy soils. If you live in a high rainfall zone with a good loam soil and never have droughts longer than four to six weeks, you need only water new plantings to establish them in the soil. Whereas if you live in a dry zone and garden on a light, sandy soil, almost any drought will put your plants under pressure, and weekly watering will be very beneficial.

Watering equipment Watering cans, hand-held hoses, and sprinkler systems are inexpensive and easy to use, but a significant amount of water is lost to evaporation, and it is easy to apply too much. A more efficient, but expensive, alternative is to install a network of pipes or buried hoses, which can be supplied as fully automatic systems complete with pop-up sprinklers.

Seep hoses and trickle irrigation devices provide a cheaper option. A seep hose is full of small perforations through which the water slowly oozes out into the soil. In trickle irrigation systems the water drips out of nozzles either onto the soil surface or just below. With these systems virtually no water is lost through evaporation, but it is not so easy to measure how much is being applied, and seep hoses, in particular, are liable to become blocked after a year or two.

Protecting plants

Winter protection Winter protection is appropriate for some plants but is not really feasible for larger shrubs and trees. Straw is ideal for wrapping plants or covering up vulnerable parts of the plant. To prevent semihardy trees and shrubs being killed by winter cold, cover over the crown of the plant (around the base) with a layer of straw or mulch. Frost damage may still cause the plant to be cut back, but new shoots will grow from the protected base in spring. To protect tender and newly planted trees and shrubs, wrap them up in straw, then hold the straw in place with a sheet of polyethylene or burlap.

The problem with winter protection is always when to remove it—too early and a cold snap or hard frost may kill the plant; too late and the plant may be making soft growth beneath the protection, which will be susceptible to fungal attack. The best advice is to keep an eye on the temperature forecasts and be prepared to act quickly to re-cover plants if a cold snap occurs.

Use straw and polyethylene wrapping for winter protection.

Protection from animals You may need to protect your trees and shrubs from animals that like to strip bark or feed on the foliage. The most effective method of protection is to fence off vulnerable plants. Use hexagonal wire netting with a mesh size just over 1in (no more than 3cm) and at a height of 3ft 3in (1m) for smaller animals, or 5ft (1.5m) for larger animals. Make sure the bottom 6in (15cm) of netting is bent outward and covered by a thin layer of soil, to prevent burrowing animals breaking through. More practical on a small scale is to use rigid or wraparound stem guards made from plastic or rubber, which come in standard sizes for small and large animals.

Wire or plastic netting will keep hungry animals at bay when a young plant is becoming established.

TIP

To protect against late spring frosts, you can either insulate plants with a lighter material, such as fleece, or spray susceptible foliage with water. This protects plants because heat is given off when water changes from liquid into ice. Always keep an eye on the weather if air frosts are forecast.

Pruners and saws handle progressive degrees of pruning.

Equipment A pair of pruners will cut through shoots up to ½in (1cm) thick and is the best tool for most pruning of shrubs and small trees. Pruners come in two styles. Bypass pruners have a sharp blade and a blunt blade, which cut by a scissor action. With anvil pruners, the sharp blade cuts against the middle of a blunt anvil, rather like using a chopping board. Bypass pruners cause less bruising to the shoot and are better for finer pruning, whereas anvil pruners will cut thicker shoots.

Pruning

Trees and shrubs vary greatly in their need for pruning. The main reasons for pruning are to control the size of the shrub and the direction of growth, to tidy up the branch structure in order to produce an open and balanced form, to maximize flowering displays, or to promote new growth from plants with attractive young stems. The principal rule to remember is that pruning is 5 percent for the benefit of the shrub and 95 percent for the benefit of the garden.

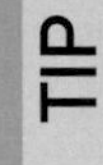

TIP Pruning can be carried out at any convenient time. However, some trees may bleed if cut at the wrong time. For this reason, avoid the late winter to early spring when pruning Acer, Betula, and Juglans.

Shrub pruners can handle branches just over 1in (up to 3cm) in thickness. Shears are useful for trimming hedges and similar bushes. Choose shears that have a notch in one blade near the base because these make cutting woody stems much easier. Use a pruning saw to remove branches from established trees, and a bow saw is useful for larger branches.

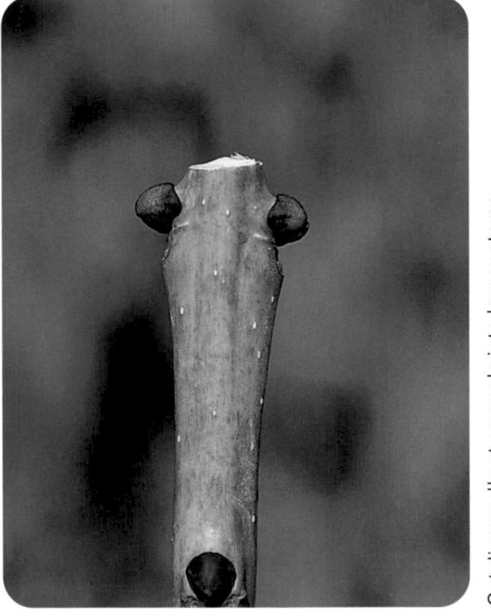

Make a straight cut with opposite buds.

Cut diagonally at an angle into larger stems.

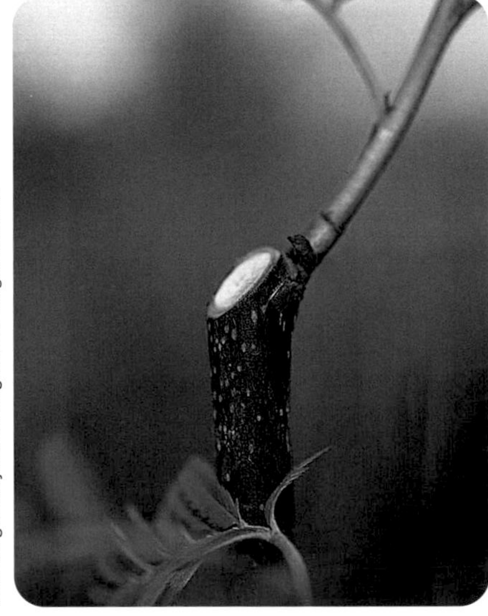

Fine pruning Pruning current or one-year wood requires fine cuts. These should be made at a point on the branch where there are identifiable buds from which new shoots will grow. Make the cut about ¼in (0.5cm) above a bud or pair of buds. Where there are opposing buds, cut straight across the stem; where there are alternate

A

C

B

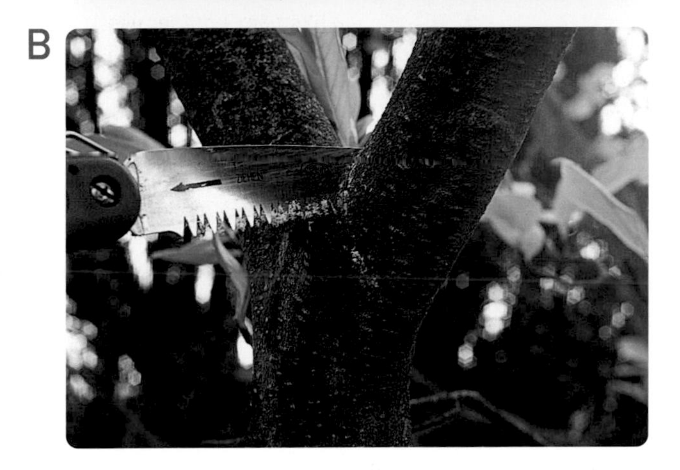

buds, cut at an angle. Choose buds that will grow outward, so that the shrub develops an open framework of branches. For cuts into larger stems, where regrowth will not be from identifiable buds but from dormant buds, make the cut at an angle so that water drains off the cut surface.

Removing a branch The main practical consideration in taking off a branch is to avoid making a tear that runs down the stem and rips the bark off, leaving a wound prone to infection. This is done by making the cut in three stages for branches over 6in (15cm).

Make an under cut upward through the branch at a point about 12in (30cm) from where you wish to remove the branch, only cutting to about a quarter of the thickness of the branch. Next, make a cut from the top of the branch 1in (2 or 3cm) beyond the first cut. When you are about halfway through the branch it should snap off without a tear. This leaves a short stump or "snag", which, because it weighs a lot less than the complete branch, is much easier to remove with a final single cut. On smaller branches less than 6in (15cm), make two cuts above [A] and below [B], to give a neat cut [C].

Most trees and large shrubs have special defenses for healing the wounds left after a branch has been removed, but for these to come into play the final cut must leave the collar intact around the base of the branch. This collar is thicker on the trunk side than on the branch side, and is normally at an angle across the branch, nearer the trunk at the top and further from the trunk at the bottom. Therefore, you will need to make the final cut at a point on the branch beyond the edge of the collar, angling the saw slightly so that the cut slopes away from the trunk.

TIP

Safety must always be your first consideration when removing a branch from a tree, especially if the branch is relatively high up. Do not use a chain saw above chest height under any circumstances unless you are a trained tree surgeon. If you cannot remove the branch with a 24in (60cm) bow saw, then employ a professional to do the job for you. And, although it may seem a little obvious, make sure you are not cutting off a branch that is supporting you or your ladder—you would be surprised at how many accidents are caused by this oversight!

Training Training is the simplest category of pruning. With established trees and shrubs, training involves cutting back a plant that has become too large for its setting or has spread in the "wrong" direction, for example if it is being trained against a wall. General maintenance to remove dead, defective, or crossing limbs is part of training. Errant branches should be removed at a suitable point, either where the branch originates on the stem, or at a side branch or bud.

Most newly planted trees will also require some initial training to promote vigorous growth and a balanced, open shape. Immediately after planting, prune back any dead or damaged stems and any stems that are crossing, and, if necessary, thin out to encourage an open branch structure.

Coppicing and pollarding With trees and shrubs that have grown too large for their setting, one option is to cut them back hard to just above ground level, a technique known as coppicing. This is a quick way both to reduce and rejuvenate a plant. Pollarding is a variant of coppicing; the main difference is that a pollard has a stem, often 8–16ft (2.5–5m) in height. Originally, the technique was used to keep the new foliage out of the reach of cattle.

To coppice a tree or shrub, cut it down to between 2–6in (5–15cm) above ground level; a variant is to leave the shrub on a short stem, or leg. You may need to thin out the new growth after the first season to form a natural shape. This will involve removing surplus stems, and possibly shortening the new growths. Coppicing is best carried out in spring, but it can be done at any time of the year. However, it is best to avoid early fall—if regrowth is made before winter, the new growth is likely to be killed by winter cold.

Not all trees and shrubs can be coppiced, however, because it requires a plant that will respond by regrowing from dormant buds in the bark. Many broad-leaved trees and shrubs will respond, but old trees of Fagus may be very sensitive and liable to die. Almost all conifers, apart from Taxus, will die if cut back hard because they must have green foliage from which to make new growth. Also, be wary of coppicing a specimen that has been propagated by grafting, as you will probably encourage the rootstock to grow, rather than the scion variety.

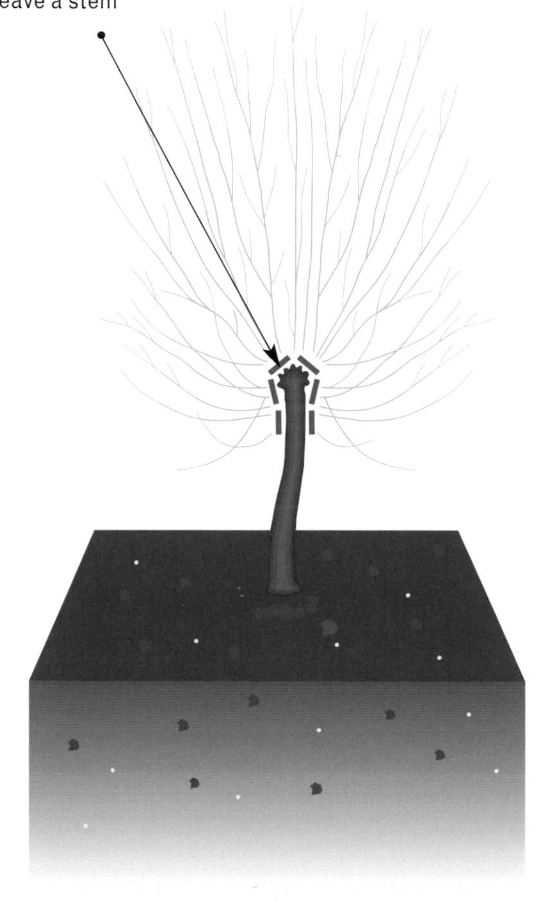

POLLARDING

In pollarding, the overgrown branches of a tree or shrub are cut right back to leave a stem roughly 8–16ft (2.5–5m) in height. Farmers often use this method to keep new foliage out of the reach of cattle.

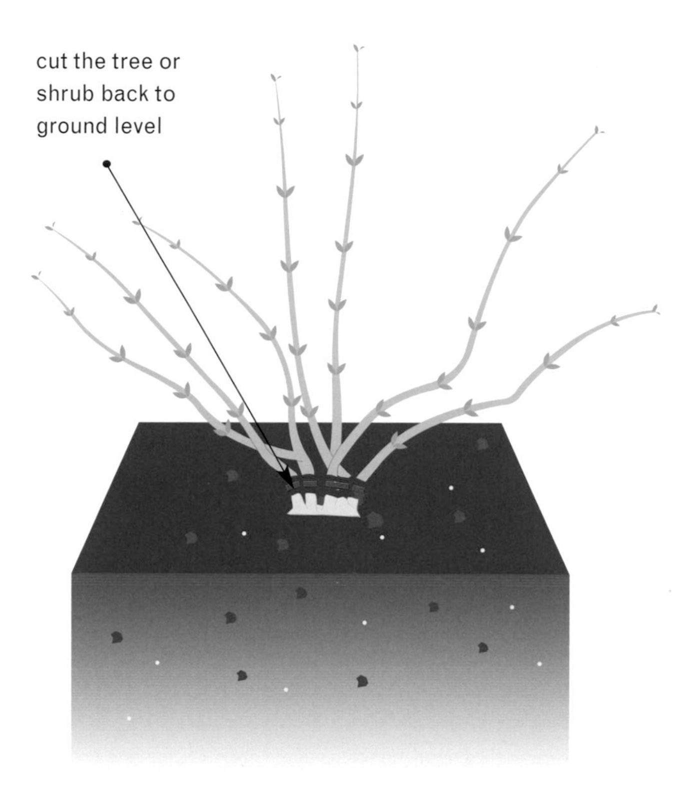

COPPICING

This is a method used both to reduce and rejuvenate a tree or shrub. Cut the branches and stems down to about 2–6in (5–15cm) above ground level. Coppicing is best carried out in late winter or early spring.

> **TIP**
>
> **Winter color**
> Trees and shrubs with beautiful colored bark can be coppiced to encourage a vigorous display of young stems. Salix, particularly *Salix alba* ssp. *vitellina* 'Britzensis', Cornus, and Corylus will all respond well to this treatment. Cut back to near ground level in early spring, removing all the stems, for a colorful display in winter.

Pruning a mature tree If you need to keep a larger tree within bounds, this can be done to some extent by pruning. Simply hacking off branches in a random fashion is not advisable, since this can promote disease from wounding and lead to excessive regrowth, which often means that in just a few years the tree becomes as large as when you started. Instead, your aim should be to reduce the density and spread of branches as unobtrusively as possible. To reduce the density, remove any surplus branches, cutting them off where they join the trunk or main stem so as not to leave a "snag." To diminish the spread of branches without spoiling the overall shape, shorten longer branches by cutting off the larger portion where there is a side branch or fork in the branch. Pruning can be carried out at any season on most trees, but if cutting back hard, it's best to prune in early spring when new growth will soon follow, rather than late summer when any new growth may not be hardy enough to survive fall frosts.

PRUNING A MATURE TREE
Do not hack off branches at random. Reduce the density and spread of branches as unobtrusively as possible, removing any surplus branches.

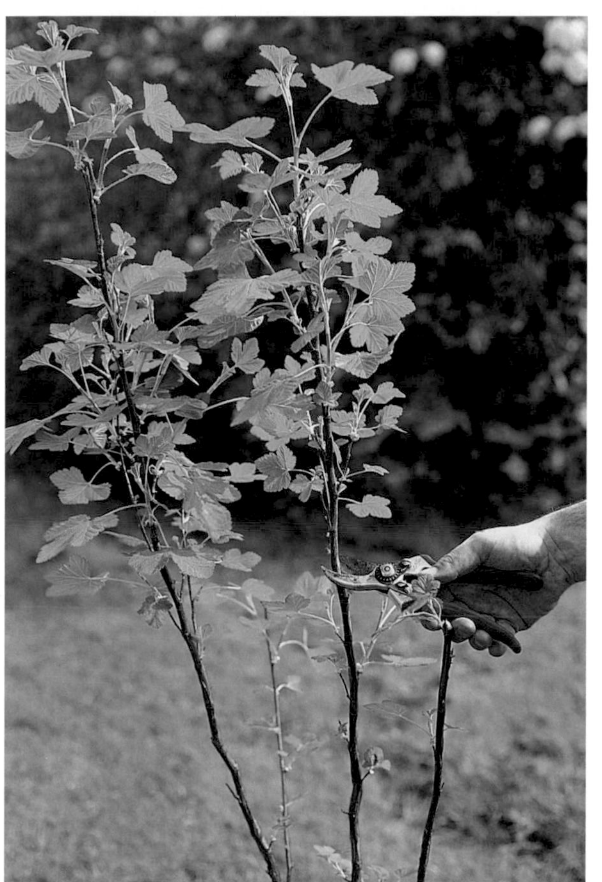

Regular pruning is essential to keep many trees and shrubs at their best.

Pruning to flower Pruning is also carried out to increase flowering. To practice this successfully requires an understanding of how each particular tree or shrub flowers. There are two main categories for this type of pruning and knowing which one you are dealing with can make all the difference between impressive floral displays and undistinguished foliage.

The difference between the two groups is whether they flower from buds laid down last year (Group 1) or whether they flower on new growth (Group 2). Generally, Group 1 trees and shrubs flower over winter, in spring, or early summer, while Group 2 shrubs flower in summer and fall.

Buddleja provides an example of a genus that includes varieties in both Group 1 and Group 2. *Buddleja globosa* flowers in spring and is a Group 1 shrub, whereas *Buddleja davidii* flowers in late summer and fall and is in Group 2. If *Buddleja globosa* is hard-pruned in late winter or early spring, it will not flower until the following season because you will have removed the previous year's growth. However, if you hard-prune *Buddleja davidii* back to two or three buds in late winter or early spring, it will produce more new growth and therefore lots more flowers.

Group 1 trees and shrubs Group 1 plants include Acacia, Chimonanthus, Cornus, Fremontodendron, Laburnum, Ligustrum, Magnolia, Mahonia, Pyracantha, Rhododendron, Sophora, and Syringa.

Group 1 shrubs should be pruned immediately after they finish flowering. However, for most of these the level of pruning will be limited to the removal of crowded shoots, and only with wall-trained Fremontodendron and Laburnum will the pruning consist of cutting back to a framework of branches. The main thing to remember with Group 1 plants is that, in general, you should restrict your pruning to the older shoots, leaving the newer shoots intact, because they tend to flower better on the spur shoots that are formed in the second year of a stem's life.

Group 2 trees and shrubs Group 2 plants include *Buddleja davidii* and Hibiscus among those treated here for flowers. They can be hard-pruned just as growth is starting in the spring, which will encourage them to make vigorous new growths and these will bear large trusses of flowers. Hard-pruning can either take the form of coppicing down to just above ground level, or cutting back to the bases of branches (see page 24); new growth will be made from dormant buds in either case.

Shrubs pruned in this manner will tend to flower later in the summer than if unpruned. This is most easily observed with *Buddleja davidii*; unpruned specimens flower in early to mid-summer with many small trusses, while hard-pruned ones flower mid- to late summer with fewer but much larger trusses. As this plant is grown both for its floral beauty and because the honey-scented nectar is a favorite food for butterflies, it is possible to extend both flowering and butterfly attraction seasons by planting two specimens, hard-pruning one as per Group 2 and lightly pruning the other as per Group 1.

Evergreen trees and shrubs Evergreen shrubs may fit either Group 1 or Group 2 but most of them require little pruning apart from "tidying up." Where they do need specific pruning is if any parts suffer from winter cold damage. This can happen when the severity of the cold kills parts of the shrub, or when there are cold dry winds that freeze roots so they are unable to provide water and the foliage dries out. As most evergreens tend to produce new leaves later than their deciduous counterparts, damage may not show until "normal" growth has been made. Evergreens damaged in this way will require minor trimming to remove any damaged areas, mainly by cutting back to suitable side branches. Otherwise, prune as per the above groups if more active pruning is appropriate.

Deadheading Deadheading refers to removing the old faded blooms. It is most often practiced on Rhododendrons where the flowers are picked off to prevent the bush exhausting itself by making seeds. By removing the flowers, energy is diverted into new growth, so that the side buds will mature in time to set flower buds for next year. To remove, hold the flower between the thumb and first two fingers just above the dormant buds in the leaf axils and snap it off. Don't worry if the leaf and bud come away with the flower because there will be several others remaining.

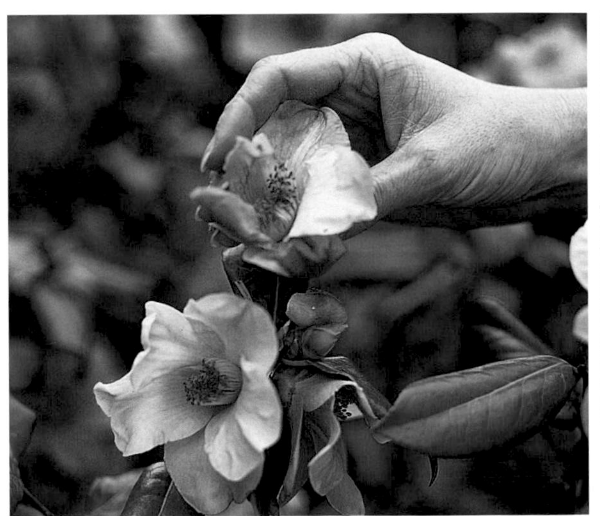

Hold the faded flower gently and just snap it off.

Deadheading is valuable where the faded flower contrasts with remaining flowers. *Buddleja davidii* 'White Profusion' and *Buddleja fallowiana* 'Alba' can be very attractive when the large trusses of white flowers first open. However, after the flowers have finished, the petals turn brown and this contrasts poorly with the bright white flowers of later flushes. Snip off the faded trusses at the base of the flowers above the last leaves and you may get a further smaller pair of trusses.

Shaping a hedge A good shape for a hedge is a narrow A-shape, wider at the bottom than the top. This is more stable than a parallel-sided hedge and allows light to fall on the lower foliage. Use a frame to mark out the shape and then cut to that template; if doing it by eye, the hedge is likely to undulate in and out.

Most hedges, however, tend to have an inverted A- or V-shape, and thus lose the lower foliage, becoming bare and ineffective at the base. This problem is often caused by cutting with the shears pointing down toward the base. Always clip with the ends of the shears pointing upward.

The right time for clipping varies with the species used for the hedge and also with the purpose of the hedge. Conifer hedges made with *Cupressus leylandii*, Taxus, and Thuja, and broad-leaved hedges made with Carpinus, Crataegus, and Fagus should only need clipping once in late summer, but can be trimmed twice if you want a particularly neat appearance.

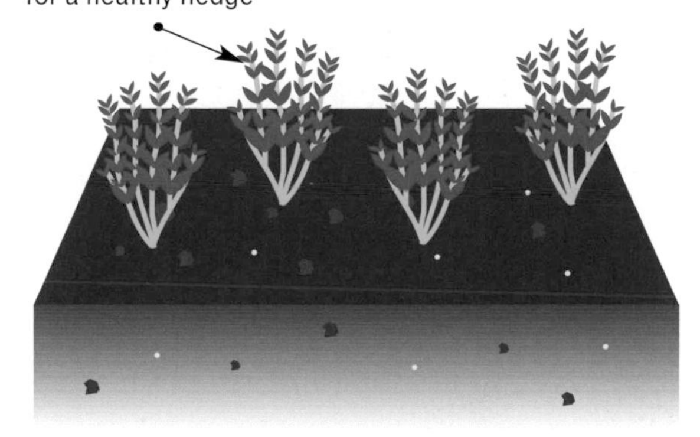

DOUBLE ROW HEDGE PLANTING AND SHAPING

If you want a much denser hedge, then plant a double row of plants, with the second row set back in the gap behind the first row.

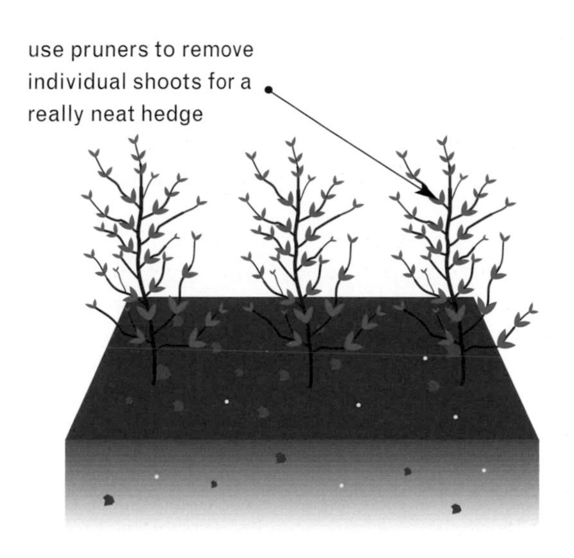

SINGLE ROW HEDGE PLANTING AND SHAPING

Fast-growing hedging plants will soon produce a neat boundary if they are trimmed or clipped at the right time and frequency.

Faster-growing hedging plants, like Ligustrum and *Lonicera nitida*, will need more frequent trimming to keep them neat, perhaps even four times during the summer months. Broad-leaved evergreens, such as Ilex and *Prunus laurocerasus*, can be clipped just before they come into growth in the spring or at the end of summer. With the large leaves of *Prunus laurocerasus*, do not use shears because these will cut leaves in half and the hedge will look odd for the next 12 months! Use pruners to remove individual shoots, or if you do still use shears, then remove any cut leaves with pruners.

Informal hedges will need much less attention when trimming. The aim should be to keep them tidy and, if the flowers are a prominent feature, to prune them in order to maximize the show of blooms. For example, if you decided to grow Crataegus as an informal hedge for the blossom in late spring, hard-prune it immediately after the blooms are over, possibly on a two-year cycle for best flowering.

TIP

Pruning for foliage

A number of trees and shrubs can be pruned to produce exotic foliage. These are mainly large-leaved ones, like Ailanthus and Paulownia, where vigorous regrowth can result in enormous leaves. The technique can also be used on plants with vividly colored new foliage, such as with most Eucalyptus.

Propagation

Trees and shrubs may be reproduced by either seeds, taking cuttings, layering, or grafting. Each method has its own particular advantages.

Sexual or asexual reproduction

Propagation by seeds is usually a sexual form of reproduction, with the parent plants having combined their genes to produce the seeds, and as a result each plant produced will be uniquely different.

Asexual reproduction of trees and shrubs is most often carried out by taking cuttings from the parent plant to produce an exact copy of the original. The main benefit of growing from cuttings is that, for many trees and shrubs, this will provide usable stock more quickly than from seed. Asexual propagation is essential if you wish to propagate a particular form or cultivar, which tend not to come "true" from seed.

By seed

Raising plants from seeds is a quick method for many shrubs and for some it is the only practical way. Seed-raised plants also have a natural root system, whereas cutting-raised plants can develop unbalanced roots, which makes them prone to being blown over. Growing plants from seed normally gives you diversity in the offspring, so that you are growing something "new" and may even create a spectacular original cultivar.

To raise plants from seed you must first obtain viable seeds. These need to be treated so that they will germinate, and the resultant seedlings must be nurtured to produce healthy plants, which can then be hardened off and planted out.

Collecting and storing seeds Seeds can be collected from your own garden, a friend's garden, bought from garden centers or nurseries, or otherwise obtained in packet form by mail order. Horticultural societies may also run seed distribution schemes.

Collect your own seed as soon as the fruit is ripe. For many Prunus, for instance, this will be in early to mid-summer when the fruits turn purple-black; any later and you will lose them to hungry birds. Most fruits ripen in the fall, and some late into the winter. For plants that produce fine seeds in capsules, such as Buddleja and Rhododendron, you will even find some seed in old capsules into spring.

The next stage is to extract the seed. Fruits that are capsules will need drying to release the seeds. Lay these out in small trays to dry, and avoid using heat except for a few items, such as pine cones. With fleshy fruits, especially juicy ones like some Sorbus, it is usually best to remove the flesh to prevent it rotting, which may kill the seeds. However, Cotoneaster fruits can be sown with the flesh intact. Larger individual fruits that contain a single seed, such as Acer, need only surface drying before being put into storage.

The seeds of horse chestnut trees are encased in spiky capsules.

Store seeds in plastic bags or small paper envelopes. Make sure the surface of the seeds is dry, otherwise the paper will disintegrate, or in plastic they may rot. Store seeds in the refrigerator to keep them for longer.

Germination Having acquired your seed, the next phase is to germinate it. Most really fine seeds will germinate immediately, but many of the larger seeds have dormant periods before germination. Since larger seeds are not produced very often, they need to be sure conditions are right before they germinate—because they have their own food reserves they can afford to wait. For example, a seed may remain dormant until several weeks of cold soil temperatures have passed. That way it can be sure the worst of the winter chill period is over and it is now safe to start putting down roots. Such seeds should be sown during fall in trays placed in a cold frame, and left over the winter to go through their cold dormancy period naturally.

Another common form of dormancy is caused by a hard or thick seed coat that must be broken down before it can germinate. The seeds of Cotoneaster and Juniperus are among the hardest and may take up to five years to germinate. The seed coats are so hard because they are designed to be eaten by birds and passed through the gut. Most species with this type of seed coat will also require a cool period of further dormancy before germinating.

The thinner waxy coat of trees and shrubs in the Legume family, such as Acacia, can be mechanically scoured, or "scarified." To do this, use a file to scratch through the waxy layer in a section of the seed, which will enable it to absorb water and so germinate.

Some seeds experience a two-stage dormancy, whereby a root is put out after one condition is satisfied, but the shoot only grows later after a further dormancy requirement is met. Some varieties of Quercus fall into this category. In practice, sow in the fall and be prepared to wait.

Sowing Seeds are usually sown in the fall in seed trays and then kept over winter in a cold frame outdoors if they can withstand the low temperatures, or under cover in a greenhouse or propagator if they are less hardy. Some temperate plants should only be raised in a greenhouse in spring.

To stimulate germination, soak larger seeds overnight before sowing. To decide if the seeds are large enough to soak, consider whether you will still be able to handle them when wetted. If the seed is fine dust, then the answer is no, but if each seed is 1/10in (2–3mm) or

TIP

Cold dormancy can be artificially broken, if you are sowing these type of seeds in spring, by putting damp seed in the refrigerator for three or more weeks. This simulates the experience of "hibernating" in cold soil.

Sow seeds in trays and cover for the winter.

larger, the answer is yes. Seeds that store their reserves as oils, including Acer, Magnolia, and Quercus, are particularly susceptible to drying out.

Seeds require a starting mix for sowing, which does not need to be rich in nutrients but should be moist and freely draining. Sow seeds with enough space in between to allow them to grow without being crowded, then cover them over according to their size. The small dustlike seeds of Betula, Buddleja, and Rhododendron will require no more than a fine dusting of sand to hold them in place, while larger seeds should be covered by a depth of starting mix equivalent to the size of the seed.

Thoroughly soak the mix before sowing and do not allow it to dry out. With fine seeds, if the mix is suitably moist from the start, then you may not need to carry out any further watering before germination occurs. If watering is required, however, do so from below by standing the pot in a bowl of water. Larger seeds protected by a layer of starting mix can be watered gently from above.

When the seeds have germinated, they can either be potted up individually, as soon as they are large enough to handle, or left to grow until the second spring. Avoid potting up until there are two adult leaves, and never hold a small seedling by its stem—always use a leaf or cotyledon (seed leaf). Pot on using a potting mix with sufficient nutrients to support growth or, failing that, provide weekly feeds.

Protect seeds from mice and birds by covering them over with wire netting. Germinating seedlings make tasty meals for slugs, while scarid flies in the soil mix will eat the roots. Fungal diseases can also be a problem, more so if the seedlings are densely packed, but this can be avoided by spraying with a fungicide.

By cuttings

Cuttings can be taken as softwood, semi-ripe, and hardwood cuttings. When raising plants from cuttings, the main requirement is to keep the cutting alive while it forms roots. The shorter this time is, the quicker and better will be the resultant plant. The speed and timing of rooting is largely determined by the presence of plant hormones, or "auxins," but these can be introduced by dipping the cuttings into proprietary hormonal rooting powders.

Potting mixes for propagating cuttings must be able to retain moisture but at the same time be free-draining, so that the cutting can absorb oxygen, and they must also be sterile to prevent rotting. Mix humus-rich soil and sand in proportions of three parts soil to one of sand, or half and half for maximum drainage. Vermiculite and perlite can also be used in combination with the humus-rich soil but are often used on their own. Proprietary potting mixes specifically tailored for propagating cuttings are also widely available.

Hardwood cuttings Deciduous shrubs do not give successful cuttings in late fall, but they can be propagated from hardwood cuttings in late winter when the shrubs are leafless or almost leafless.

Select a bed in a shaded part of the garden and dig a trench about 7in (17cm) deep to hold the cuttings [A]. Place sand in the bottom of the trench to assist with drainage. Select healthy, fully matured sideshoots and cut them off just above the junction with the older wood of the main stem. Remove remaining leaves and trim each cutting to a length of 10in (25cm) [B]. Treat the base with rooting hormone, cutting a wound if necessary. Place in the trench and drag soil over the cuttings [C], burying them to two-thirds of their length at a spacing of 8in (20cm) apart [D]. Lift the cuttings the following fall and either plant them out or grow them on in a nursery bed for a year.

A

B

C

D

Semi-ripe cuttings Propagating with semi-ripe cuttings works especially well with conifers and some evergreen trees and shrubs. Semi-ripe cuttings are taken from new shoots later in the growing season, in late summer or early fall, which are woody at the base but still soft at the tip. They can either be cut with a "heel" of the old wood at the base, or just below the node of a leaf, shoot, or bud on the stem. Making a cut below a node or with a heel will assist with rooting as growth hormones concentrate in these areas.

TIP

Take leafy cuttings early in the day rather than late afternoon because plants tend to be fully erect in the morning and slightly wilted by the evening. Also, make sure the parent plant is healthy and not suffering from drought.

The method of propagation is similar to softwood cuttings but with a few differences. As well as removing the lower sets of leaves, you may need to cut off the soft tip or it may rot. If there are sideshoots, these should also be removed. In addition, the base of the cutting can be wounded to improve rooting. To cut a wound, remove a thin sliver of bark at the base of the stem on one or both sides, just over 1in (about 3cm) long. The wound increases the cut surface, so that water and rooting hormone are more readily absorbed, and it also increases the production of hormones. Dip the cutting into rooting hormone, then plant in a ready-made hole in the potting mix and lightly water in.

If propagating with pots in a cold frame, keep them covered over winter and insulate if necessary. Then, harden off over the next growing season and either plant out in the fall or pot on and wait until the following spring. Cuttings grown in a propagator over winter can usually be potted on or planted out the following spring.

Softwood cuttings Softwood cuttings are taken from shoots in late spring or early summer when the current season's growth is soft and has not become woody at the base. Using a knife, cut off a young shoot

A

B

C

about 4–6in (10–15cm) in length, or shorter for slower-growing shrubs. Ensure the bottom is cut off neatly. Then remove the lower leaves, leaving 2–4 pairs of leaves at the tip.

Dip the base of the cutting into rooting hormone, then insert the cutting into a tray or pot filled with suitable potting mix and gently water it in. Do not push the cutting directly into the soil or you will rub off the rooting hormone. Use a dibber to make the planting hole instead. Keep the planted cuttings in a humid atmosphere by placing them in a propagator or by covering them with polyethylene sheeting—pots can be covered with a polyethylene bag.

Cuttings may root within two weeks but it can take several months, particularly for slow-growing shrubs. After rooting has occurred, pot on the cuttings into separate pots and, after a few days, gradually harden them off by letting in more air. If at any time they become wilted, place them under cover once again.

Layering

Layering involves holding a section of a shoot in the ground so that over the course of a year or so it develops roots and forms a new plant. This propagation technique is particularly useful for slow-to-root trees and shrubs.

Select a vigorous stem whose tip can be bent down to ground level. On the top side of the stem, about 16in (40cm) from the tip, make a slanting cut in the direction of the tip; if the cut is made on the bottom side, the stem snaps. Apply rooting hormone. Dig out a shallow hole, then hold down the wounded portion of the stem and backfill with well-drained potting mix, staking the shoot tip with a split cane and holding the branch firm with a stone. A year later the shoot should have put down roots, and it can be severed from the parent plant and grown on.

Grafting

The technique of grafting comprises attaching a piece of the plant you wish to propagate, called the scion, onto the roots of another, the rootstock. The result should be that they end up growing as a single plant with the characteristics of the scion and, often, the growth habit of the rootstock.

Grafting is used for difficult-to-root subjects, for example Picea and Pinus cultivars, but is also useful where a rootstock can be used to convey an advantage to a tree or shrub, such as a particular resistance to disease or a dwarfing growth habit for ornamental trees.

Scions and rootstocks from the same genus or family of plants are likely to be compatible, but it comes down to trial and error. Scions should be selected from vigorous stems, usually one-year-old and with at least three buds, trimmed down to between 4–8in (10–20cm) in length. Grow your own rootstocks from young plants propagated from seed or by cuttings a year or so in advance, or buy them directly from a garden center or nursery.

Grafting is mainly carried out in late winter on dormant scions but when the rootstocks are starting to grow, or in late summer when the scion variety has made the current year's growth. However, both the scion and the rootstock are still capable of quickly forming a callus over the wound.

Side-veneer grafting

The most common form of grafting is with a side-veneer. As with all grafting, the object is to match up as accurately as possible the "cambium" of the scion with that of the rootstock. The cambium is the layer between bark and wood made up of cells that divide to make wood on the inside and bark on the outside. Hence the thickness of the scion and rootstock should be the same, so that the cambiums can be matched on both sides of the cuts.

Take a sharp knife and at a point 2–4in (5–10cm) from the top of the rootstock make a shallow, downward slanting cut just over 1in (about 3cm) in length into the bark and surface wood of the rootstock, then remove the sliver of wood with a nick at the base of the cut [A]. Remove an equivalent sliver from the bottom of the scion so that it fits into the cut on the rootstock [B]. Hold the scion in place by binding with a tie [C].

Keep the graft in a moist environment to encourage callus formation to unite the scion and rootstock, which will take from two to six weeks. Then, in stages, slowly admit more and more air into the environment, and at the same time cut off bits of the rootstock down to the callus to encourage the scion to make growth.

Planting Combinations

Some plants go well together; equally, it is very obvious, at least after the event, that some combinations do not. The success of any combination is partly a matter of taste, but also a question of whether the planting scheme actually "works." A great variety of different colors, forms, and foliages mixed together can be very discordant, although occasionally it works. So how can we increase the chances of a scheme looking as good in practice as when we first conceived it?

I think there are several elements, but your personal taste may suggest others.

Seasonal considerations are important in any garden scheme.

Evergreens

The first consideration is that the planting scheme will be in your garden year-round. Therefore, it must take account of the changing seasons and look good in all of them. The right use of evergreens is invaluable here. Too few and the garden looks bare for half the year; too many and it is too dark for the other half. My opinion is that the garden landscape is enhanced by between 10 and 40 percent evergreens, with probably 20 to 25 percent being ideal. Evergreens exist as broad-leaved trees, shrubs, and many conifers. Most bamboos are also evergreen, for although the foliage may turn brown in cold periods, the shoots fulfill much the same function.

The next stage is to plan how to provide this evergreen element—should it be a few tall trees, or evergreen shrubs, and will evergreen conifers fit the situation better than broad-leaved evergreens, or is a combination best?

Scale

Scale is very important because each part of a feature in the garden needs to relate to the space available. Sometimes we can "borrow" space from our neighbors, perhaps using their tree or large shrub as a focal point, but generally we have to use the space within the garden. Therefore, large trees with rounded crowns—say a mature oak or *Platanus hispanica*—need space around them if they are to be specimen trees. There is little point in having the most beautifully proportioned oak if all except the branch on the far left is hidden from view by other features in the garden.

Shape is also important. A garden full of narrow spiky trees, such as *Juniperus communis* 'Hibernica', will look dull.

Use of features

Our eyes are used to the fall of land from a mountain top into a valley, whether seen from above (even if you live somewhere that is not especially mountainous), or from

Color and form are key elements in any planting combination.

beneath, or the view over water and marginal vegetation. This style of landscape can be utilized on a small scale in the garden. For instance, if your garden slopes, put the larger items at the top of the slope unless this causes some other problem. Rarely will it be wise to put the largest plants in a valley bottom if they are going to fill the valley. Similarly, it is common sense to put the larger items on the far side of a pond so that they can be seen reflected in the water, rather than on the nearside where they will hide the pond. If the site is level, such as a flat lawn, the view can be stopped by a bed of shrubs; this is similar to the hedge around a meadow and therefore has a certain rustic charm.

When planning combinations, consider when trees look their best.

Variety but conformity

Too much variety can be uncomfortable, like a choppy sea making one seasick. However, although a placid flat sea may suit those of a nauseous disposition, it soon tires for those seeking a modicum of stimulation.

A good planting scheme will achieve a combination of variety, so that each particular aspect of the scheme has its own character, while holding together as a planned setting.

Timing

Plants do their things at different times. This has two benefits; for instance, two plants whose flowers would clash if in bloom at the same time can be grown together because they come into flower at different times of the year. The other benefit of timing is that you can plant a variety to give color over an extended season. A garden should be designed to look good throughout the year, not just for one short period.

Quality plants

Always use quality plants. Just because a garden center will sell you a plant does not mean it is a good one for your garden. Many plants are selected for ease of propagation as much as they are for quality of flower, fruit, and foliage; an example is the common form of Leyland cypress, which is inferior to some of the other clones, but these are harder to raise and not commercially viable.

Select plants that look good after they have been grown in a garden for several years, not because they look good in a garden center. *Picea abies* is the common Christmas tree, but it is one of several spruces susceptible to a severe infestation by a sap-sucking aphid. Every now and then, the trees are devastated for a couple of years, so they are really not worth having; there are more beautiful spruces that are not affected by these aphids, such as *Picea breweriana* and *Picea omorika*.

Be prepared to be different

Finally, be different. Too much of modern culture is based on having (or wanting) whatever everyone else has. But never forget that your garden is your own, not anyone else's. And be prepared to experiment; if it doesn't work, there is always the compost heap...

Trees & Shrubs

This section includes most of the trees and shrubs included in the book. There are separate sections for Bamboos (pages 129–132), Tree ferns & Palms (page 133) and Conifers (pages 134–151). The plants covered range from medium shrubs, such as Cotinus and Euonymus, to large trees, such as Fagus and *Tilia* 'Petiolaris'. The main unifying feature in this section is their general suitability for use in the garden.

The size and spread after five years and ten years are indicative of what may be expected if the soil is well drained and reasonably fertile. If given lush conditions, many plants can exceed the suggested dimensions; similarly, on weedy or barren sites, they may take twice as long to grow to any size. The sizes assume that the planting stock is of a normal size for the individual shrub. Most of the time, shrubs will be planted as stock at around 16in (40cm) in height. Many trees will be available at this size. However, trees are also available (at increasing cost) at much larger sizes. Many trees may only be available as feathered trees 5–8ft (1.5–2.5m) in height or standard trees around 8–12ft (2.5–3.7m) tall. This can make quite an impact upon the height, especially after five years, and the most likely planting height is used as a starting point for the size and spread tables. Larger planting stock can give an immeditate impact and has its place in planting schemes. However, it is often slow to get established and may not be any larger over a five- or ten-year period than smaller trees.

Acacia

Wattle

The wattles characterize the savannas of East Africa and are also a major component of the forests of Australia. The hardy species of wattle originate from these areas in Australia.

The flowers are mainly yellow and carried over the winter/spring period. The species featured here have flowers in globular heads, but others have them in cylindrical "bottlebrushes." Although they are members of the legume family, they do not have typical pealike flowers with five arranged petals; instead, the main attraction of the flowers is the massed stamens.

The foliage of Acacia is also interesting. The standard foliage is bipinnate, with masses of small leaflets—⅙in (4mm) by less than 1/25in (1mm) in *Acacia dealbata*. However, this form persists only in species from moist environments. In drier climates, leaves are soon abandoned in favor of modified leaf-stalks, which are tough and often oblong.

Acacia retinodes

Acacia pravissima

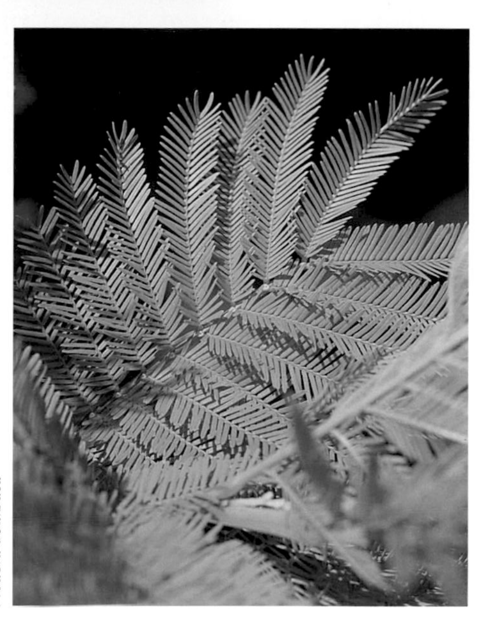

Acacia dealbata

soil 	Plant in any suitable well-drained soil but avoid limy conditions.
site 	Plant in sun with side shelter away from any cold winds
pruning 	Not much pruning required, except to remove any unsightly dieback
general care 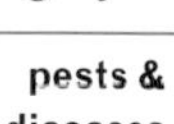	Fast-growing but half-hardy to frost tender and likely to be trimmed back by cold conditions every few years
pests & diseases 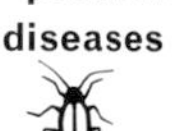	Relatively trouble-free; pests and diseases do not usually cause any particular problems

Wattles are mainly trees or large shrubs for open sites in full sun. They are not reliably hardy, even in mild areas, so choose a sheltered site or grow them against a wall. More than light shade will result in fewer flowers. They thrive in any well-drained soil but will not flourish on shallow chalky soils.

Acacia can be propagated from seed (pour boiling water over them, equal to the volume of the seeds, and leave to cool down) and by semi-ripe cuttings in summer. Some species sucker and these can be lifted with care and grown on.

	SPRING			SUMMER			FALL			WINTER			height 5yrs (ft)	height 10yrs (ft)	spread 5yrs (ft)	spread 10yrs (ft)	flower color	
Acacia baileyana	✹	✹									✹	✹	10	20	8		☐	Vivid blue foliage, long drooping wands
A. dealbata	✹	✹									✹	✹	16	33	13		☐	Silvery downy leaves, common tree form
A. pravissima	✹	✹									✹	✹	16	36	13		☐	Leaves absent, phyllodes present
A. retinodes				✹	✹								5	10	3	4	☐	Phyllodes gray-green, tolerant of alkaline soils

✹ *flowering*

Acer

Maple

The maples are a large genus of over 100 species and many cultivars. The species range in size from shrubs to the largest of broad-leaved trees. The species are mainly deciduous, although in warm temperate and tropical areas there are evergreen ones. Maples offer a range of attractive features, particularly with their foliage.

Acer shirasawanum 'Aureum'

Foliage can vary from boldly lobed leaves to the delicately cut or dissected leaves of some selections of Japanese maple. The color of the foliage is golden green in a number of selections, such as *Acer shirasawanum* 'Aureum' and *Acer cappadocicum* 'Aureum', purple in many forms of *Acer palmatum* and *Acer platanoides*, and various hues of green in others. In the fall, the colors can be spectacular, from a butter-yellow in *Acer cappadocicum* to brilliant red in *Acer rubrum*.

Flowers are not their strongest feature but in *Acer platanoides* they open before the leaves. By contrast, the bark of maples can be the most striking feature, such as with the various snake-bark maples.

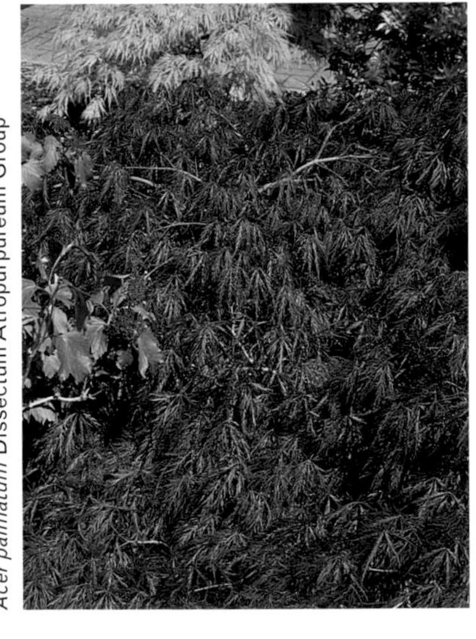

Acer palmatum Dissectum Atropurpureum Group

Maples divide into those that are naturally under-story trees, and those that are dominant forest trees. The former will tolerate some shade, whereas the forest types will only tolerate shade while young. However, they will all grow happily in full sun. They generally grow on all soil types but not waterlogged soils. Some species do not like much chalk or lime in the soil, especially if the soil is thin—Japanese maples come into this category.

Maples can be propagated from seed, by cuttings, and also grafting. Seed can be sown as soon as it is ripe and kept in a cool greenhouse or frame, where it should germinate in the first spring. However, if allowed to dry out, it may become dormant and germinate only in the second spring. Seed that is bought has often been dried and will therefore have a dormancy period. The simplest way to treat the seeds is to soak overnight, then sow with a covering of grit or seed starting mix and wait. Or else mix with damp starting mix in a polyethylene bag and place in the refrigerator; after three months, sow or wait until the seeds start to germinate and then prick them out.

Cuttings are an effective way of propagating maples if you can get them to make growth before they become dormant. Take them as softwood cuttings as soon as the leaves are fully expanded. Keep the rooted plants on the dry side (not bone dry) over the first winter and increase the water only after they have come into leaf in the spring—they will die if too wet.

soil	Any well-drained soil, preferably fertile and deep if the soil is chalky
site	Will tolerate being planted in areas that receive sun or dappled shade
pruning	Maples tend to bleed if cut; this is reduced if they are pruned in mid-summer
general care	Mulch the soil to aid moisture retention in the summer, and also to control weeds
pests & diseases	Verticillium wilt and coral spot can affect many species. Tar spot and aphids can affect leaves but do little harm

Grafting is also simple, as long as you get the conditions right. Use similar species: for example, for Japanese maples, use *Acer palmatum* seedlings. The simplest method is to graft in mid- to late summer. Dry the stock plant so that it is not quite wilted and remove the top half; use a side-veneer technique with a two-year-old scion whose leaves are cut off at the petiole, tying in gently and place in a cold frame. After 10 days, if the graft has taken, the petioles will fall off. Slowly increase the water. The graft may shoot in the fall but most will not move until spring. Cut back the rootstock in spring and grow on.

Japanese maples

Acer palmatum 'Butterfly'

These are mainly cultivars of *A. palmatum* but also include two other Japanese species (*Acer japonicum* and *Acer shirasawanum*) and the closely related *Acer circinatum* (Vine maple) from western North America. They make large shrubs, to about 13ft (4m) in 10 years, but will grow on to make trees 20–50ft (6–15m) in 50–100 years. They are understory trees in broad-leaved or conifer woodland. Accordingly, they will tolerate light to moderate, but not dense, shade. They also like protection from spring frosts and cold dry winds, which woodland conditions give. In the garden, you can use hardy screening plants, such as bamboos or other shrubs, to give the necessary shelter.

Japanese maples are the structural plants of most Japanese-style gardens, and are particularly effective if planted to reflect over water. They can also make useful plants for containers. Care with watering is important, otherwise the foliage will become brown between the veins—this can be a symptom of drought or an indicator of overwatering. Also, vine weevil can be a bugbear to maples in containers.

Acer palmatum

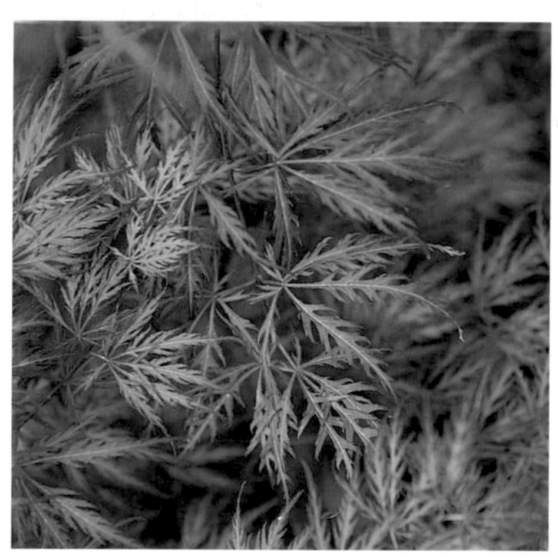

Acer palmatum 'Garnet'

Snake-bark maples

Acer davidii

Snake-bark maples belong to a distinct section in the genus that includes about 20 species. Their chief horticultural character is in the bark. This is some form of green (or red in one-year shoots and candy-pink in *Acer pensylvanicum* 'Erythrocladum'), which fissures to reveal pure white striations running up and down the trunk like a snake. The bark feature is present throughout the year, but at its best for the winter season. It is shown off to best effect in vigorously growing trees. The foliage is usually lobed, except in *Acer davidii*, and in some species turns a clear yellow in the fall. *Acer forrestii* has particularly attractive leaves which are three lobed.

Snake-bark maples attain 20–26ft (6–8m) in about 15 years but only slowly growing taller thereafter. They make excellent specimen trees, either in the lawn or in light woodland. The habit is arching, with weeping outer branchlets.

Remember, when planting into lawns, however, to keep a good 3ft (1m) radius clear of grass because the bark is easily damaged by mowers and weed wackers.

Small tree maples

Small tree maples offer a number of characteristics, and are small to medium trees making 25–40ft (8–12m). The paperbark maple, *Acer griseum*, is outstanding in two ways: the cinnamon-colored bark peels off in thin, paperlike flakes, looking attractive throughout the year. Resist the temptation to peel off the flakes—it is much better with a shaggy coat than "close shaved." The other outstanding feature is excellent fall color, turning red and scarlet. It grows better in well-drained acidic loams but will grow slowly on quite thin soils over chalk.

Acer cappadocicum 'Aureum'

Acer griseum

Another species with trifoliate leaves is *Acer maximowicziana* (syn. *Acer nikkoense*). The bark is tight, but in fall the foliage colors orange and red. Another species with leaves composed of leaflets, not single leaves, is *Acer negundo*, the inappropriately named "box elder." It can look good, especially the male forms when the male flowers hang down from the shoots before the leaves.

In *Acer cappadocicum* 'Aureum', the leaves soon become golden yellow. *Acer cappadocicum* is also unusual among maples in that it produces suckers from the roots and these offer a method of propagation. *Acer ginnala* is a shrubby tree, which turns orange and crimson in the fall.

Large tree maples

Large tree maples are bold specimen trees, rather too large for the average modern garden but well suited to the distant parts of larger gardens, and also much used in public parks. They have the potential to reach around 65ft (20m) in height with domed crowns 65ft (20m) across. *Acer platanoides*, the Norway maple, is one of the few maples worth planting for the flowers—these are pale yellow and open just before the leaves. In the purple-leaved forms the flowers are tinged with red. Several selections have leaves that are crimson-purple.

The sycamore maple, *Acer pseudoplatanus*, is a pet hate of many gardeners, due to its ability to seed freely. However, provided their heads are chopped off at the stage when only the pair of cotyledons show, they are easily controlled. When mature, the sycamore maple can be majestic, with a domed crown of billowing branches. Young trees, however, are

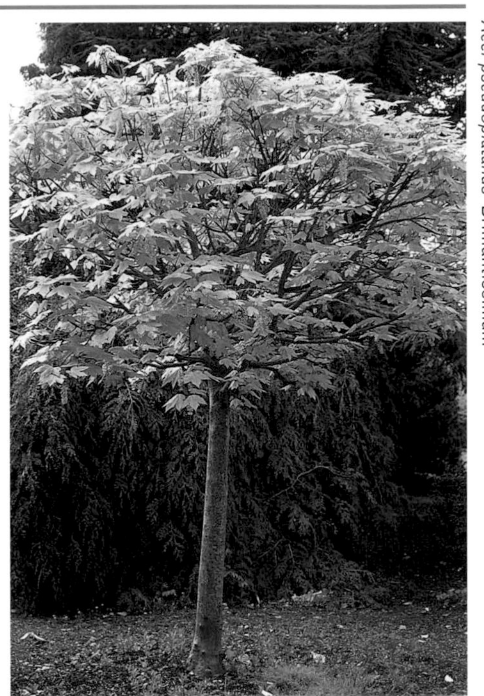
Acer pseudoplatanus 'Brilliantissimum'

spiky. 'Brilliantissimum' is a slow-growing form whose foliage opens a brilliant shrimp-pink, before passing through yellow-green to (a slightly mottled) green.

The red maple, *Acer rubrum*, has leaves silvery beneath, which turn brilliant red and scarlet in the fall. It will grow on chalky soils but tends to be somewhat chlorotic and not

Acer palmatum 'Sango-kaku'

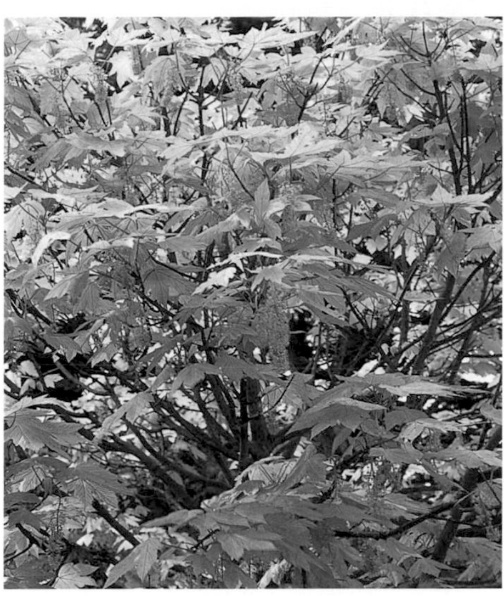

Acer pseudoplatanus 'Brilliantissimum'

to color well. Silver maple, *Acer saccharinum*, also has leaves glaucous beneath but they are deeply dissected. The fall color is fair, and it makes a fast-growing, more upright dome above the trees. Both red and silver maples flower early.

	SPRING			SUMMER			FALL			WINTER			height 5yrs (ft)	height 10yrs (ft)	spread 5yrs (ft)	spread 10yrs (ft)	color of blossom	
[JAPANESE] *A. japonicum* 'Vitiifolium'			flowering										4	8	4	8		Large leaves to 6in, good fall color
A. palmatum			flowering										5	8	5	8		5–7 lobed leaves, can slowly make a tree 26ft+
A. palmatum f. *atropurpureum*			flowering										4	6½	4	6		Leaves mainly 5-lobed, rich reddish color
A. palmatum 'Garnet'			flowering										3	5	3	5		Red-orange during summer, scarlet in fall
A. palmatum 'Sangu Kaku'			flowering										5	8	5	8		Yellowish-green leaves; small tree in 30 years
A. shirasawanum 'Aureum'			flowering										8	20	8	20		Leaves golden yellow
[SNAKE-BARK] *A. capillipes*			flowering				harvest	harvest					8	16	8	16		Leaves with reddish petioles, bright green
A. davidii			flowering				harvest	harvest					8	16	8	16		Leaves unlobed, sometimes yellow
A. forrestii			flowering				harvest	harvest					8	16	8	16		Shoots red in first year, then jade-green
A. pensylvanicum 'Erythrocladum'			flowering										8	16	8	16		First year shoots pink, crimson late fall
A. rufinerve			flowering				harvest	harvest					8	16	8	16		Leaves rusty hairy beneath, bark green
[SMALL TREE] *A. campestre*		flowering											13	23	10	20		Yellow fall color, grows well on chalky soil
A. cappadocicum 'Aureum'		flowering											13	20	13	16		Gold-yellow foliage in summer, gold in fall
A. griseum		flowering					harvest	harvest					10	16	6½	13		Fall color red and scarlet
A. negundo	flowering												13	23	10	20		Leaves with 5 or 7 leaflets
[LARGE TREE] *A. platanoides*		flowering					harvest	harvest					20	30	13	20		Tall tree, good fall color
A. pseudoplatanus			flowering				harvest	harvest					20	30	13	20		Makes a majestic tree with time
A. pseudoplatanus 'Brilliantissimum'			flowering										6½	10	6½	10		Brilliant shrimp-pink new foliage
A. rubrum	flowering			harvest									16	26	13	20		Good red fall color
A. saccharinum	flowering			harvest									20	26	13	20		Leaves silvery beneath

flowering *harvest*

Aesculus

Horse chestnut *or* Buckeye

Horse chestnut (*Aesculus hippocastanum*) is widely grown for the large candles of white flowers with pink, red, or yellow spots that rise from buds on last year's shoots in mid- to late spring, and for its shiny, nutlike seeds.

It grows at a steady 12–16in (30–40cm) a year until 70ft (20m) in height, by which time it is a large tree with a high domed crown. It will tolerate a wide range of soil types, from chalk to damp, heavy clays. To flower, it needs full sun but it will grow in shade. The leaves are digitate or palmate with 5–7 leaflets. The cultivar 'Baumannii' is sterile, setting no seed. It is useful for sites where it is unsafe for children to hurl sticks to get the seed cases down. But if you have space for *Aesculus hippocastanum* in your garden, plant the fertile form. The red horse chestnut (*Aesculus* x *carnea*) has rose-pink flowers. *Aesculus* x *carnea* makes a smaller tree, which is interesting in flower but otherwise the foliage is rather dull and the trunk is inclined to suffer from canker.

soil	Will grow well in any good, moist but well-drained garden soil, including chalk
site	Grow in sun or partial shade; suitable only for large gardens
pruning	None needed except to maintain a good shape or thin out the dense foliage
general care	Apply mulch to retain moisture in the soil during the summer and prevent early leaf-fall
pests & diseases	A leaf blotch can cause unsightly foliage and early leaf loss, also prone to canker, coral spot, and scale insects

However, there are other species to choose from. *Aesculus neglecta* 'Erythroblastos' is a small tree whose new foliage is a brilliant shrimp-pink, slowly fading to yellow-green. As a spring foliage plant, it is outstanding. It is slow growing and must be sheltered from spring frosts. The flowers are a peachy pink, but plant it for the spring foliage. *Aesculus parviflora* is a suckering shrub. It will not grow taller than 6½–8ft (2–2.5m) but with time may spread 16–18ft (5–6m). No garden is too small to have this species. However, the best species is the medium-sized Indian horse chestnut, *Aesculus indica*. The flowers are some six weeks later than the horse chestnut. However, beware that this superior tree can be damaged by spring frost when young.

Aesculus indica

Horse chestnuts should be propagated by seed, except for 'Baumannii', which has to be grafted, and *Aesculus parviflora*, which will grow from root cuttings taken in late winter.

	SPRING			SUMMER			FALL			WINTER			height 5yrs (ft)	height 10yrs (ft)	spread 5yrs (ft)	spread 10yrs (ft)	color of blossom	
Aesculus carnea 'Briottii'			flowering										13	20	3	6		"Red" flowers but dull foliage
A. hippocastanum		flowering					harvest	harvest					16	23	4	7		Dense foliage; fall color variable
A. hippocastanum 'Baumannii'		flowering											16	23	4	7		No seeds
A. indica				flowering	flowering				harvest				16	23	4	7		Excellent medium-sized tree; fall color good
A. neglecta 'Erythroblastos'			flowering										10	16	2	4		Shrimp-pink new foliage; fall color good
A. parviflora					flowering	flowering							3	6½	1.5	3		Valuable late summer flowering shrub

flowering harvest

Ailanthus

Tree of heaven

***Ailanthus altissima,* the most interesting species, is a fine tree with large leaves composed of many leaflets. The flowers are carried in the summer on large terminal clusters on the current season's shoots. They are greenish-white with a fetid smell on male trees. The foliage also has a somewhat unpleasant smell if touched.**

The female trees produce the seeds, which have a twisted wing; immature fruits are red or green, with the red ones showing up well, even on a tall tree. Ailanthus makes a vigorous specimen tree, ideal for a large garden when a bold tree is required, probably making 50ft (15m) in 20–25 years. The foliage is red colored in spring and is normally 1–2ft (30–60cm) in length. However, on vigorous young trees it can be 3ft (90cm).

To grow the tree, even in small gardens, coppice the plant in late winter. It will produce one to several shoots; select the most vigorous and remove the others. Feed, mulch, and water this shoot to make a stem 6½–10ft (2–3m) in length with leaves up to 3ft (90cm) or more by the end of the summer.

It will grow in a wide range of soil types, tolerating poor and barren city center soils better than many trees. The fall color is negligible, although the bark is interestingly fissured with buff streaks.

Ailanthus can be propagated by seed. It suckers freely in some situations and these can be removed, or you could try root cuttings in late winter.

soil 	Not suitable for water-logged sites but otherwise plant in any garden soil
site 	Plant in sun or partial shade; needs space so suitable for large gardens
pruning 	No pruning needed except to restrict size; will grow as a shrub if pruned hard annually
general care 	Watch out for suckers growing in the wrong places; manure and mulch for best foliage
pests & diseases 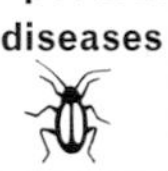	Relatively trouble-free; pests and diseases do not usually cause any particular problems

Ailanthus altissima

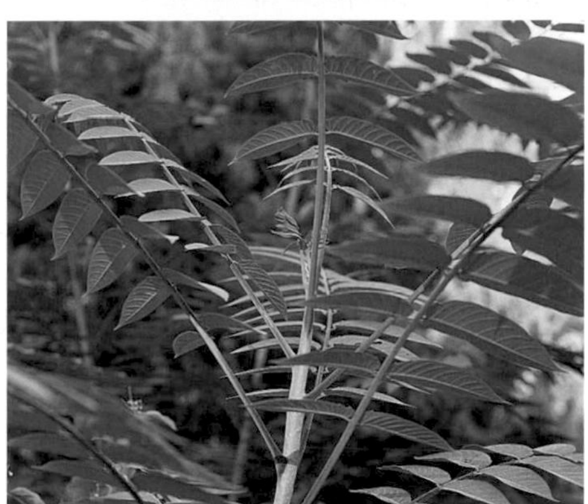

Ailanthus altissima

Alnus
Alder

Alders are often found growing beside water, especially the common alder, *Alnus glutinosa*. However, they will thrive in any normal garden soil except shallow chalky ones, but they are able to tolerate the poor conditions found in swampy sites.

Alders are at home in the water garden but are useful in a number of other locations. Their chief horticultural merit is in the male catkins. These expand in late winter or early spring, giving a purple (*Alnus glutinosa*), red (*Alnus incana*), or yellow (*Alnus cordata*) haze to the tree. The woody cones follow and often persist; they can be used for festive decorations or in flower arrangements. The fall color is usually poor. The forms of gray alder, *Alnus incana*, include the 'Aurea' with yellow-green foliage, and also the weeping 'Pendula'.

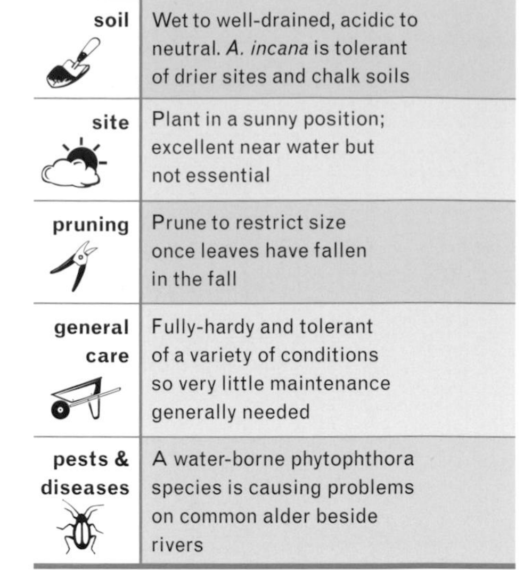

soil	Wet to well-drained, acidic to neutral. *A. incana* is tolerant of drier sites and chalk soils
site	Plant in a sunny position; excellent near water but not essential
pruning	Prune to restrict size once leaves have fallen in the fall
general care	Fully-hardy and tolerant of a variety of conditions so very little maintenance generally needed
pests & diseases	A water-borne phytophthora species is causing problems on common alder beside rivers

Alnus incana

In addition to the trees featured here, there are a number of shrubby species that can make tanglewoods for the wild garden. Alders are used for shelter plantings in orchards as they come into leaf and flower earlier than apples and other fruit trees, thereby giving protection against spring frosts. They are also small trees that do not spread widely.

Alders can be propagated by seed; sow the small seeds on the surface of damp starting mix and cover with a thin layer of sand or grit no deeper than the seeds' own depth. Cuttings of semi-ripe shoots in summer should root. *Alnus incana* will produce suckers, which can be separated.

	SPRING	SUMMER	FALL	WINTER	height 5yrs (ft)	height 10yrs (ft)	spread 5yrs (ft)	spread 10yrs (ft)	color of blossom	
Alnus cordata	flowering		harvest harvest harvest	flowering	20	33	13	20		Fast-growing tree with narrow habit
A. glutinosa	flowering		harvest harvest harvest	flowering	13	23	6½	13		Good for waterlogged sites; no fall color
A. incana	flowering		harvest harvest harvest	flowering	16	26	10	13		Neat habit, suckers
A. incana 'Aurea'	flowering			flowering	13	20	6½	10		Yellow-green leaves, reddish shoots

flowering   harvest

Amelanchier

Snowy mespilus

These are deciduous shrubs or small shrubby trees. They are grown mainly for the snowy white flowers in late spring that emerge with, or just ahead of, the foliage. The new foliage is a coppery red for a few days, especially in *Amelanchier lamarckii* where it contrasts with the flowers to good effect.

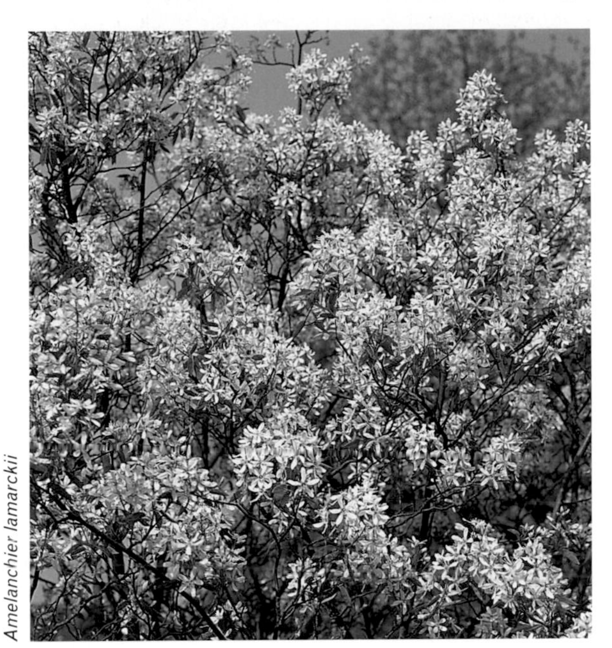

Amelanchier lamarckii

The fruits ripen in early to mid-summer but are normally eaten by the birds before you notice them. They are black or purplish-red and like miniature apples. Fall color is excellent—red and orange—especially on bushes grown in the full sun.

Snowy mespilus is at home on sandy heaths, as well as in fertile garden soils. They make excellent large shrubs for a border, as a backcloth or boundary planting, or as a specimen in the lawn. They can be propagated by seed sown as soon as it is ripe or by layers. Cuttings can be attempted but are rather difficult to root.

soil	Both trees: well-drained to moist. Amelanchier: acidic to neutral; avoid chalk soils
site	Amelanchier: sun to moderate shade. Aralia: sun to dappled shade
pruning	Amelanchier: only to restrict. Aralia: likewise or as coppicing for bold foliage
general care	Amelanchier: easy to grow. Aralia: On too fertile sites, the wood is pithy and liable to frost damage over winter
pests & diseases	Amelanchier: can get fire blight. Aralia: fairly trouble-free from pests and diseases

Aralia

Devil's walking stick *or* Japanese angelica tree

This tree is so named because of the suckers it produces. These do not branch until 6½ft or so (around 2m) in height. Instead, and particularly after the leaves have fallen, they appear as stout rods or walking sticks—apart, that is, from the dense and sharp spines.

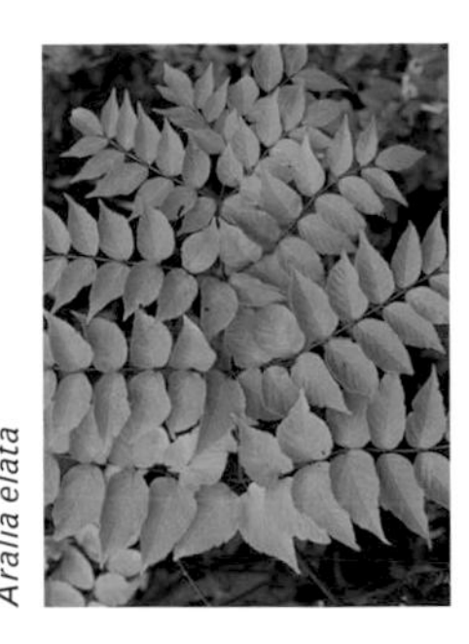

Aralia elata

The foliage consists of enormous compound leaves, which are bipinnate and rather deltoid in shape. The leaves can be 3ft (90cm) long by 2ft (60cm) wide, but if the plant is cut back and mulched and manured, they can reach up to 4ft (1.2m) long. The flowers are white, in large showy panicles in the fall. In the garden, the woody Aralia should be sited in a shrub bed, as a specimen small tree where it can be viewed from many angles, or in the wild garden.

It can be propagated from seed but the best method is to separate off a root sucker or take root cuttings.

	SPRING	SUMMER	FALL	WINTER	height 5yrs (ft)	height 10yrs (ft)	spread 5yrs (ft)	spread 10yrs (ft)	flower color	
Amelanchier grandiflora 'Ballerina'	flowering	harvest			5	8	5	8		Flowers—large racemes, blue-black, edible fruit
A. lamarckii	flowering	harvest			5	8	5	8		Flowers in small racemes, can make 20–26ft
Aralia elata			flowering, flowering, harvest		10	16	3	10		Grown for its bold foliage

flowering harvest

Arbutus

Strawberry tree *or* Madroño

These evergreen trees and large shrubs are members of the heather family, which is shown by their bell-shaped flowers. However, unlike most members of the family, they thrive on chalk and limy soils, as well as on acidic sands and anything else that is freely drained.

Of the species featured, *Arbutus unedo* is the best one for flowers and fruits. The white blooms are carried in the fall at the same time as the fruits from last year ripen. Thus it brings the two seasons of flower and fruit together in one strong display.

Arbutus menziesii

The form *rubra* has flowers that are tinged pink. This may sound more impressive than the normal white but it isn't. The delight of the white form is that the flowers contrast with and complement the yellow, orange-red, or scarlet ½–¾in (1.5–2cm) across "strawberry" fruits, but this is lost in f. *rubra.*

The fruits are edible and can be used for preserves, but they are quite bland. The bark is finely shredded but in the other two species it is outstanding—smooth and peeling in large sheets, which are red or yellow-pink in *Arbutus menziesii* and ruby-red or orange-red peeling to reveal orange-brown in *Arbutus andrachnoides.*

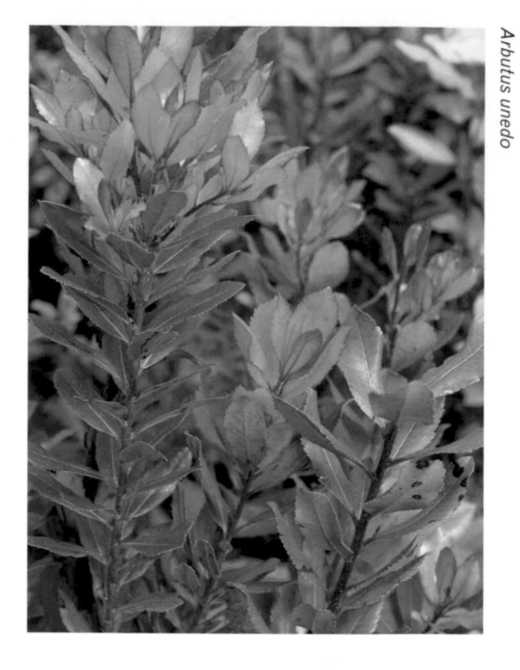

Arbutus unedo

Arbutus menziesii can make a large tree, albeit slow growing, whereas the other two are basically shrub trees, 20–26ft (6–8m) over 20–30 years. They should be used as specimen trees or as focal points in the garden, and *Arbutus unedo* can fit into a shrub bed for its evergreen foliage and season of display.

Propagation is by basal cuttings taken in late winter and rooted with some bottom heat, by layering, or by seed. Young plants of *A. andrachnoides* and *A. menziesii* can be tender and will need some initial winter protection.

soil	Prefers well-drained soils but can tolerate chalk, lime, and acid sands
site	The trees and shrubs of this family grow best in sun to light shade
pruning	None is required. *A. unedo* will coppice if it needs severe reshaping
general care	They need shelter as young plants, especially the seed-raised variety *A. menziesii*
pests & diseases	A fungus can cause blotches on the leaves but is not significant and causes no real damage

	SPRING	SUMMER	FALL	WINTER	height 5yrs (ft)	height 10yrs (ft)	spread 5yrs (ft)	spread 10yrs (ft)	flower color	
Arbutus andrachnoides	flowering		flowering, harvest		4	8	4	8	white	Hybrid between *A. andrachne* and *A. unedo*
A. menziesii	flowering		harvest		5	10	4	8	white	Wonderful bark, 50ft+ over a century
A. unedo			harvest, flowering, harvest, flowering		4	8	4	8	white	Evergreen and autumnal interest
A. unedo f. *rubra*			harvest, flowering, harvest, flowering		4	8	4	8	pink	Pink flowers—not as successful as white form

flowering · harvest

Aucuba

Spotted Aucuba is one of the hangovers from 19th-century shrubberies found in many inner city parks.

A worthwhile bush that grows in almost any soil, and in full sun to dense shade, deserves our consideration. Aucuba is one of the few shrubs that can make a pleasing display beneath the dense canopy of lime, beech, or even horse chestnut. The main requirement is either to plant hermaphrodite forms, such as 'Rozannie', or ensure that you plant both male and female selections. 'Variegata' will not be at her best without a male. Put the two together and the large red fruits of 'Rozannie' and the variegated foliage and red fruits of 'Variegata' will enliven any dead spot, or provide screening below the canopy of large trees. Propagate by basal cuttings in the fall and plant in the spring.

Aucuba japonica 'Crotonifolia'

Aucuba japonica 'Variegata'

soil	Aucuba: any freely drained soil. Azara: any, but best on deep humus-rich soils
site	Aucuba: dense shade to sun. Azara: prefers sun to dappled shade
pruning	For both shrubs, none is required except to reshape or restrict
general care	Aucuba: best planted in spring. Azara: keep sheltered from cold, drying winds
pests & diseases	Both are fairly trouble-free from pests and diseases, although Aucuba can suffer from scale insects

Azara

These evergreens have flowers that lack petals. The display is from the many stamens and its delicious scent.

Azara lanceolata

In *Azara microphylla*, the flowers are strongly vanilla-scented but borne beneath the level of the leaves and modestly hidden; whereas with *Azara lanceolata* the flowers are much more showy but not nearly as fragrant. Azaras grow on most soil types but need shelter in cold climates, especially against cold drying winds. They are excellent in mild areas in shrubberies, and in colder ones if grown against the wall of a house, especially where the aroma emanating from the flowers can be appreciated. Propagate by semi-ripe cuttings or by layers.

	SPRING			SUMMER			FALL			WINTER			height 5yrs (ft)	height 10yrs (ft)	spread 5yrs (ft)	spread 10yrs (ft)	color of blossom	
Aucuba japonica 'Crotonifolia'							harvest	harvest					4	6½	4	7		Female yellow-speckled leaves
A. japonica 'Rozannie'			flowering				harvest	harvest					4	6½	4	7		Self-fertile, freely berrying; broad green leaves
A. japonica 'Variegata'			flowering				harvest	harvest					4	6½	4	7		Leaves speckled with yellow
Azara lanceolata		flowering	flowering										4	8	4	8		Floriferous, masses of small flowerheads
A. microphylla	flowering												5	8	3	5		Fragrant small flowers
A. microphylla 'Variegata'	flowering												4	6½	2½	4		Leaves with a variable creamy white margin

 *flowering*  *harvest*

Betula

Birch

The birches include some of the most "garden worthy" of small trees. The male catkins in spring provide an attractive display before the leaves emerge, but other assets include their bark, foliage, habit, or spectacular fall color.

Betula nigra 'Heritage'

In many birches, the bark is rich in betulin, a compound that gives it a vivid whiteness. The bark of the European white birch (*Betula pendula*) is silvery white at the top of the tree, giving it a ghostlike aspect on a moonlit night, where as *Betula jacquemontii*, *Betula ermanii*, and *Betula papyrifera* have vivid white or creamy white barks. However, all birch barks aren't white, and for those who like something special, there are birches with copper and mahogany barks; some forms of *Betula utilis* are outstanding, with peeling sheets of burnished copper to almost shiny back, but these are less readily available.

All the forms listed will make trees 33–50ft (10–15m) in height over 20 to 30 years. They are surface rooting and will compete for soil moisture with other plants. They like well-drained soils, preferably not shallow, chalk ones. Propagate from seed, but if home-collected or where there are several species growing together, expect hybrids; sow on the starting mix surface and cover with a thin layer of sand or grit. Varieties can be grafted but this requires keeping the rootstock on the dry side while the union joins.

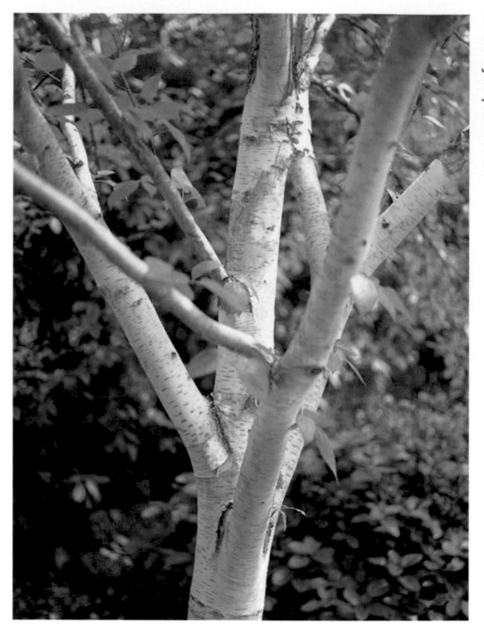

Betula jacquemontii

soil	Freely drained. *B.nigra*, *B. papyrifera*, and *B. pubescens* tolerate wet sites and clays
site	These trees prefer sun but no more than dappled shade if full sun is not possible
pruning	Minimal pruning. Avoid cutting in late winter/early spring as they will bleed
general care	Keep moist during dry periods in summer. In particular, do not allow the roots to dry out when transplanting trees
pests & diseases	No major problems: moribund and recently dead trees host the birch polypore bracket fungus (*P. betulinus*)

	SPRING	SUMMER	FALL	WINTER	height 5yrs (ft)	height 10yrs (ft)	spread 5yrs (ft)	spread 10yrs (ft)	color of blossom	
Betula albosinensis	flowering				13	23	10	16		Excellent orange-red, purple, or copper bark
B. ermanii	flowering				13	23	10	16		Creamy white to pink bark on branches/trunk
B. jacquemontii	flowering				13	23	10	16		Creamy white bark on trunk/main branches
B. nigra	flowering				13	20	10	13		Bark buff-pink/orange—brown peeling flakes
B. nigra 'Heritage'	flowering				13	23	10	16		Dark green leaves, light brown to cream bark
B. papyrifera	flowering				13	23	10	16		Stiff habit; good white bark and fall color
B. pendula	flowering				13	23	6½	13		Neat habit with variable weeping branches
B. pendula 'Laciniata'	flowering				13	23	6½	13		Drooping branches; also called 'Dalecarlica'
B. pendula 'Purpurea'	flowering				10	16	3	6½		Purple leaves; purple-tinged bark
B. pendula 'Tristis'	flowering				13	26	6½	13		Outstanding tree with narrow crown
B. pubescens	flowering				13	23	10	16		Dense leafy crown but poor bark
B. utilis	flowering				13	23	10	16		Best forms have peeling copper bark

flowering

Buddleja

Butterfly bush

These are chiefly grown for the very colorful and fragrant flowers, which have a strong honey scent and whose nectar attracts butterflies. The principal species in cultivation is *Buddleja davidii*, with a number of different color selections.

The attraction of the larger-growing group of Buddleja is that they provide fast-growing, medium shrubs or even small trees, which require very little in the way of maintenance. Left to its own devices, *Buddleja davidii* makes a small semi-evergreen tree perhaps 20ft (6m) in height and 13ft (4m) across. Having reached this size it virtually stops growing. In most situations where screening is wanted, it is only needed to a height of around 16ft (5m). Consider how much aggravation and hedge trimming could be

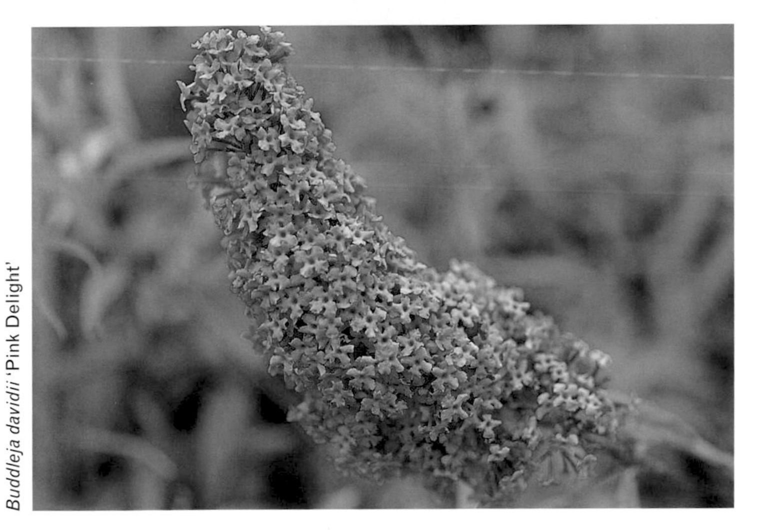

Buddleja davidii 'Pink Delight'

obviated if everyone planted *B. davidii* rather than Leyland cypress. Simplistic? Maybe, but just think of all those fragrant blooms and the butterflies they would attract. Untrimmed bushes also flower earlier in the summer than the heavily trimmed ones.

soil	Quite happy in most soils—acidic or chalky—as long as they are well drained
site	For the best results, plant these in a hot sunny position in the garden
pruning	They can all be coppiced and pruned either according to Group 2 or Group 1
general care	Make sure you know when your particular buddleja flowers, so that you can prune accordingly
pests & diseases	Relatively trouble-free. Pests and diseases do not usually cause any problems

Buddleja globosa starts flowering in late spring and is more fully evergreen. It makes a wider spreading bush, to 16ft (5m). *Buddleja weyeriana* is the hybrid between *globosa* and *davidii*. *Buddleja lindleyana* has racemes of purple-violet flowers. The other two species are for milder gardens or the shelter of a south-facing wall. *Buddleja colvilei* has individual flowers, which are over ½in (1cm) in length, carried in long drooping sprays of deep rose. *Buddleja salvifolia* has sagelike leaves and white or pale lavender blooms.

Buddleja thrive on any well-drained soil—*B. davidii* readily seeds itself on freely drained gravels and chalk cuttings. They can be propagated from semi-ripe cuttings taken in summer with a heel of older wood.

	SPRING			SUMMER			FALL			WINTER			height 5yrs (ft)	height 10yrs (ft)	spread 5yrs (ft)	spread 10yrs (ft)	flower color	
Buddleja colvilei				●	●	●							6	10	5	10		Best trained against a wall
B. davidii				●	●	●							6	10	5	10		Good nectar source for butterflies
B. globosa			●	●	●	●							6	10	5	10		Flowers in globose heads, leaves evergreen
B. lindleyana				●	●	●							6	8	5	6½		Small green leaves
B. salvifolia								●	●	●			6	10	5	10		Sagelike leaves
B. weyeriana					●	●	●						6	10	5	10		Fragrant, rounded, yellow to violet flowers

● *flowering*

Broussonetia
Paper mulberry

This is a relative of the mulberry, and similarly has a milky sap in the leaf stalk. It makes a small tree with a domed crown.

The flowers are carried on separate male and female trees. The male flowers are in long curly, yellow, pendulous catkins and release the pollen explosively. The female flowers are in pendulous, globose heads and are followed (if pollinated) by red or orange mulberrylike fruits. The leaves are lobed, with the lobes separated by deep rounded sinuses. The bark has been used for papermaking. This tree will grow in a wide range of soils, including chalky ones. It can be propagated from semi-ripe cuttings in summer, taken with a heel of older wood.

Broussonetia papyrifera

soil	Both plants like any well-drained soil. Buxus: slight preference for alkaline soils
site	Broussonetia: prefers sun to light shade. Buxus: moderate sun to shade
pruning	Broussonetia: none, except to restrict. Buxus: likewise but tolerated wonderfully
general care	Broussonetia: feed and mulch for vigor. Buxus: full sun and strong winds can lead to foliage scorch
pests & diseases	Both shrubs are relatively trouble-free. Pests and diseases do not usually cause any problems

Buxus
Box

Box has small, evergreen leaves and much smaller, insignificant flowers. It is valuable in the garden because it is very tolerant of clipping.

This makes it one of the best shrubs to use for topiaries and living sculptures. It is also excellent for hedges of all sizes. The wild or normal form of the species

Buxus sempervirens 'Latifolia Maculata'

can make a narrow crowned tree over time, able to make 33ft (10m) but more often a rounded bush to 20ft (6m). Box is often found in the wild on soils derived from chalk and limestone, but it is happy over a wide range of soil pH, from about 5.5 to 7.4. It is also very tolerant of shade. However, it prefers good drainage. Box is easily raised from cuttings taken in spring or fall. (See page 12 for a picture of the species form.)

	SPRING	SUMMER	FALL	WINTER	height 5yrs (ft)	height 10yrs (ft)	spread 5yrs (ft)	spread 10yrs (ft)	color of blossom	
Broussonetia papyrifera	flowering (late)	flowering (early)	harvest		10	16	6½	13	white	Fruit only if male and female trees present
Buxus sempervirens	flowering (early)			flowering (late)	3	6½	3	6½	pale green	Evergreen shrub

flowering   harvest

Carpinus

Hornbeam

The name hornbeam is Anglo-Saxon in origin, with horn being hard and beam meaning tree. The timber is very tough and is often used for chopping boards.

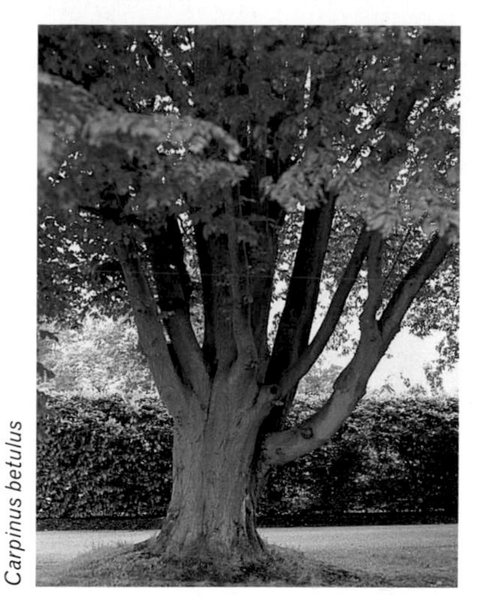

Carpinus betulus

In the garden, hornbeams are used either as specimen trees for the neat foliage, smooth silvery gray bark, and attractive fall color or for hedging. Although deciduous, the leaves on juvenile plants are retained over winter to give the plant winter protection, and regular clipping keeps it in the juvenile phase. Carpinus is well adapted to heavy clay soils but it is also at home on light gravels. The male catkins are yellow and open in advance of the leaves. Propagate Carpinus by seed or grafting. Sometimes seed may germinate only in the second year, so keep the pots for at least 18 months. The less common species can be struck from semi-ripe cuttings in summer.

soil	Carpinus: heavy clays to light gravels. Castanea: well-drained; dry, acidic sand
site	Carpinus: sun to moderate shade. Castanea: prefers sun to light shade
pruning	Carpinus: avoid in spring as they will bleed. Trim hedges in summer. Castanea: none
general care	Carpinus: no particular problems. Castanea: Coppice on a 10–15-year cycle for firewood or poles
pests & diseases	Carpinus: fairly trouble-free. Castanea: can be troubled by phytophthora root disease and chestnut blight

Castanea

Sweet chestnut *or* Spanish chestnut

This genus is related to the oaks. It is widely cultivated in temperate regions for the very tasty fruit—the chestnut. The flowers in mid-summer are quite showy and formed at the end of the current season's shoots.

Castanea sativa

The flowers consist of a spike of whitish-yellow male flowers with the female flowers at the base. The fruits ripen in the fall to a burr of vicious spines, which protect the 1–3 nuts. Castanea is adapted to hot dry summers, and flourishes in such years. A coppice plantation is cut down to the stump (stool) on a cycle of 10 to 15 years and quickly regrows.

In the garden, Castanea is useful as a specimen tree and as a coppice tree. Castanea requires a well-drained soil, being well adapted to acidic sandy soils but not tolerant of chalky ones; it will grow on hard limestones.

On waterlogged or poorly drained soils, it is susceptible to root death by the fungus phythophthora. Chestnut blight (caused by *Chrysonectria parasitica*, syn. *Endothia parasitica*) can also be extremely harmful for Castanea.

Propagation is by seed for the species but the cultivars should either be grafted or layered.

	SPRING	SUMMER	FALL	WINTER	height 5yrs (ft)	height 10yrs (ft)	spread 5yrs (ft)	spread 10yrs (ft)	flower color	
Carpinus betulus	flowering		harvest		13	20	6½	13		Good for heavy clay soils
C. betulus 'Fastigiata'	flowering				13	20	6½	13		Conical habit when young, ascending branches
Castanea sativa		flowering	harvest, harvest		13	23	10	16		Fall color russet, edible fruits
C. sativa 'Albomarginata'		flowering	harvest, harvest		10	16	6½	13		Leaves with a creamy white margin

flowering · harvest

Catalpa

Indian bean tree

Indian bean trees are excellent for the large erect panicles that are carried in mid- to late summer like candles or lanterns above the fresh green foliage. The bell-shaped flowers are usually white with spots of red, yellow, and purple, and are often fragrant.

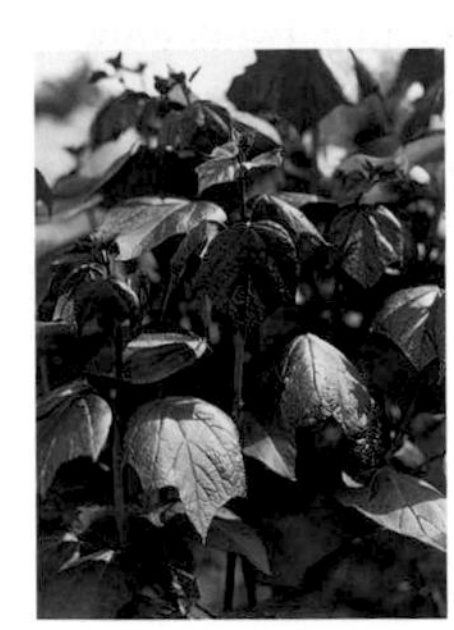

Catalpa erubescens 'Purpurea'

The fruits are long slender pods, which hang down like strands of spaghetti or clusters of green beans, persisting long into the winter, and opening to release the small two-winged seeds. Catalpa have large, heart-shaped leaves, which are thin in texture. The leaves are very susceptible to damage by strong winds and can end up being torn to shreds in exposed gardens. It is important, therefore, to site Catalpa in a sheltered spot during the growing season.

The fall color of the leaves is negative, turning black at the first frost. Most form squat spreading trees with short stout trunks. Catalpa are ideal trees for parkland settings and large gardens. They can be coppiced, and well-manured trees that are looked after in this manner will produce enormous foliage; *Catalpa erubescens* 'Purpurea' treated in this way will make a good foliage plant for a shrubbery, with the new foliage (particularly in spring) very deep purple, almost black.

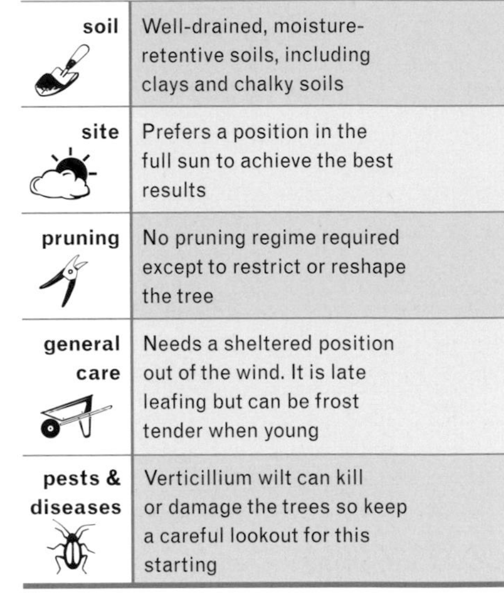

soil	Well-drained, moisture-retentive soils, including clays and chalky soils
site	Prefers a position in the full sun to achieve the best results
pruning	No pruning regime required except to restrict or reshape the tree
general care	Needs a sheltered position out of the wind. It is late leafing but can be frost tender when young
pests & diseases	Verticillium wilt can kill or damage the trees so keep a careful lookout for this starting

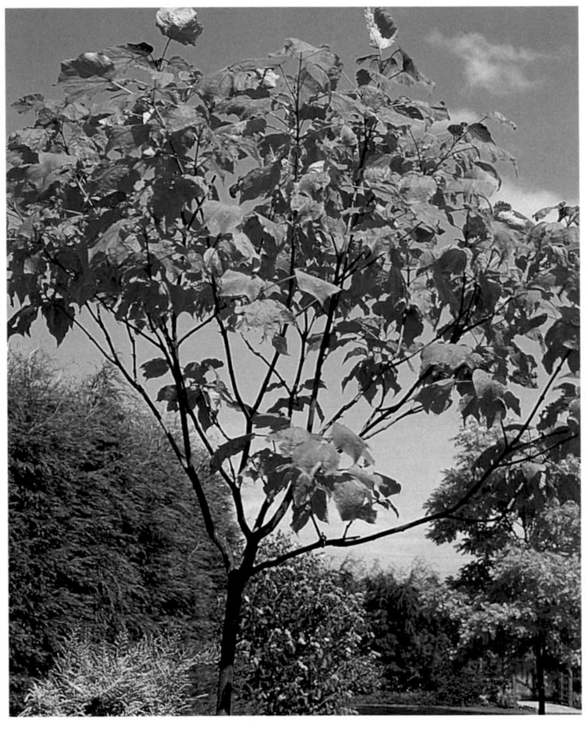

Catalpa bignonioides

Catalpa tolerate a wide range of soils, including chalk soils. Generally they like well-drained and moisture-retentive soils, but *Catalpa bignonioides* will tolerate heavy clays. They can be propagated by seed, which germinates readily, grafting in late winter, softwood cuttings in summer, and root cuttings in late winter.

	SPRING	SUMMER	FALL	WINTER	height 5yrs (ft)	height 10yrs (ft)	spread 5yrs (ft)	spread 10yrs (ft)	flower color	
Catalpa bignonioides		flowering, flowering	harvest		10	16	6½	16	white	Wonderful tree bearing mass of white blooms
C. bignonioides 'Aurea'		flowering, flowering			10	13	6½	16	white	Yellow leaves throughout the summer
C. erubescens 'Purpurea'		flowering, flowering	harvest		10	16	6½	16	white	Leaves initially deep purple or black
C. speciosa		flowering	harvest		10	16	6½	16	white	White flowers, glossy green leaves

flowering · harvest

Cercidiphyllum

Katsura tree

This tree, originating from China and Japan, is grown for the rounded, heart-shaped leaves, attractive habit and, most of all, for the brilliant fall color. The color is a mixture of yellows, scarlets, crimsons, pinks, and golds.

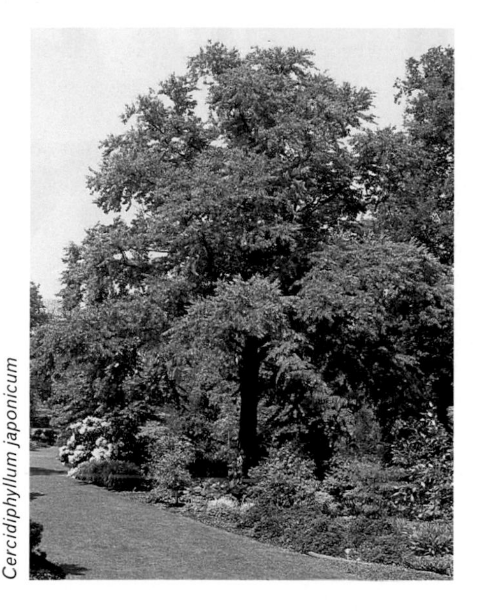

Cercidiphyllum japonicum

The new foliage, however, is usually bronzed. The flowers are insignificant—you may notice some red ones if you look carefully, and the small green podlike fruits are carried only on female trees. Cercidiphyllum makes a good specimen tree, capable of growing to a medium to large size, between 33–65ft (10–20m). The new foliage is tender to spring frosts, although there is always a second (and third) flush to replace those lost or damaged. It will grow happily on any reasonable garden soil, including chalky and heavy soils, although fall color will be better in acidic soils.

Cercidiphyllum can be propagated by seed, which should be sown as soon as ripe, and by cuttings in early summer.

soil	Cercidiphyllum: humus-rich, moisture-retentive. Cercis: any well-drained soil
site	Cercidiphyllum: sun to light shade. Cercis: also sun or very light shade
pruning	None needed for either tree, except for restricting or reshaping
general care	Cercidiphyllum: shelter from spring frosts if possible. Cercis: mulch to keep soil moist in summer
pests & diseases	Cercidiphyllum: no particular problems. Cercis: verticillium wilt and coral spot can cause problems

Cercis

Judas tree

Cercis has pink or white pealike flowers, which are carried on the older branches, often directly on the trunk.

The flowers are followed by the typical legume pod, showing it as a member of this family, but it is almost unique in having simple heart-shaped leaves. It has no reliable fall color but sometimes turns a clear yellow. It is best used as a specimen tree in a lawn area, by the driveway or in a shrub bed. It needs full sunlight, or at most light dappled shade. It will slowly make 26–40ft (8–12m) over 30 years or so. Cercis can tolerate acid sands and chalky soils but it will not stand waterlogged or very heavy soils. Propagation is by seed or semi-ripe cuttings in summer.

Cercis canadensis 'Forest Pansy'

Ceris canadensis 'Forest Pansy'

	SPRING	SUMMER	FALL	WINTER	height 5yrs (ft)	height 10yrs (ft)	spread 5yrs (ft)	spread 10yrs (ft)	color of blossom	
Cercidiphyllum japonicum	flowering				13	23	6½	13		Excellent fall color and neat habit
C. japonicum 'Pendulum'	flowering				10	16	6½	13		Mound-forming plant with pendulous shoots
Cercis canadensis 'Forest Pansy'	flowering				10	16	6½	10		Deep reddish-purple leaves
C. siliquastrum	flowering		harvest		13	20	10	13		Colorful when bearing flowers on bare branches

 *flowering*  *harvest*

Chimonanthus
Wintersweet

Chimonanthus praecox **is a deciduous shrub widely grown for its winter flowers. These are yellowish-green with a hint of purple. The flowers are extremely fragrant and their pleasant aroma will waft a good distance away from the plant.**

The foliage of *C. praecox* is dark, shiny green and lanceolate in shape. Wintersweet is usually grown as a wall shrub, which needs protection in colder areas, but in warmer climates it can be grown as a free-standing bush. It needs to be situated where the pleasing aroma from the foliage can be enjoyed to good effect. It will tolerate some shade but is better in full sun. It thrives on a wide range of soils, provided they are freely drained. Chimonanthus can be propagated by seed and by layers.

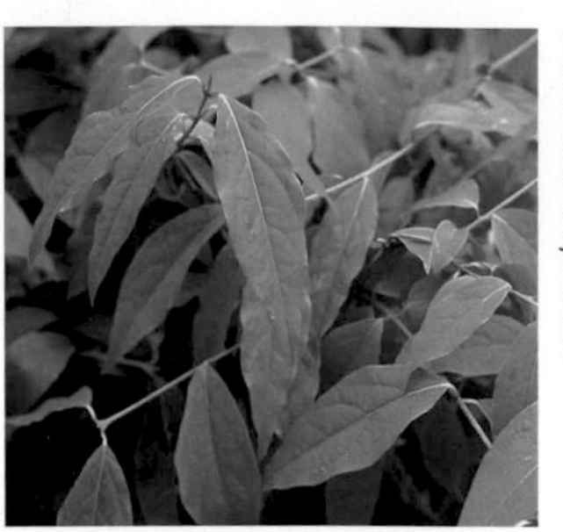
Chimonanthus praecox

Cladrastis
Yellowwood

The Latin name Cladrastis translates as "yellow wood," and this tree is a member of the legume family.

Cladrastis kentukea has fragrant white flowers, which are carried in enormous pendent clusters, but these are only produced following a hot, dry summer and are rare in gardens. It has pinnate foliage and a yellow-orange autumnal color. *Cladrastis sinensis* produces bluish-white, fragrant flowers very freely and is a worthy summer-flowering tree. Both species will thrive on a wide range of well-drained soils, especially friable loams, and tolerate chalk and limestone. Propagate by seed and by root cuttings in late spring.

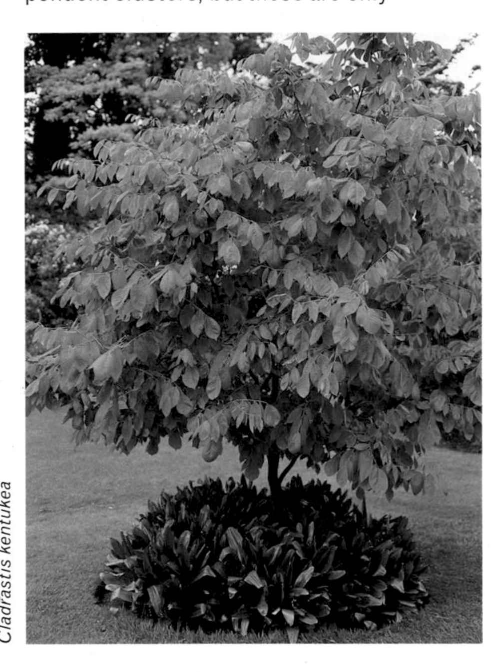
Cladrastis kentukea

soil	Chimonanthus: well-drained, moisture-retentive. Cladrastis: well-drained loams
site	Chimonanthus: sun to dappled shade. Cladrastis: enjoys sun to light shade
pruning	Chimonanthus: wall-trained specimens. Cladrastis: not in winter/spring as it will bleed
general care	Chimonanthus: easy to look after. Cladrastis: branches are brittle and liable to fracture in strong winds
pests & diseases	Cladrastis is likely to suffer from verticillium wilt, but apart from this, both are fairly trouble-free

	SPRING			SUMMER			FALL			WINTER			height 5yrs (ft)	height 10yrs (ft)	spread 5yrs (ft)	spread 10yrs (ft)	flower color	
Chimonanthus praecox										✿	✿	✿	6½	10	5	10		Excellent wall shrub; grow alone in milder parts
Cladrastis kentukea					✿								13	20	10	16		Synonym is *Cladrastis lutea*
C. sinensis					✿								10	16	10	16		In flower this gives the whole area a lilac tinge

✿ *flowering*

Cornus

Cornel *or* Dogwood

This is a large group of plants. Botanically there are several, albeit related, genera, but in horticultural terms they are generally all listed as Cornus.

The species here are best considered as belonging to three genera: Cornus in the narrow sense, in which the flowers are in dense umbels enclosed by two or more bracts and which appear before the leaves (for example, *Cornus mas*); Swida, with the flowers in large heads without bracts (including *Cornus alternifolia* and *Cornus controversa*), along with other shrubby species; Benthamidia, with the clusters of small flowers subtended by four (or six) large white or reddish bracts.

Cornels are useful in the garden. *Cornus mas* is one of the earliest woody harbingers of spring, opening its yellow flowers in late winter. *Cornus alternifolia* and *Cornus controversa* flower in early summer. Where they excel is in the tiered foliage—flat or slightly drooping plates of foliage on which the flower clusters are supported above the leaves. They are worth planting for this architectural form alone.

All three species have variegated forms: *Cornus mas* 'Variegata' has leaves with creamy white variegation, whereas 'Aureoelegantissima' has leaves margined with yellow, sometimes pink, and with occasional whole yellow leaves; *Cornus alternifolia* 'Argentea' has leaves variegated with white; and *Cornus controversa* 'Variegata' with yellow-white. *C. alternifolia* 'Argentea' is perhaps better for small settings, as it is more of a multistemmed shrub to 16–20ft (5–6m), whereas *C. controversa* 'Variegata' makes a single stemmed tree 20–33ft (6–10m) for larger settings. *C. mas* and its forms are ideal for shrub beds, whereas *C. alternifolia* and

Cornus kousa var. *chinensis* 'Satomi'

Cornus kousa var. *chinensis*

soil	Likes well-drained soils, including chalky soils (except *C. florida*)
site	Prefers to be kept in a position where there is sun to light shade
pruning	No particular pruning requirements, except for restricting or reshaping
general care	Fairly straightforward to cultivate and maintain—mulch to keep soil moist during the summer
pests & diseases	Relatively trouble-free. Pests and diseases do not usually cause any problems

C. controversa are at their best as specimen trees in a lawn setting. *C. mas* is the cornelian cherry, bright red and cherry-like—the flesh around the single seed is edible and can be used for jellies. The fruits of *C. alternifolia* are black.

Cornus florida 'Rainbow'

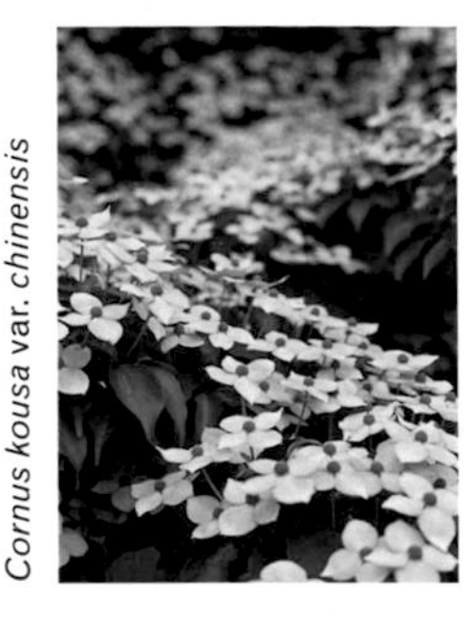
Cornus kousa var. *chinensis*

The large-flowered Cornus are showy for the bracts that form a plate below the cluster of totally inconspicuous flowers. There are usually four bracts, but *Cornus nuttallii* often has six. The bracts cover the flowers in bud, slowly expanding in spring. Initially they are green and lost in the foliage but as the flowers open they become white or pink. Because they are derived from leaves, the bracts tend to last, slowly withering and providing a display for three to six weeks.

At its best, the branches can be wreathed in flowers and the leaves almost entirely hidden. *Cornus kousa*, especially the var. *chinensis*, forms a broad conical large shrub to small tree, making 26–33ft (8–10m) after 20 to 30 years. It is the most reliable of this group, tolerating most garden soils, including chalky ones provided they are not too shallow.

Cornus florida is a smaller shrub, attaining only 13–16ft (4–5m) in the average garden. It can be stunning in full bloom but never quite lives up to the quality when wild in its native eastern North America. It also dislikes chalky soils. *C. nuttallii* makes a tall tree, 50–80ft (15–25m) when wild in its native western North America, but more usually 26–40ft (8–12m) in cultivation. It prefers a well-drained, moisture-retentive soil, but will grow on chalk soils.

Cornus 'Eddie's White Wonder' is a hybrid of *C. florida* and *C. nuttallii*. It makes a large shrub or small tree and is spectacular in spring. *Cornus* 'Norman Haddon' is a hybrid of *C. kousa* with *Cornus capitata* (an evergreen, yellow-flowered species). Cornus can be propagated by seed and by softwood cuttings in summer.

	SPRING			SUMMER			FALL			WINTER			height 5yrs (ft)	height 10yrs (ft)	spread 5yrs (ft)	spread 10yrs (ft)	flower color	
Cornus alternifolia 'Argentea'				flowering	flowering	harvest							10	16	5	10		Multistemmed habit, tiered branching
C. controversa				flowering	flowering								10	23	6½	13		Single-stemmed tree, tiered branching
C. controversa 'Variegata'				flowering	flowering								10	20	6½	13		Leaves with creamy white margins
C. mas						harvest						flowering	6½	13	5	10		Flowers at end of winter; bright red fruits
C. mas 'Variegata'												flowering	6½	13	5	10		Flowers at end of winter; leaves white margin
C. 'Eddie's White Wonder'			flowering										10	13	6½	10		Large white flowers
C. florida			flowering										10	13	6½	10		Good fall color; not for chalk
C. florida 'Cherokee Chief'			flowering										10	13	6½	10		Dark, ruby-pink bracts
C. florida 'Rainbow'			flowering										10	13	6½	10		Leaves margined deep yellow, upright bush
C. florida f. *rubra*			flowering										10	13	6½	10		Pink bracts
C. kousa				flowering	flowering								10	16	6½	13		Not for shallow, chalk soils; good fall color
C. kousa var. *chinensis*				flowering	flowering								10	16	6½	13		Purple fall color, better in chalk
C. kousa var. *chinensis* 'China Girl'				flowering	flowering								10	16	6½	13		Crimson-purple leaves in fall
C. kousa var. *chinensis* 'Gold Star'				flowering	flowering								10	16	6½	13		Leaves with a central blotch of golden yellow
C. kousa var. *chinensis* 'Satomi'				flowering	flowering								10	16	6½	13		Deep purple-red leaves in fall
C. 'Norman Haddon'				flowering	flowering	harvest							10	16	6½	13		Semi-evergreen, fruits 1in strawberry-like
C. nuttallii			flowering	flowering	flowering								10	20	6½	13		Large flowers with six bracts

flowering *harvest*

Corylus

Hazel

Corylus includes the hazel (*Corylus avellana*), which is a major understory tree in forests and forest margins. This is one of the species that provides hazel nuts, the other being the filbert, *Corylus maxima*.

All the hazels are valuable for their showy male catkins. These open sometime in late winter, lasting into early spring. The color of the catkins ranges from lemon-yellow to a more browny yellow. The female flowers are modest, comprising only 12–15 crimson stigmas of which only less than 1⁄10in (1–2mm) poke out from a green bud. *Corylus avellana* 'Contorta' is a form with twisted branches. It is a genetic oddity that has lost the ability to grow shoots in a straight line. It can look good in the winter tracery of the branches, especially when laden with pendent catkins. *Corylus maxima* 'Purpurea' is a purple-leaved form, with the catkins also purple. It is particularly useful used in a shrub border as a backdrop for plants with light golden foliage.

C. avellana and *C. maxima* are shrubs, growing to a maximum of 20–26ft (6–8m) and are usually multistemmed. By contrast, the Turkish hazel, *Corylus colurna*, is a tree with a single straight bole, making 50ft (15m) in a garden setting. It is attractive in catkin but also has an interesting bark—ash-gray or buff-brown, and flaking in thin scaly flecks. Hazels can be propagated by seed, which is best sown fresh, or by layering.

Corylus avellana

Corylus avellana 'Contorta'

Corylus maxima 'Purpurea'

soil	Any type of soil except waterlogged ones, from acidic to alkaline
site	Enjoys a situation where there is sun to moderate shade
pruning	Will coppice readily; best when stems are replaced every five or so years
general care	Easy to manage. Fruiting forms produce excellent nuts, which squirrels may get to before you!
pests & diseases	A variety of insects and mites affect these trees, but not seriously enough to cause lasting damage

	SPRING			SUMMER			FALL			WINTER			height 5yrs (ft)	height 10yrs (ft)	spread 5yrs (ft)	spread 10yrs (ft)	flower color	
Corylus avellana	flowering						harvest	harvest			flowering	flowering	10	20	10	20		Cultivars can produce edible nuts
C. avellana 'Contorta'	flowering						harvest	harvest			flowering	flowering	6½	13	6½	13		Corkscrew hazel, with contorted branches
C. colurna	flowering						harvest	harvest				flowering	13	23	6½	10		Turkish hazel, forming a strong-growing tree
C. maxima 'Purpurea'	flowering						harvest	harvest			flowering	flowering	10	20	10	20		Purple-leaved filbert, one of the best purples

flowering harvest

Cotinus

Smoke tree

The common name is derived from the way in which the bushes are smothered by the flowers from early summer onward. These are expanded panicles, which contain many sterile flowers, each with long, threadlike plumose stalks.

The stalks persist as summer turns into fall and the flowers into far fewer fruits. However, it makes them worth their spot in the shrub border or as a specimen at the edge of a sea of grass. Most of the forms in cultivation have purple foliage, and in these the flower stalks have a purplish tinge. Whereas in the natural green form they start a shade of fawn and end as a smoky gray. The fall color is even better, normally a strong, vivid red but in some forms orange-red.

Cotinus 'Grace'

Cotinus coggygria 'Royal Purple'

Smoke trees are tolerant of well-drained and moisture-retentive soils of moderate fertility. Overfeeding or planting on very fertile sites should be avoided for the simple reason that on these soils the fall color is less than exemplary.

Cotinus coggygria will thrive on chalk but the native species, *Cotinus obovatus*, requires a neutral or acidic soil. They all need full sun. The genus used to be included in Rhus and may feature in old books and catalogs under this name. Propagate by semi-ripe cuttings with a heel of older wood in summer, by layering, and by seed.

soil	An unfussy shrub. Will tolerate any type of soil, as long as it is well drained
site	Enjoys being grown in a position in the garden where there is lots of sun
pruning	Prune only to remove damage or to shorten wayward stems
general care	Avoid overfertile sites, resulting in a proliferation of foliage, no flowers, and less fall color
pests & diseases	Powdery mildew can be a problem on purple forms; verticillium wilt occasionally kills branches

	SPRING			SUMMER			FALL			WINTER			height 5yrs (ft)	height 10yrs (ft)	spread 5yrs (ft)	spread 10yrs (ft)	flower color	
Cotinus coggygria				flowering	flowering	flowering	flowering						6½	13	6½	13		Brilliant red fall color
C. coggygria 'Notcutt's Variety'				flowering	flowering	flowering	flowering						6½	13	6½	13		Maroon-purple leaves
C. coggygria 'Royal Purple'				flowering	flowering	flowering	flowering						6½	13	6½	13		Darker leaves than 'Notcutt's Variety'
C. 'Flame'				flowering	flowering	flowering	flowering						10	16	6½	13		Hybrid of *C. coggygria* and *C. obovatus*
C. 'Grace'				flowering	flowering	flowering	flowering						6½	16	6½	16		Hybrid of *C. coggygria* and *C. obovatus*
C. obovatus				flowering	flowering	flowering	flowering						8	16	6½	16		Long leaves, taller tree

flowering

Cotoneaster

The Cotoneaster considered here are the taller-growing forms, making large shrubs or small trees. These forms all have masses of white flowers, which, while individually small, produce quite a display—and make them attractive to bees.

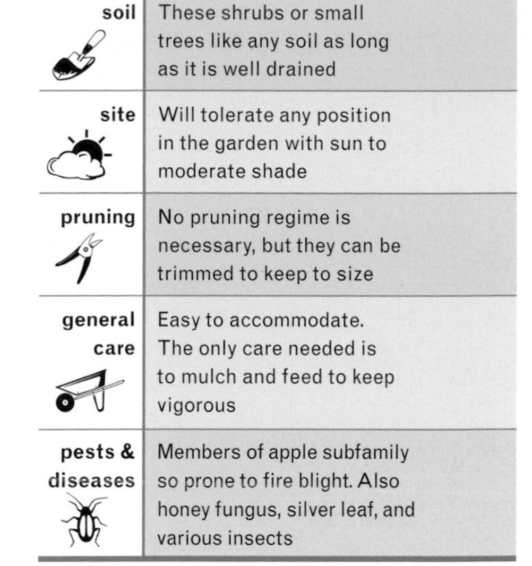

soil	These shrubs or small trees like any soil as long as it is well drained
site	Will tolerate any position in the garden with sun to moderate shade
pruning	No pruning regime is necessary, but they can be trimmed to keep to size
general care	Easy to accommodate. The only care needed is to mulch and feed to keep vigorous
pests & diseases	Members of apple subfamily so prone to fire blight. Also honey fungus, silver leaf, and various insects

Although there are larger-growing deciduous Cotoneaster, these are all evergreens. They have lots of uses in the garden, apart from the obvious color of their flowers and fruits. As berrying plants, they provide winter food for many birds. When the individual fruit is eaten depends upon a number of factors. Location is an important consideration—if the bush is close to shelter where birds can feel secure, it tends to be stripped sooner than if it is in an exposed position.

Cotoneaster watereri 'John Waterer'

Some species ripen much later than others. It is possible to manipulate the choice of species and siting so that natural bird food is available for much of the winter. The red-fruited forms, such as 'Cornubia' and 'John Waterer', tend to be eaten more quickly than the yellow-fruited forms 'Exburyensis' and 'Rothschildianus'.

The larger Cotoneaster are also useful in the shrub bed as evergreen screens, as small specimen trees, and as an effective hedge. *Cotoneaster lacteus* is excellent both as a screen and as a wall shrub. They grow in almost any well-drained soil, including chalky ones and acidic sands. Propagation is by cuttings, semi-ripe taken in summer, or from seed. The main disadvantage with seed is that it can take up to five years for the seeds to germinate (although most pop up in the second or third spring).

Cotoneaster salicifolius

	SPRING			SUMMER			FALL			WINTER			height 5yrs (ft)	height 10yrs (ft)	spread 5yrs (ft)	spread 10yrs (ft)	color of blossom	
Cotoneaster frigidus 'Cornubia'				flowering			harvest	harvest	harvest				10	20	10	16		Large red fruits in fall/early winter
C. 'Exburyensis'				flowering			harvest	harvest	harvest				10	16	10	16		Fruits apricot-yellow, tinged pink later
C. lacteus				flowering					harvest	harvest	harvest		10	16	10	16		Evergreen, flowers in clusters of 100 or more
C. salicifolius				flowering			harvest	harvest	harvest				6½	13	6½	13		Evergreen shrub with rugose leaves
C. salicifolius 'Rothschildianus'				flowering			harvest	harvest	harvest				10	16	10	16		Creamy yellow fruits in fall, spreading habit
C. watereri 'John Waterer'				flowering			harvest	harvest	harvest				10	16	10	16		Semi-evergreen or evergreen

flowering *harvest*

Crataegus

Hawthorn

The singleseed hawthorn (*Crataegus monogyna*), especially the wild white form, is one of the most attractive small flowering trees. It makes a domed crown with pendent branches, which are wreathed with small clusters of white flowers, followed by maroon-red fruits in the fall (and often persisting into late winter).

The flowers are scented, although the scent does not please all noses! The cultivar 'Biflora' (sometimes known as 'Glastonbury Thorn') produces some flowers during mild periods in winter, plus a "normal" flush in late spring. The forms of *Crataegus laevigata* (*C. oxycantha* in many lists and older books) with pink or scarlet, single or double flowers have a similar habit but never seem to have the quality of *C. monogyna*. Still, they make attractive small trees.

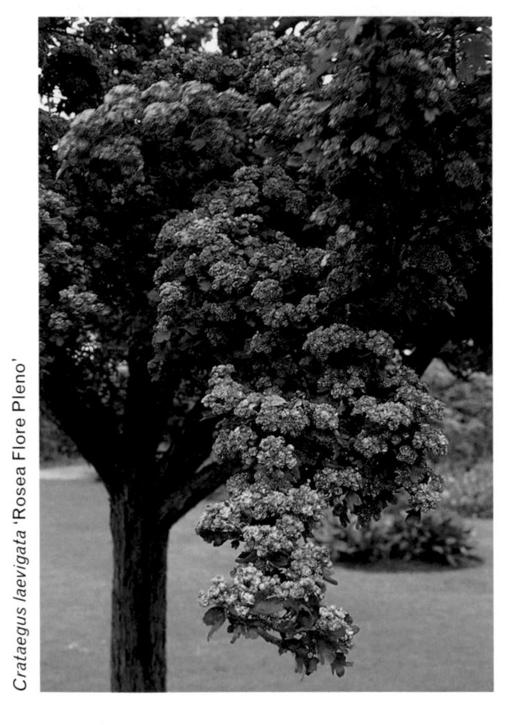

Crataegus laevigata 'Rosea Flore Pleno'

C. lavallei 'Carrierei' has leaves that persist into mid-winter and orange-red fruits that hang on through much of the winter, if not into spring. By contrast, the attraction of *Crataegus persimilis* 'Prunifolia' is that the leaves do not persist. Instead the glossy leaves turn from green to orange, then red and finally crimson, and make a greater splash of color than the large red fruits, which fall almost as soon as they are ripe. These small trees are useful as specimens. They also make excellent hedges, tolerating clipping. They all have thorns to a greater (*C. persimilis*, where they may be ¾in/2cm) or lesser (*C. lavallei* 'Carrierei', ¼in/½cm) extent. They require sun for best effect but will grow happily, although flowering less readily, in moderate shade. They tolerate all soils except seriously wet ones, and are happy on clays and chalky soils. They can be propagated by seed, which will take two or more years to germinate, or by grafting.

soil	Will grow in any heavy to well-drained soil, including chalk
site	Prefer sun for best results, but also happy in moderate shade
pruning	Very tolerant of clipping but do not need a specific pruning regime
general care	These are easy to look after. However, be aware of the thorns, which can be quite big on some varieties
pests & diseases	A number of insect and fungal problems (including fire blight) but generally not adversely affected

	SPRING			SUMMER			FALL			WINTER			height 5yrs (ft)	height 10yrs (ft)	spread 5yrs (ft)	spread 10yrs (ft)	color of blossom	
Crataegus laevigata 'Crimson Cloud'			flowering	flowering				harvest					10	16	10	16	dark red	Sometimes known as 'Punicea'
C. laevigata 'Paul's Scarlet'			flowering	flowering				harvest					10	16	10	16	dark red	Also known as 'Coccinea Plena'
C. laevigata 'Plena'			flowering	flowering				harvest					10	16	10	16	white	Double white flowers
C. laevigata 'Rosea Flore Pleno'			flowering	flowering				harvest					10	16	10	16	pink	Double pink flowers
C. lavallei 'Carrierei'			flowering	flowering				harvest	harvest	harvest	harvest		10	16	10	16	white	Orange-red fruits; semi-evergreen
C. monogyna			flowering	flowering			harvest	harvest	harvest				10	16	10	16	white	Common native tree, widely used in hedges
C. monogyna 'Biflora'			flowering	flowering				harvest	harvest		flowering		10	16	10	16	white	Some flowers mid-winter, most late spring
C. persimilis 'Prunifolia'			flowering	flowering				harvest					10	13	10	20	white	Excellent fall color, thorns to ¾in

flowering harvest

Crinodendron

These two species are evergreen and make large shrubs. The flowers of *Crinodendron hookerianum* are held pointing down on long stiff peduncles. The flowers are urn-shaped with fleshy petals of a rich crimson. The flower stalks expand in the fall but the flowers themselves don't swell until late spring.

Crinodendron hookerianum

Crinodendron patagua has more bell-shaped flowers. They are white and less showy but have a stronger scent. Both species need some shelter, especially in cold gardens. For this reason, they do better in light woodland or against a wall. They do not take kindly to any lime in the soil, needing acidic to neutral and well-drained sites.

They can be propagated by seed, or by cuttings in summer.

soil	Crinodendron: acidic to neutral, avoid lime or chalk. Cydonia: well-drained, acidic
site	Crinodendron: prefers light shade. Cydonia: enjoys sun or dappled shade
pruning	No pruning necessary for either, except to restrict or reshape
general care	Crinodendron: protect from cold winds. Cydonia: seeds are poisonous. Mulch on light soils
pests & diseases	Crinodendron: no particular problems. Cydonia: can get the usual range of orchard apple bugs

Cydonia

Quince

This is the classical quince, which is the source of the original (Portuguese) marmalade. It makes a small deciduous tree, which, in late spring, carries large, single white flowers.

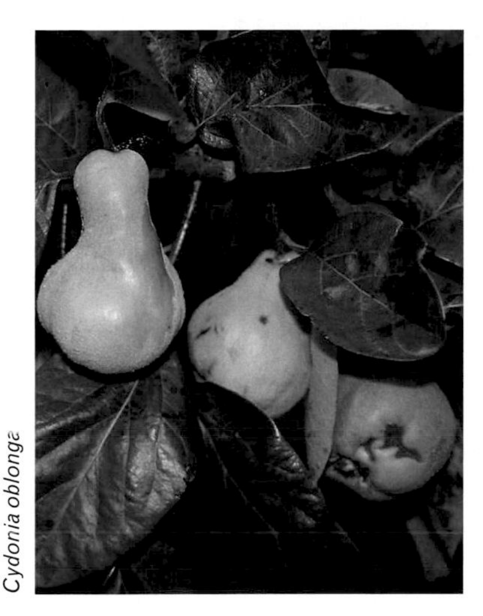
Cydonia oblonga

In the fall, the fruit follows the flowers. These are pear-shaped, ripening from green to light golden yellow, with wonderfully fragrant flesh. The bark is attractive in its own right, smooth and purplish-gray, which flakes to reveal orange beneath. And in the fall, the foliage turns yellow. Quince should not be restricted to the orchard or, as is commonly the case, as a rootstock for orchard pears, but used within the garden as a small specimen tree. It requires full sun in order to flower and fruit well, but will grow in some shade. It will thrive on any well-drained soil, including chalky ones. Propagate by seed, grafting, or by removing suckers.

	SPRING	SUMMER	FALL	WINTER	height 5yrs (ft)	height 10yrs (ft)	spread 5yrs (ft)	spread 10yrs (ft)	color of blossom	
Crinodendron hookerianum	flowering	flowering			5	10	5	10	dark	Dark, evergreen lanceolate foliage
C. patagua	flowering	flowering			6½	13	5	10	white	Dark, evergreen oval foliage, shrub to 20ft
Cydonia oblonga	flowering		harvest harvest		10	13	10	13	white	Excellent small tree, can make 26ft

flowering *harvest*

Davidia

Dove tree

The large white bracts that make this tree special are in pairs, flopped over the cluster of male flowers containing only stamens with a single female flower near the tip.

The bracts give the appearance of doves resting in the tree. They open just as the new fresh green leaves are nearly fully expanded and when in full bloom there can appear to be almost as many white bracts as there are green leaves. The leaves are similar to those of the European linden tree, turning yellow in the fall. The fruit is a hard oblong green drupe, which hangs down from the boughs in the fall, usually persisting until spring. The typical form, *Davidia involucrata*, has velvety-down leaves on the underside, instead of being hairless and glaucous in var. *vilmoriniana*. It is as attractive but harder to establish because young plants are prone to suffer more from spring frosts.

Davidia involucrata var. *vilmoriniana*

Dove trees thrive on heavy, water-retentive soils, including those overlying chalk and limestone as well as acidic soils. They require full sun or a light woodland setting. Davidia can be propagated by seed (plant the whole fruit and allow nature to break down the hard shell; this will take 2–3 years before germination occurs) or by semi-ripe cuttings in summer.

soil	Davidia: heavy to well-drained, acidic or alkaline. Decaisnea: well-drained
site	Davidia: sun to light shade. Decaisnea: likewise—preferably overhead shade
pruning	No special pruning regime is required for either Davidia or Decaisnea
general care	Davidia: takes a year or two to establish; mulch and water as needed. Decaisnea: site to avoid spring frost risk
pests & diseases	Both Davidia and Decaisnea do not have any particular problems with pests and diseases

Decaisnea

The glory of *Decaisnea fargesii* is in the fruit. This is a stout pod of about 3–4in (8–10cm), which is metallic blue in color with a glaucous waxy layer.

Decaisnea fargesii

Embedded in the flesh, which is edible, are masses of flattened dark brown or black seeds. The flowers are in long drooping panicles and have six yellowish-green sepals but no petals. They are borne slightly early in the year and, like the new foliage, are liable to damage by spring frosts, so site with overhead shelter to minimize this problem. Each pinnate, bold leaf is usually 2–3ft (60–90cm) in length and has 13–25 leaflets. As there are six or more clustered toward the tips of the shoots and radiating out like the spokes of an umbrella, it is quite attractive as a foliage plant, even if the frost does get the flowers. It requires full sun to moderate shade and likes moisture-retentive but well-drained soils. Propagate by seeds, which germinate readily.

	SPRING	SUMMER	FALL	WINTER	height 5yrs (ft)	height 10yrs (ft)	spread 5yrs (ft)	spread 10yrs (ft)	color of blossom	
Davidia involucrata var. *vilmoriniana*	flowering		harvest		10	20	6½	16		Flowers in two unequal bracts up to 8in
Decaisnea fargesii	flowering		harvest harvest		6½	10	6½	13		Bold pinnate leaves radiating out from shoots

flowering harvest

Drimys

Winter's bark

This is an evergreen genus with aromatic leaves, and it is grown for the fragrant ivory–white flowers that terminate the shoots in early summer. There are separate male- and female-flowered bushes.

Drimys winteri

The fruit of the Drimys is a fleshy carpel containing a number of seeds, and can also be used as a pepper substitute. Plant these shrubs with side and overhead shelter in lime-free soils.

They can be propagated by seed or by cuttings in late summer.

soil	Drimys: well-drained, moisture-retentive. Elaeagnus: light/sandy, avoid rich soil
site	Drimys: light shade. Elaeagnus: sun for deciduous; sun/light shade for evergreens
pruning	Drimys: if needed, prune after flowering (Group 1). Elaeagnus: only to reshape
general care	Drimys: plant in spring after risk of frosts is passed. Elaeagnus: vigorous growths may need tying in
pests & diseases	Both Drimys and Elaeagnus do not have any particular problems with pests and diseases

Elaeagnus

Oleaster

This genus includes both deciduous and evergreen species. The evergreens have some rich leaf markings, with speckles of gold or white, while the deciduous species have silvery leaves.

Elaeagnus ebbingei 'Limelight'

The flowers are not overtly showy but are fragrant. The fruits are an oblong drupe with a single seed. The fleshy layer is sweet and juicy. All parts of the plants are covered with silvery or brownish scales. Elaeagnus are good for coastal sites. They are better on poorer soils, especially for the deciduous ones, but like good drainage. They have an association with a bacterium that enables them to fix atmospheric nitrogen to make fertilizer. The deciduous species need full sunlight, but the evergreens will tolerate some shade. They can be propagated by cuttings in summer or by seed.

	SPRING			SUMMER			FALL			WINTER			height 5yrs (ft)	height 10yrs (ft)	spread 5yrs (ft)	spread 10yrs (ft)	flower color	
Drimys lanceolata		flowering	flowering		harvest								5	8	3	6½		Flowers with buff-colored stamens
Drimys winteri				flowering		harvest							6½	13	5	10		Leaves aromatic, bright glaucous on underside
Elaeagnus angustifolia				flowering				harvest	harvest				10	16	10	16		Deciduous, narrow dark green leaves
E. angustifolia 'Quicksilver'				flowering				harvest	harvest				10	13	10	13		Pyramidal habit, deciduous, not for chalk soils
E. commutata			flowering					harvest	harvest				5	10	3	6½		Elliptic leaves, deciduous, silvery scaly
E. ebbingei	harvest	harvest						flowering					3	8	3	8		Dark green or metallic leaves; evergreen
E. ebbingei 'Coastal Gold'	harvest	harvest						flowering					3	8	3	8		Dark green evergreen leaves splashed with gold
E. ebbingei 'Gilt Edge'	harvest	harvest						flowering					3	8	3	8		Evergreen leaves, dark green in center
E. ebbingei 'Limelight'	harvest	harvest						flowering					3	8	3	8		Evergreen leaves, with yellow/pale green center
E. pungens 'Maculata'	harvest	harvest						flowering					3	8	3	8		Evergreen, center of leaf dark yellow

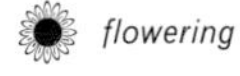 flowering  harvest

Embothrium

Chilean fire bush

The tubular waxy flowers, which are scarlet and borne in axillary and terminal racemes in late spring, are reminiscent of fire. Despite its common name, however, the Chilean fire bush usually makes a narrow crowned tree rather than a bush.

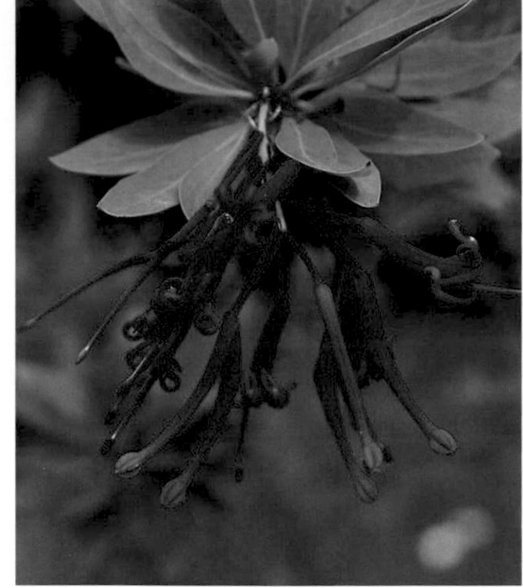

Embothrium coccineum

It is one of the most flamboyant of evergreen flowering trees when at its prime. It is a member of the Proteaceae family, and like other species in the family, does not like excess phosphate in the soil or added fertilizer. Embothrium needs an acidic site. In colder or more exposed gardens, offer shelter, but in milder locations they will flourish in the open. Use it as an exclamation plant where it will be prominent when in leaf and flower.

Propagate by softwood or semi-ripe cuttings in summer.

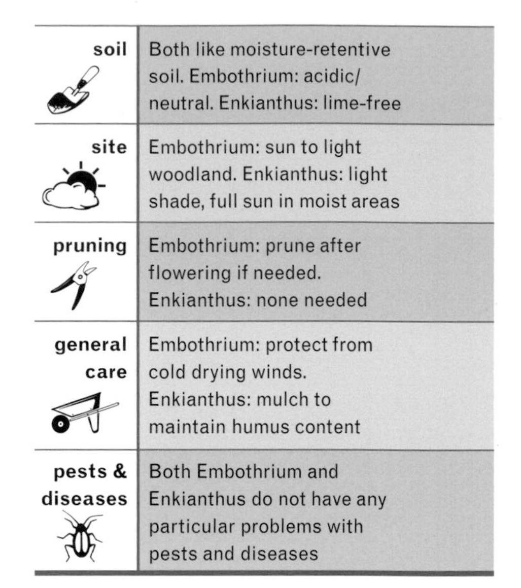

soil	Both like moisture-retentive soil. Embothrium: acidic/neutral. Enkianthus: lime-free
site	Embothrium: sun to light woodland. Enkianthus: light shade, full sun in moist areas
pruning	Embothrium: prune after flowering if needed. Enkianthus: none needed
general care	Embothrium: protect from cold drying winds. Enkianthus: mulch to maintain humus content
pests & diseases	Both Embothrium and Enkianthus do not have any particular problems with pests and diseases

Enkianthus

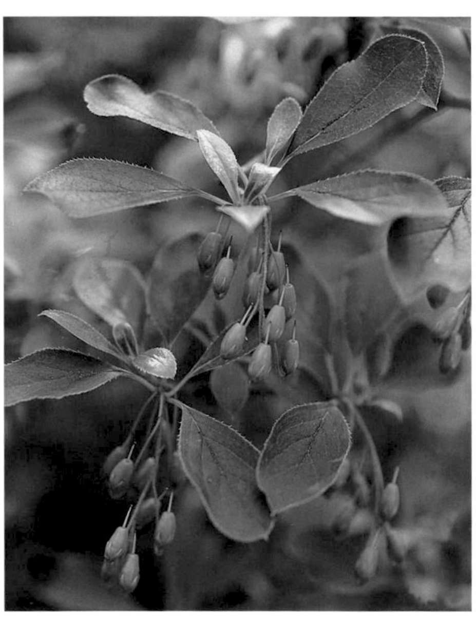

Enkianthus campanulatus

These are deciduous shrubs grown for the clusters of bell- or urn-shaped flowers in late spring from buds on last year's shoots.

The flower color can vary from white to pink. The flowerheads are small but the fall color is usually a stunning scarlet-red. They are excellent for a sheltered or shaded shrub border, or in light woodland. Like other members of the heather family (Ericaceae) they do not tolerate chalky sites. They can be propagated by semi-ripe cuttings in summer, layering, or by seed.

	SPRING	SUMMER	FALL	WINTER	height 5yrs (ft)	height 10yrs (ft)	spread 5yrs (ft)	spread 10yrs (ft)	flower color	
Embothrium coccineum	flowering				10	16	3	6½		Evergreen, showy flowers
Enkianthus campanulatus	flowering				5	10	3	10		Excellent form, gold and red leaves in fall
E. campanulatus 'Red Bells'	flowering				½	1	½	1		Dwarf form, red fall color
E. cernuus f. *rubens*	flowering				3	6½	3	6½		Fall color deep reddish-purple
E. perulatus	flowering				3	6½	3	6½		Fall color scarlet

flowering

Eucalyptus

This genus contains about 600 or so species originating from Australia. Most are not hardy but quite a few are, leaving a large number from which to choose.

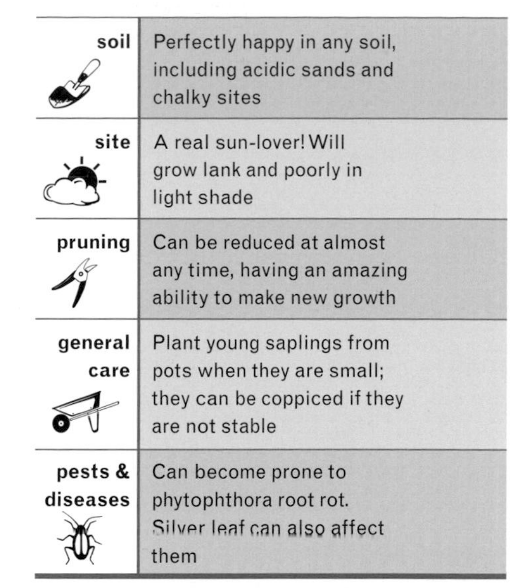

soil	Perfectly happy in any soil, including acidic sands and chalky sites
site	A real sun-lover! Will grow lank and poorly in light shade
pruning	Can be reduced at almost any time, having an amazing ability to make new growth
general care	Plant young saplings from pots when they are small; they can be coppiced if they are not stable
pests & diseases	Can become prone to phytophthora root rot. Silver leaf can also affect them

Most of the hardy species, colloquially known as "gums," have a bark that exfoliates, revealing white, green, and yellow at different stages. The leaves are evergreen. In the adult phase they are identical on both sides and usually hang down on a petiole. In the juvenile phase, they are usually sessile, sitting directly on the shoot and in opposite pairs. In some, the juvenile foliage is a bright glaucous blue, much loved for flower arrangements. The flowers have a cap that fits over them at the bud stage; this is derived from the petals and falls off as the flower opens. The time of flowering varies with the weather but is generally mid-summer.

Eucalyptus 'Debeuzevillei'

In the garden, eucalyptus make excellent and fast-growing specimen trees. They tolerate a wide range of soils, from acidic to chalky, but resent being transplanted. Buy small, container-grown plants. Plant them in late spring at 12–18in (30–45cm) in height, and species like *E. dalrympleana* and *E. gunnii* can be 8ft (2.5m) by the fall. Never try to make them stand up by staking. Indeed, cut them back to half their height—if the regrowth still flops over, repeat the cutting back, but hopefully you will only need to take a third off. Propagate also by seed; pot on when large enough to handle, and plant out as soon as the risk of frost is past.

Eucalyptus niphophila

Eucalyptus glaucescens

	SPRING	SUMMER	FALL	WINTER	height 5yrs (ft)	height 10yrs (ft)	spread 5yrs (ft)	spread 10yrs (ft)	flower color	
Eucalyptus archeri		flowering			8	16	3	6½		Small tree, to circa 26ft
E. coccifera		flowering			10	20	3	6½		Will grow to about 33ft, peppermint scent bark
E. dalrympleana		flowering			20	33	6½	16		Bark shed in large flakes; tolerant of chalk
E. 'Debeuzevillei'		flowering			8	16	6½	16		Related to *E. niphophila* and just as good
E. glaucescens		flowering			13	26	6½	13		White bark, darkening to gray
E. gunnii		flowering			20	33	6½	13		Can make 50–65ft in 25 years. Pale green bark
E. niphophila		flowering			8	16	6½	16		Grows to circa 20ft by 20ft, trunk often leans.
E. parvifolia		flowering			13	23	6½	13		Bark smooth, graying, dark green leaves, small
E. perriniana		flowering			10	20	6½	13		Gray and brown bark

flowering

Eucryphia

These have large white flowers with a showy boss of stamens in mid- to late-summer. *Eucryphia glutinosa* is deciduous with the leaves turning orange and red, giving two pronounced seasons of display.

Eucryphia glutinosa

Eucryphia glutinosa makes a bush ultimately 13–16ft (4–5m) in height and spread. The other forms also have two main seasons, one lasting all year because they are evergreen, with the flowers also lasting for several weeks. These forms make upright trees, especially *Eucryphia nymansensis*, which can make 50ft (15m) in 30 years. *E. mulliganii* also has a narrow upright habit, but is dwarf, making 20ft (6m) in height but only 3ft (1m) wide in 30 years. In the garden, position *E. glutinosa* in a shrub bed or as a specimen shrub at a focal point. *E. milliganii* makes a feature plant among smaller shrubs, and flowers from a young age. *E. intermedia* and *E. nymansensis* make specimen trees or large upright shrubs.

All the forms appreciate being shaded and kept cool at the roots, but with as much light as possible for the crown. In more temperate climates, they need protection from cold dry winds. The ideal soil is a well-drained but fertile and moisture-retentive acidic loam.

They can be raised from seed but this often produces hybrids if more than one species is grown. Cuttings offer the best route for propagation, using semi-ripe cuttings in late summer. *E. glutinosa* will sucker and these can be removed and grown on.

soil	Well-drained, moisture-retentive acid/neutral; *E. nymansensis* tolerates chalk
site	Needs sun for the top but also side shelter, with the roots shaded
pruning	No special pruning regime is required; it can be reduced for size and reshaping
general care	Protect from cold dry winds. For propagation, try cuttings rather than attempting to grow from seed
pests & diseases	Relatively trouble-free. Does not have any particular problems with pests and diseases

Eucryphia intermedia 'Rostrevor'

	SPRING			SUMMER			FALL			WINTER			height 5yrs (ft)	height 10yrs (ft)	spread 5yrs (ft)	spread 10yrs (ft)	flower color	
Eucryphia glutinosa					●	●							5	10	5	10	☐	Deciduous shrub, orange and red in fall
E. intermedia 'Rostrevor'						●	●						8	13	5	8	☐	Evergreen leaves glaucous beneath
E. mulliganii				●	●								3	6½	1½	3	☐	Dwarf form, slow-growing
E. nymansensis 'Nymansay'						●	●						8	13	5	8	☐	Fast-growing, forming a columnar tree

● *flowering*

Euonymus

Spindle tree

These make shrubs or small trees. The fruit is a capsule, which has four or five segments. It ripens to yellow-green or pink, when the segments open to show the seeds. These are white but have a fleshy, orange covering.

The capsule covering is intended to be eaten by birds, with the seed surviving the gut and passing through the system to be "laid" with a little pot of fertilizer. The species featured here are deciduous and provide excellent fall color. Other species are evergreen.

soil	Well-drained soils of good to moderate fertility, especially good on shallow chalk soils
site	Prefers a position in the garden where there is sun or dappled shade
pruning	No pruning necessary except when reshaping or resizing is required
general care	Fairly easy to manage and cultivate. Mulch to maintain humus content in soil
pests & diseases	Occasionally caterpillars pay a visit and can cause slight damage, but fairly trouble-free otherwise

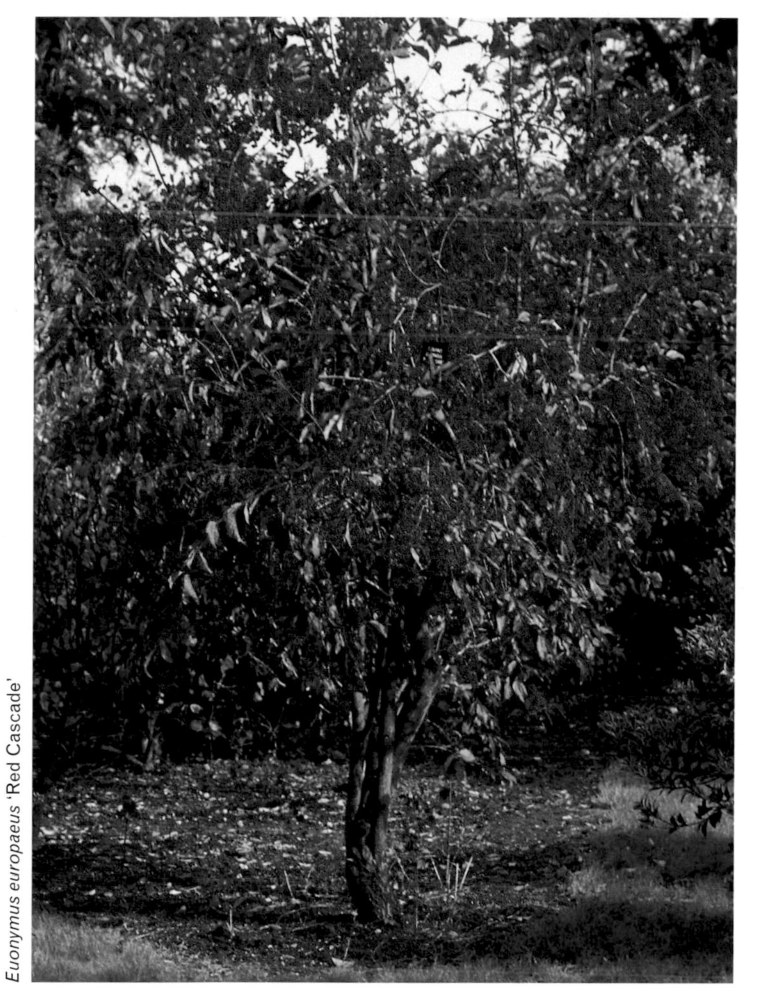

Euonymus europaeus 'Red Cascade'

The flowers are rather nondescript, usually greenish-yellow but some of them have a touch of purple or white. In the garden Euonymus can be used in shrub and mixed borders or as spot plants in the lawn.

E. europaeus is found in hedgerows and makes a small tree. It is a good size to make a screen between houses with little space between them without getting out of control.

Euonymus thrive in full sun to moderate shade, although fruiting will always be more reliable in full sun. They like well-drained soils, and are especially good on shallow soils overlying chalk. They can be propagated by seeds sown as soon as ripe, or from cuttings. Cuttings should be taken as semi-ripe cuttings in early summer. The wood is white and easily "worked" or carved. It was the favorite wood used in making spindles for the spinning industry.

	SPRING	SUMMER	FALL	WINTER	height 5yrs (ft)	height 10yrs (ft)	spread 5yrs (ft)	spread 10yrs (ft)	color of blossom	
Euonymus europaeus	flowering (late)		harvest (mid, late)		5	10	5	10		Native small tree/shrub; good for chalk soils
E. europaeus 'Red Cascade'	flowering (late)		harvest (mid, late)		5	10	5	10		Superior form with branches pendent at tips
E. planipes	flowering (late)		harvest (mid, late)		4	6½	3	6½		Brilliant red fall color and scarlet fruits

 *flowering*  *harvest*

Fagus
Beech

Beech has a number of uses in the garden. Specimen trees give shape, color, and texture. Mature beech trees form rounded domed crowns, usually as broad as they are high. However, *Fagus sylvatica* 'Dawyck' has a narrow columnar crown very reminiscent of the Lombardy poplar but a little broader.

Beech foliage often contains large quantities of xanthocyanins, which give the tree its purple foliage. Another attractive feature of beech is the wonderful, fresh green new foliage, with the leaves turning russet colors in the fall. The silvery gray bark is also quite stunning. Most bark cells live for only a few years before dying, but in beech the cells in the bark can live for 100 years or more.

Because beech is an aggressive surface rooter, few other plants can survive under an established beech. A beech woodland, therefore, is open with an attractive leaf litter of fallen beech leaves.

The other major use of beech is as a hedging plant. It can be trimmed to almost any height. Because trimming makes the foliage juvenile, a beech hedge will retain the old dead leaves until they drop off in spring when the buds expand. Beech will grow in sun to medium shade. It does not mind whether the soil is acidic or alkaline, but must have good drainage to thrive.

Propagate by seed sown as soon as it is ripe, and protect the seed from mice. Selected forms can be grafted in spring.

Fagus sylvatica 'Purple Fountain'

Fagus sylvatica 'Dawyck Purple'

soil	Any well-drained soil—will not tolerate waterlogging or heavy soils
site	Prefers a site where there is both sun and medium, but not complete, shade
pruning	Clip hedges in late summer. Old plants do not respond to severe pruning
general care	It is surface rooting and so can be aggressive on other plants. It also casts a dense shade where planted
pests & diseases	Gray squirrels can cause damage to the bark of the stem and major branches; bracket fungi can rot the heartwood

	SPRING	SUMMER	FALL	WINTER	height 5yrs (ft)	height 10yrs (ft)	spread 5yrs (ft)	spread 10yrs (ft)	color of blossom	
Fagus sylvatica	flowering		harvest		6½	13	3	6½		Large-growing tree or for hedging
F. sylvatica 'Asplenifolia'	flowering		harvest		6½	13	3	6½		Leaves narrow and deeply cut into lobes
F. sylvatica f. *atropurpurea*	flowering		harvest		6½	13	3	6½		Includes all the forms with purple foliage
F. sylvatica 'Dawyck'	flowering		harvest		6½	13	3	5		Narrow upright habit, green leaves
F. sylvatica 'Dawyck Gold'	flowering		harvest		6½	13	3	5		Narrow upright habit, leaves open bright yellow
F. sylvatica 'Dawyck Purple'	flowering		harvest		6½	13	3	3		Narrow upright habit, leaves purple
F. sylvatica 'Pendula'	flowering		harvest		6½	13	3	10		Foliage green, branches pendulous
F. sylvatica 'Purple Fountain'	flowering		harvest		6½	13	3	6½		Purple leaf form, narrow upright crown
F. sylvatica 'Purpurea Pendula'	flowering		harvest		6½	6½	3	6½		Purple foliage, make a mopheaded tree
F. sylvatica 'Riversii'	flowering		harvest		6½	13	3	6½		Dark purple leaves
F. sylvatica 'Rohanii'	flowering		harvest		6½	13	3	6½		Purple cut-leaf foliage form

Fatsia & Fatshedera

***Fatsia japonica* is native to Japan, Korea, and Taiwan. In cultivation it has hybridized with *Hedera hibernica* (Atlantic ivy) to produce *Fatshedera lizei*.**

Fatsia japonica is an evergreen shrub to about 6½–16ft (2–5m) in time. It has palmately lobed leaves 12–16in (30–40cm) across with around nine deep lobes. The leaf has a petiole up to 12in (30cm) in length. Milky white panicles of flowers are produced in the fall and are followed by black pea-shaped berries. *Fatshedera lizei* is a smaller shrub, which has inherited a somewhat scandent habit from the ivy parent and can benefit from staking. It has smaller leaves, only 4–10in (10–25cm) across, with five or seven shallow lobes, and shorter petioles. Both species are fine architectural plants and are valuable as they are late flowering. They will grow in sun or shade, but *Fatshedera lizei* is especially useful for tolerating dry shade. They will tolerate very hot conditions, especially *Fatshedera lizei*, and can be useful in sunrooms or on sun-drenched patios, and are good in polluted atmospheres or coastal exposure. Both have variegated forms, which tend to be less vigorous, needing more sunlight.

Fatsia japonica and *Fatshedera lizei* can be propagated by softwood cuttings in early summer. These should include two nodes of the shoot but only one leaf. *F. japonica* can also be raised from seed and root cuttings.

Fatshedera lizei

soil 	Fertile, well-drained, moist if in full sun. Will tolerate drier soils if in shade
site 	Extremely tolerant of sunny sites and fairly heavy shade
pruning 	No special pruning is required, except possibly to keep to size
general care	Fairly easy to manage and cultivate. Keep pot-grown plants slightly dry over winter
pests & diseases 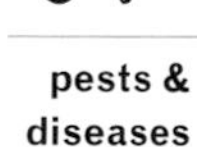	Frost can damage the leaves but otherwise there are no particular problems

F

Trees & Shrubs

Fatsia japonica

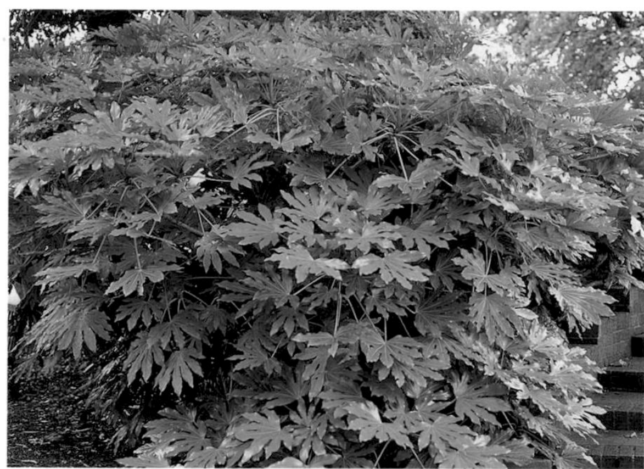

Fatsia japonica

	SPRING	SUMMER	FALL	WINTER	height 5yrs (ft)	height 10yrs (ft)	spread 5yrs (ft)	spread 10yrs (ft)	flower color	
Fatshedera lizei			flowering, flowering		3	5	3	6½		Sterile; glossy foliage, evergreen
F. lizei 'Variegata'			flowering, flowering		3	5	3	6½		Gray-green leaves with irregular creamy margin
Fatsia japonica			flowering, harvest		4	8	4	8		Black fruits in early winter; leaves deeply lobed
F. japonica 'Variegata'			flowering, harvest		4	8	4	8		Leaves with broad white margin at tips of lobes

 *flowering*  *harvest*

Ficus
Fig

This large genus contains mainly tropical evergreen species, including several indoor plants such as the rubber plant (*Ficus elastica*) and the banyan tree (*Ficus benghalensis*).

For the garden, the common fig (*Ficus carica*) is hardy and will ripen its fruits. It is a deciduous shrub with large, deeply lobed leaves on stout shoots. It is often grown against a wall, which helps ripen the fruits.

Ficus carica 'Brown Turkey'

However, it is hardy as a foliage shrub, although it may be cut to ground level by hard winters.

The fruits can take longer than a year to ripen. Two flushes are usually produced. The early summer flush invariably fails over winter, but the later flush is much smaller and hardier, and it is these that expand and ripen in late summer the following year. Figs are tolerant of any well-drained soil, in sun or light shade. Propagate by removing suckers, layering, or by hardwood cuttings.

soil 	Both: any well-drained soil. Ficus: including chalk. Fraxinus: preferably fertile
site 	Ficus: sun to light shade, sun-drenched wall for fruit. Fraxinus: sunny position
pruning 	Ficus: thin to prevent becoming too dense and overcrowded. Fraxinus: none
general care 	Ficus: growth quite thick, so thin bushes heavily. Fraxinus: gross feeders that do compete with choice plants
pests & diseases 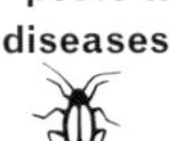	Ficus: susceptible to a few pests and diseases but not major. Fraxinus: old trees can suffer from wood-decay fungi

Fraxinus
Ash

Ashes are deciduous trees with pinnate leaves. They mainly form substantial trees suited as specimens for the largest gardens or as peripheral screening.

Fraxinus ornus

The European ash (*Fraxinus excelsior*) fits here with foliage and habit but little flower and only a yellow fall color in good years. However, the Manna ash (*Fraxinus ornus*) makes a very floriferous tree at a young age and has considerable beauty when the foliage is obliterated by the white flowers.

Ashes thrive on rich, well-drained soils, including those overlying chalk and limestone, but can grow on less fertile sites. Propagate by seed or by grafting.

	SPRING	SUMMER	FALL	WINTER	height 5yrs (ft)	height 10yrs (ft)	spread 5yrs (ft)	spread 10yrs (ft)	flower color	
Ficus carica 'Brown Turkey'		harvest harvest			5	8	5	8		Doesn't really have flowers! Can reach 20–30ft
Fraxinus excelsior	flowering		harvest harvest		13	23	3	10		Flowers without petals, not showy
F. excelsior 'Pendula'	flowering				6½	10	6½	16		Weeping habit, little height above grafting
F. ornus	flowering		harvest harvest		10	16	3	6½		Flowers showy, best ash for gardens
F. oxycarpa 'Raywood'	flowering				13	23	6½	16		Good fall color; flowers barely worthwhile

flowering harvest

Fremontodendron

This small genus is grown for the bright yellow flowers. The flowers have no corolla but the calyx looks just like the petals of any other flower.

The flowers are carried singly from axillary buds in the shoots. The first flush of flowers, in late spring, come from the buds in last summer's shoots, but later blooms are on the current season's extension growths. The season of flowering extends into the summer. In warmer areas this can continue into the fall, although the best display is in late spring/early summer.

Fremontodendron 'California Glory'

Fremontodendron is best represented by the form 'California Glory'. This is a hybrid between the two species and is hardier than either parent. 'Pacific Sunset' is very similar but has flowers of a brighter yellow. *Fremontodendron californicum* tends to open the flowers in a more concentrated flush.

Fremontodendron are best as wall shrubs, since they are too tender for all except mild gardens without the shelter of a wall. They are fast growing and will quickly attain 16–20ft (5–6m). They should not be overfed or planted on the most fertile soils because they produce foliage at the expense of flowers in these conditions. Unfortunately, these shrubs are not long-lived.

Propagate by seed or by softwood or semi-ripe cuttings in the summer, rooting them in a freely drained, sandy substrate soil.

soil 	Well-drained soils, including chalky ones, of low to moderate fertility
site 	Full sun, on a sun-drenched wall, for summer heat and winter protection
pruning 	No special requirements. Prune only to restrict growth or to reshape
general care	Fairly easy to cultivate and maintain. As a general rule, tie in any wayward branches
pests & diseases	Relatively trouble-free. Does not have any particular problems with pests and diseases

	SPRING			SUMMER			FALL			WINTER			height 5yrs (ft)	height 10yrs (ft)	spread 5yrs (ft)	spread 10yrs (ft)	flower color	
Fremontodendron 'California Glory'			✹	✹	✹	✹							20	26	13	20		Fast-growing, evergreen shrub
F. californicum			✹	✹	✹	✹							20	26	13	20		Semi-evergreen; saucer-shaped flowers
F. 'Pacific Sunset'				✹	✹	✹							20	26	13	20		Upright, evergreen shrub

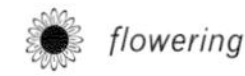 *flowering*

F

Trees & Shrubs

Garrya

Silk-tassel bush

These evergreen bushes are grown for the catkins in mid-winter through to early spring. The catkins are best on the male forms. On *Garrya elliptica* 'James Roof' they can be 8in (20cm) or more in length, hanging like silk tassels and brightening up what can be a rather gloomy time of the year.

soil	Well-drained soils of moderate fertility, including chalk soils
site	Prefers a sunny to shady position—good for more temperate aspects
pruning	No pruning needed but, if necessary, prune after flowering
general care	Fairly easy to maintain and cultivate. Any winter damage can be cut out and tidied up
pests & diseases	Relatively trouble-free. Does not have any particular problems with pests and diseases

The catkins are green with yellow anthers. In *Garrya issaquahensis* 'Glasnevin Wine' the catkins are ruby colored at the base of the green bracts. Garrya is excellent if sited next to the home or where the winter flowering will attract attention. Another reason for siting them in such positions is that they can be damaged by cold dry winds in winter, and will benefit from the protection given by walls in cold areas. They are also very tolerant of urban pollution and maritime exposure.

The female forms have shorter catkins, only 1½–4in (4–10cm) in length and are not as decorative in winter. The catkins develop into deep purple-brown fruits, providing interest in the fall. However, apart from flowering time, Garrya can be rather dull evergreens. They can grow to 13ft (4m) in height and spread, and thrive on a wide range of soil types, including chalk soils. They resent root disturbance, and should be planted from pots in the spring after the worst of the weather is past.

Propagate by semi-ripe cuttings taken with a heel of older wood in late summer.

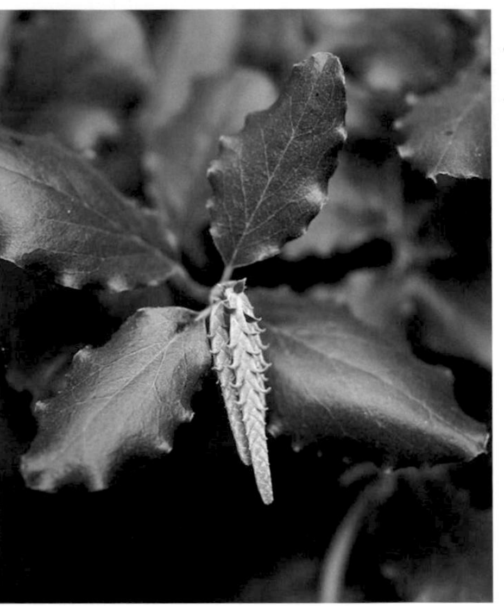

Garrya elliptica

Garrya elliptica

	SPRING			SUMMER			FALL			WINTER			height 5yrs (ft)	height 10yrs (ft)	spread 5yrs (ft)	spread 10yrs (ft)	flower color	
Garrya elliptica	flowering							harvest		flowering	flowering	flowering	5	10	5	10		Evergreen bush
G. elliptica 'James Roof'	flowering							harvest		flowering	flowering	flowering	5	10	5	10		Evergreen bush, very long catkins
G. issaquahensis 'Glasnevin Wine'	flowering							harvest		flowering	flowering	flowering	4	6½	4	6½		More compact than *G. elliptica*

flowering harvest

Genista

Mt Etna broom

The brooms include a number of small shrubs but they also include one outstanding tree. *Genista aetnensis* is found in the wild on Mt Etna in Sicily at around 6,500ft altitude, as well as in Sardinia, but it can be grown successfully in the garden.

Genista aetnensis

Genista aetnenesis starts life as a bush, and because of its intolerance of transplanting must be grown in a pot until planted out. It will form a tree with an upright domed crown, ultimately making 20–40ft (6–12m) in height. The leaves are transient, usually lasting a few days before falling. Photosynthesis is carried out by the gray-green shoots. The flowers are small, yellow, and pealike; they are carried in mid- to late summer, and are followed by small pods.

This tree should be more widely planted. It is one of the best of all flowering trees, colorful at a time when most other woody plants have ceased flowering and before the delights of autumnal color arrive. It is also attractive when placed in a mixed or shrub border toward the rear, where it can look down on lesser shrubs. Also, it does not cast a dense shade; instead it provides light dappled shade, making it excellent for small gardens.

It is ideal for many low-intensity screening situations. It will grow on any well-drained soil, being happy on chalk and also soils of low fertility.

Propagate by seed or by semi-ripe cuttings in summer.

soil	Tolerates well-drained soils, whether acidic, neutral, or limy
site	Much prefers a sunny site—not suitable for shaded positions
pruning	Does not tolerate pruning; trim only to remove damaged shoots or restrict
general care	This provides best results in soils of low fertility; can fix atmospheric nitrogen to make fertilizer
pests & diseases	Relatively trouble-free. Does not have any particular problems with pests and diseases

Gleditsia

Honeylocust

This is a genus of legumes that does not have the showy, pealike flowers of Genista and Robinia but shares the characteristic legume pod.

The foliage of Gleditsia is variable; it is usually doubly pinnate with each of the leaflets (there can be up to eight of them) divided into about 11 pairs of very small leaflets. However, if less vigorous, it may only be pinnate, with 7–18 pairs of undivided leaflets. More confusingly, both leaf types can occur on the same leaf. The net result is very fine foliage, which gives the tree a hazy appearance unless you are very close.

The spines of *Gleditsia triacanthos*, so named because of the three-pronged spines, really are quite lethal, so thornless forms have been highlighted. These have been bred to give the two forms featured here. 'Sunburst' has leaves that are golden yellow into summer when they change to a fresh green, before turning in the fall to a warm gold color before dropping. 'Rubylace' has leaves that open wine-red, greening in mid-summer before giving fall tints.

soil	Grows best in acidic sands to alkaline soil but requires good drainage
site	Only really suited to sunny sites and does not tolerate much shade
pruning	When pruning off branches, late summer is best since it reduces risk of bleeding
general care	A very easy tree to care for and cultivate—with plenty of sunshine. Late into leaf, they cast only a light shade
pests & diseases	Relatively trouble-free. Does not have any particular problems with pests and diseases

Gleditsia triacanthos 'Sunburst'

Both of these forms will make small to medium trees over 30 or more years. They are useful as specimen trees, and for providing fresh color. Gleditsia will grow on any well-drained soil, being just as well suited to chalky ones as to acidic sands. They do need full sun, or light side shade at most, and are not suited to shady sites.

They are propagated by grafting, but the parent species (and the rootstocks) are raised from seed. This has a hard coat that needs to be broken either by scarifying it or by mixing the seeds with an equal quantity of boiling water and allowing to cool.

	SPRING	SUMMER	FALL	WINTER	height 5yrs (ft)	height 10yrs (ft)	spread 5yrs (ft)	spread 10yrs (ft)	flower color	
Gleditsia triacanthos 'Rubylace'		flowering			10	16	6½	13		Bronze-red leaves until mid-summer
G. triacanthos 'Sunburst'		flowering			10	16	6½	13		Golden yellow leaves, changing in mid-summer

flowering

Halesia

Snowdrop tree

These two trees have white bell-shaped flowers in late spring as the leaves are expanding. The flowers hang down under last summer's growth. They are much underused deciduous trees and shrubs.

Halesia monticola should be considered when proposing to plant a small ornamental tree. It is the largest growing of the species, likely to attain 33ft (10m) in 30 or so years. In some forms the flowers have a rose tinge. *Halesia caroliniana* is a smaller tree or spreading shrub, attaining 20ft (6m) in 30 years but twice as wide. It is more suitable as a shrub. The fruit provides interest after the flowers have faded—an interest that really lasts until the next flowering period because they tend to hang on the bushes.

The fruit is hard and woody but has four wings running along the full length, and an awl-like projection at the tip. Initially green, the fruit is light brown when ripe.

Halesia are from a species of streamside vegetation and prefer a soil that is moist while being well drained. Unfortunately, they are not suited to chalk or limy soils. They thrive in either full sun or moderate shade.

The seeds can be slow to germinate because they need a warm period in the fall to break down the hard, woody coat, and then a cold winter period to stimulate germination. Cuttings of the new growths with a heel taken in late spring should root, but the resulting plants will need overwinter protection to get them through to next year.

Halesia monticola f. vestita

soil	Performs well in moist, well-drained acidic to neutral soils
site	This grows equally well in both the sun or moderate shade
pruning	No special pruning needed. However, if reducing a tree, prune after flowering
general care	Easy to maintain. Mulch to maintain humus content in the soil and conserve soil moisture
pests & diseases	Relatively trouble-free. Does not have any particular problems with pests and diseases

	SPRING			SUMMER			FALL			WINTER			height 5yrs (ft)	height 10yrs (ft)	spread 5yrs (ft)	spread 10yrs (ft)	color of blossom	
Halesia caroliniana			flowering				harvest	harvest	harvest	harvest			6½	13	10	16	white	Shrub or small tree, to 26ft eventually
H. monticola f. *vestita*			flowering				harvest	harvest	harvest	harvest			10	20	6½	16	white	Tree to 40ft

 *flowering*  *harvest*

Hamamelis

Witch hazel

Witch hazels are the source of the preparation used in eye lotions, which is distilled from the twigs. In the garden, however, their use is as winter-flowering shrubs.

The first form of *Hamamelis intermedia* can be in bloom well before early/mid-winter, and the season extends into early spring. The flowers of *H. intermedia* and *H. mollis* are carried on the bare, leafless branches. The petals are long and very narrow, and tolerate extreme weather conditions. The flowers are also fragrant, especially in *H. mollis*. They are generally yellow, but in 'Jelena' the flowers seem to be a bright copper-orange due to the base of the petal being red and the tip, yellow ocher.

The fall color of the hazel-like foliage is generally a rich yellow. However, with *Hamamelis vernalis* 'Sandra' the leaves turn orange, scarlet, and red. The new foliage of this plant is suffused with a plum-purple, before becoming green with a purplish tinge to the underside. The flowers are yellow and tend to open on sunny days, but remain shut on less pleasant days.

Hamamelis make large shrubs, attaining 13–20ft (4–6m) and as wide or wider in 20 or so years. The habit is generally open, which helps display the flowers. Hamamelis like neutral to acidic well-drained soils, but can be grown on deep soils overlying chalk. Mulch to maintain a humus-rich soil. They can be raised from seed, which often takes two years to germinate but the selected forms are grafted onto seedling rootstocks of *Hamamelis virginiana* (which are inconsequential flowerers in the fall). They can also be layered.

Hamamelis intermedia 'Jelena'

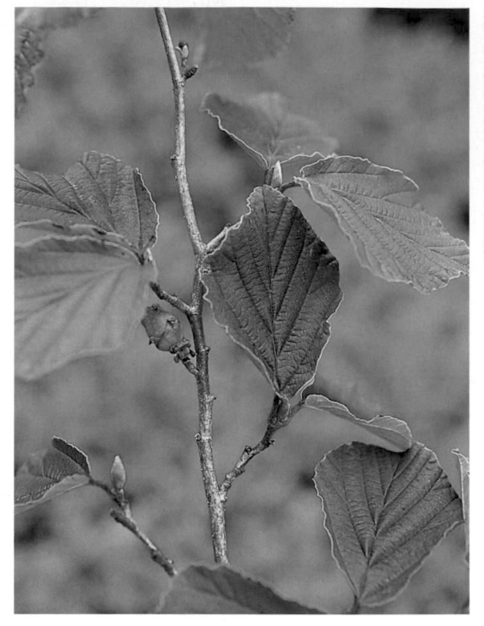

Hamamelis intermedia 'Pallida'

soil	Neutral to acidic, humus-rich soils, or deep soils overlying chalk or limestone
site	Sun to medium shade. Shelter from cold, drying winds if possible
pruning	None, except to reshape or restrain; can be difficult to break from old wood
general care	Mulch to maintain soil moisture and humus. Watch out for suckers on grafted plants
pests & diseases	Relatively trouble-free. Does not have any particular problems with pests and diseases

	SPRING	SUMMER	FALL	WINTER	height 5yrs (ft)	height 10yrs (ft)	spread 5yrs (ft)	spread 10yrs (ft)	flower color	
Hamamelis intermedia 'Arnold Promise'	flowering			flowering, flowering	6½	13	6½	13		Reddish fall color
H. intermedia 'Jelena'	flowering			flowering, flowering	6½	13	6½	13		Orange, red, and scarlet fall color
H. intermedia 'Pallida'	flowering			flowering, flowering	6½	13	6½	13		Yellow fall color
H. mollis	flowering			flowering, flowering	6½	13	6½	13		Flowers fragrant; yellow fall color
H. vernalis 'Sandra'	flowering			flowering, flowering	6½	13	6½	13		Good fall color of orange, red, and scarlet

flowering

Hibiscus

Woody mallow

Lots of mallow-type flowers (with the stamens attached to the style) carried in late summer or early fall characterize these deciduous shrubs, provided they are given a warm and sunny position in the garden.

The principal species is *Hibiscus syriacus* (which is actually a native of India and China, not Syria). The blooms are carried on the current season's growth. The shrubs can be hard pruned back to a branch framework in spring to maximize the number of flowers.

Establishing a framework to which they are pruned is important if you are going to go for maximum flower production. The flowers are generally some form of blue, white, or pink. The typical flower has a single row of five petals, which appear to form a trumpet; I find these forms more attractive than the doubles or semi-doubles. The following forms all have single flowers: 'Hamabo' is a white-flowered selection whose petals have a pinkish tinge and bronze-colored markings in the throat; 'Meehani' has lilac-mauve-colored flowers and a low habit but is more notable for the yellow margin to the leaves; 'Oiseau Blue' ('Blue Bird') has large flowers which are mauvish-blue with a deeper center; 'Woodbridge' has flowers that are a deep rosy crimson with a darker throat; 'Pink Giant' has blooms clear pink with dark red eyes. They thrive on a wide range of soils, provided they are freely drained. Propagate them by semi-ripe cuttings in summer.

Hibiscus syriacus 'Hamabo'

Hibiscus syriacus 'Pink Giant'

soil	Any well-drained soil, including chalky ones and acidic sands
site	Much prefers the sun. In colder climates, locate on a warm and sunny wall
pruning	Prune back last season's growth in late winter to the main branch structure
general care	Mulch to protect the roots, especially in cold areas, and to maintain a high humus content in the soil
pests & diseases	Can get various insect pests if grown in a sunroom, but in the garden there are no particular problems

	SPRING	SUMMER	FALL	WINTER	height 5yrs (ft)	height 10yrs (ft)	spread 5yrs (ft)	spread 10yrs (ft)	flower color	
Hibiscus syriacus 'Hamabo'		✹ ✹	✹ ✹		5	8	4	6½	white	Best white variety
H. syriacus 'Meehani'		✹ ✹	✹ ✹		3	6½	5	6½		Leaves with a yellow margin
H. syriacus 'Oiseau Blue'		✹ ✹	✹ ✹		5	8	4	6½		Also known as 'Blue Bird'; blue variety
H. syriacus 'Pink Giant'		✹ ✹	✹ ✹		5	8	4	6½		Large flowers
H. syriacus 'Woodbridge'		✹ ✹	✹ ✹		5	8	4	6½		Large-flowered, excellent pink variety

 *flowering*

Hippophae

Sea buckthorn

Hippophae rhamnoides makes a bushy shrub or occasionally a small slender-crowned tree. It is dioecious—that is, there are separate male and female plants. The attractive but acidly juicy berries are only carried on the female shrubs.

soil	Any garden soil—chalk, clay, sand, or loam. Excellent for coastal sites and on sands
site	At their best in full sun but can tolerate a moderate amount of shade
pruning	No special pruning regime required, except to restrict or reshape
general care	Fairly easy to cultivate and maintain. Remove any suckers that spring up where they are not needed
pests & diseases	Relatively trouble-free. Does not have any particular problems with pests and diseases

It is important to have one male *Hippophae rhamnoides* for every three to five or so females, to ensure adequate pollination of the flowers. The male plants are not without their own attractive feature, as the male flower buds are in clusters of a metallic bronze color over winter.

Hippophae fruits are orange-colored, measuring a little less than ½in (1cm) across. They color in early fall but often remain on bushes until the spring, especially if they are located in the open where birds feel vulnerable when eating the berries.

The foliage of this shrub is willowlike, greyish-green above and silvery gray on the underside due to a dense covering of scales. The spur shoots tend to terminate in a stout spine.

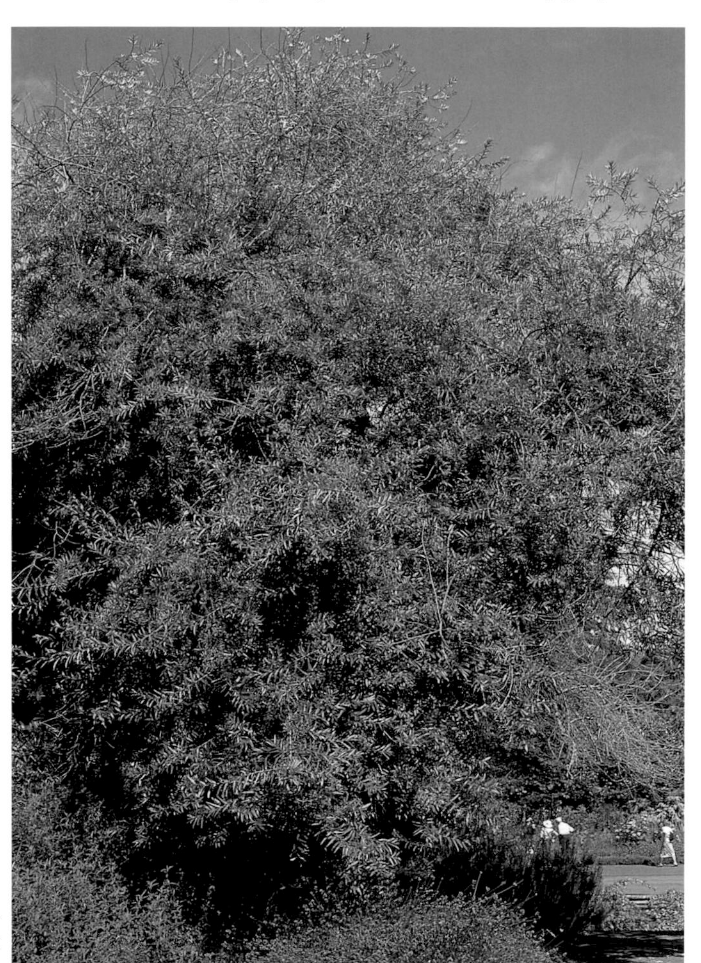

Hippophae rhamnoides

As the common name—sea buckthorn—implies, these shrubs thrive on maritime sites in the wild in the northern hemisphere. Indeed, in many coastal areas this plant is used for windbreaks, stabilizing sand dunes and as protective hedging. It is particularly useful for the latter purpose since the habit is vigorous and spreading to as much as 20ft (6m). However, *Hippophae rhamnoides* also occurs inland across Asia to western China, well away from the sea.

These shrubs will tolerate almost all garden soils, whether sand, clay, or chalk. They are at their best in full sun but are almost as good in moderate shade.

Hippophae rhamnoides can be propagated by seed, sown as soon as they are ripe. They sucker freely (some would say too freely) and these can be removed and grown on. Hardwood cuttings in the fall and semi-ripe cuttings in late summer should also root. The advantage of cuttings and suckers is that you know the sex of the plant and can ensure you get sufficient (but not too many) males.

Hoheria

Lace-bark

Hoheria give us showy white flowers on deciduous or evergreen small trees, and is one of the jewels of New Zealand. The flowers have a delicate boss of stamens, which are set off by the paper-white petals.

Hoheria's flowers are honey-scented and attractive to butterflies, providing nectar in late summer. The flowers are carried on the current season's growths and more generously as the tree matures. The foliage is variable as the tree matures, being lobed in young trees but unlobed in adult ones—a feature of a large number of New Zealand trees. They make excellent specimen trees or large shrubs when set in a lawn, or as a background tree in a shrub or mixed border. They are better in milder gardens, and will need woodland shelter in colder areas.

soil	Neutral or alkaline but well-drained. Best on humus-rich soils of moderate fertility
site	Better in milder areas where they do well in sun or light shade
pruning	If pruning is necessary, prune in spring to remove dead wood or to reshape
general care	Mulch both to protect the root system against hard winters and to maintain the soil's organic matter
pests & diseases	Coral spot can be a problem where there are lush or underripened shoots but trouble-free apart from this

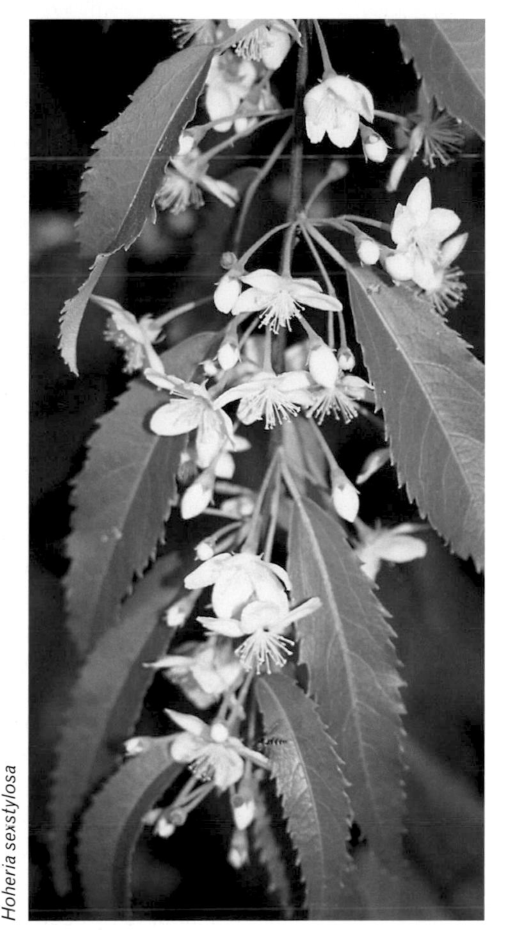

Hoheria sexstylosa

The deciduous species *Hoheria lyallii* is somewhat hardier than the evergreen *Hoheria sexstylosa* but they all like protection from cold dry winds. Hoheria is tolerant of neutral to alkaline soils, including chalk or limy ones, provided they are well drained. However, they are best on deep, moderately fertile soils with a high organic matter content. If grown in too much shade or on very fertile soil, they are more prone to coral spot on the branches since they need the summer heat fully to ripen the wood.

They can be propagated by semi-ripe cuttings in summer and also by seed. These should be sown as soon as they ripen in the fall.

	SPRING	SUMMER	FALL	WINTER	height 5yrs (ft)	height 10yrs (ft)	spread 5yrs (ft)	spread 10yrs (ft)	flower color	
Hoheria 'Glory of Amlwch'		flowering, flowering			6	10	5	6½	white	Semi-evergreen, narrow crown
H. lyallii		flowering, flowering			6	10	5	6½	white	Deciduous
H. sexstylosa		flowering, flowering			6½	10	5	6½	white	Evergreen

 *flowering*

Idesia

Idesia has several attractive attributes that can enhance any garden. The most important has to be the large, heart-shaped leaves. These are like Catalpa leaves but thicker, and therefore much tougher for windy sites.

Idesia polycarpa

The flowers are pale yellow and strongly fragrant. They are carried in early to mid-summer in erect or pendulous panicles. Provided there is a male to pollinate them, these are succeeded on female trees by the orange-red berries (see opposite page for chart). These ripen in the fall and persist after the leaves drop. Idesia can make a sizeable tree with time but flowers at a young stage if planted in a hot, sunny position. In the garden it is good in a shrub or mixed border or in a hot, sunny corner. It will grow on both acidic to alkaline soils, tolerating thin soils over chalk, but is best on fertile, well-drained, neutral soils. The fruits contain many small seeds and these can be sown in spring, or Idesia can be propagated by softwood or semi-ripe cuttings in summer.

soil	Idesia: happy in any well-drained soil, including shallow soils over chalk
site	Will perform its best if it is positioned in a hot, sunny site
pruning	No special pruning regime required, except to restrict or reshape
general care	Fairly easy to cultivate and maintain. Needs both male and female plants for good fruiting
pests & diseases	Relatively trouble-free. Does not have any particular problems with pests and diseases

Ilex
Holly

There are very many holly species scattered around the continents, including both deciduous and evergreen species and a few small shrubs.

Hollies are valuable as fruiting trees and for their foliage. The flowers are small, whitish-green and only of merit as the precursor of the fruit. This is carried only on female trees, although *Ilex aquifolium* 'J.C. van Tol' is hermaphrodite and will fruit on its own. Planting both sexes is important; however, you cannot go wrong if you plant *Ilex altaclerensis* 'Golden King' and either *Ilex aquifolium* 'Golden Queen' or 'Silver Queen'—strangely, the 'King' is female and the 'Queen' male! The berry is generally red, although *Ilex aquifolium* 'Bacciflava' has heavy crops of bright yellow berries.

Hollies are as valuable for their foliage, perhaps more so, since the berries last a few months (depending on how many

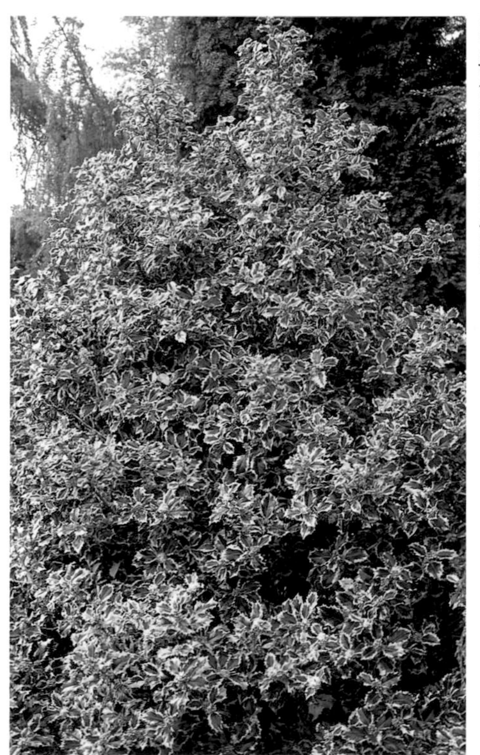
Ilex aquifolium 'Golden Queen'

birds you are feeding) but the foliage is evergreen. Wild hollies have leaves that are dark green and lustrous above with spiny margins, but of those listed here only the natural form of *Ilex aquifolium* and the cultivar 'Pyramidalis Aureomarginata' will have this type of foliage; *Ilex altaclerensis* 'Camelliifolia' and *Ilex aquifolium* 'J.C. van Tol' have leaves with few spines. However, these two species have given rise to a large number of variegated forms. These have leaves that are creamy white, creamy yellow, or gold to a greater or lesser degree.

soil	Ilex: very unfussy. Will perform in any type of garden soil
site	Very good plant to have since it thrives in both sun and fairly dense shade
pruning	Best pruned before new growth in late spring—will tolerate pruning at any time
general care	Very easy to maintain. Industrial pollution and maritime exposure will not affect its growth
pests & diseases	Leaf miners can be a small problem, otherwise reasonably unaffected by pests and diseases

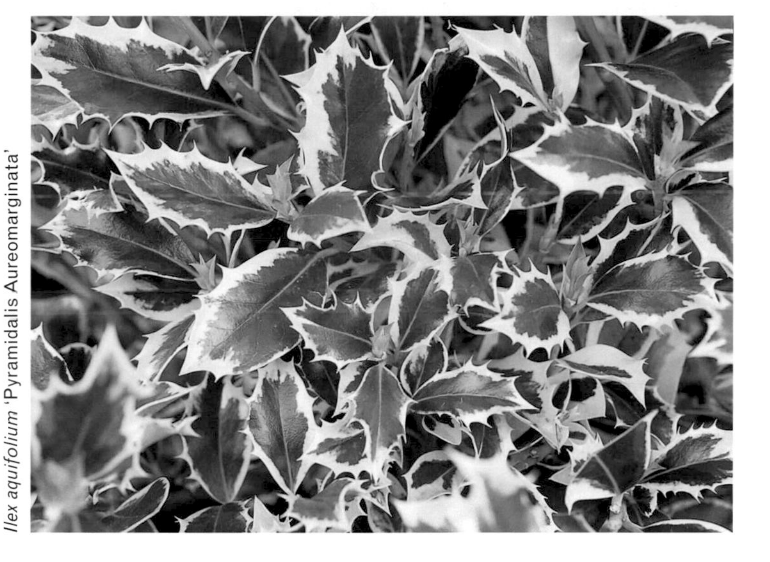

Ilex aquifolium 'Pyramidalis Aureomarginata'

In the garden, hollies are useful for specimen trees and to make dense screens. They make excellent hedges, requiring clipping only once a year. They are also extremely shade-tolerant, and are naturally understory trees. They can be propagated by cuttings taken at the end of summer and rooted in a cold frame. Seed can be used for the species but is slow to germinate.

	SPRING			SUMMER			FALL			WINTER			height 5yrs (ft)	height 10yrs (ft)	spread 5yrs (ft)	spread 10yrs (ft)	color of blossom	
Idesia polycarpa				flowering	flowering		harvest	harvest	harvest	harvest			6½	16	6½	13		Large heart-shaped leaves
Ilex altaclerensis 'Belgica Aurea'			flowering					harvest	harvest	harvest	harvest	harvest	5	11½	3	6½		Deep green leaves with pale/gray areas; female
I. altaclerensis 'Camelliifolia'			flowering					harvest	harvest	harvest	harvest	harvest	5	11½	3	6½		Large leaves, shiny dark green; female
I. altaclerensis 'Golden King'			flowering					harvest	harvest	harvest	harvest	harvest	5	11½	3	6½		Green leaves with a bright yellow margin; female
I. altaclerensis 'Lawsoniana'			flowering					harvest	harvest	harvest	harvest	harvest	5	11½	3	6½		Leaves splashed yellow in center; female
I. aquifolium			flowering					harvest	harvest	harvest	harvest	harvest	5	11½	3	6½		Leaves spiny near ground—fewer in upper crown
I. aquifolium 'Argentea Marginata'			flowering					harvest	harvest	harvest	harvest	harvest	5	11½	3	6½		Leaves white margined, young growth pink; female
I. aquifolium 'Bacciflava'			flowering					harvest	harvest	harvest	harvest	harvest	5	11½	3	6½		Leaves typical; female, fruit bright yellow
I. aquifolium 'Ferox Argentea'			flowering										5	11½	3	6½		Leaves ferociously spiny; male
I. aquifolium 'Golden Queen'			flowering										5	11½	3	6½		Dark green leaves abroad yellow margin; male
I. aquifolium 'J.C. van Tol'			flowering					harvest	harvest	harvest	harvest	harvest	5	11½	3	6½		Shiny dark green leaves, almost spine-less
I. aquifolium 'Madame Briot'			flowering					harvest	harvest	harvest	harvest	harvest	5	11½	3	6½		Dark green leaves, strongly spiny; female
I. aquifolium 'Myrtifolia Aureomaculata'			flowering										3	6½	2½	4		Dense compact form; male;
I. a. 'Pyramidalis Aureomarginata'			flowering					harvest	harvest	harvest	harvest	harvest	5	11½	3	6½		Bright green leaves; habit conical; female
I. aquifolium 'Silver Queen'			flowering										5	11½	3	6½		New foliage shrimp-pink; male

 *flowering*  *harvest*

Juglans

Walnut

Walnuts are grown in gardens partly for their nuts. They can be pickled whole, provided they are picked before the shell has become hard and woody, normally sometime around the second month of summer. They are even tastier if left to mature as walnuts, although squirrels like them at some intermediate stage and will quite merrily attempt to devour the lot.

Juglans nigra

The outer case of the nut is green but gives a strong yellow dye, which stains the hands. The flowers open with the new leaves in late spring and are susceptible to spring frost damage at this stage. Walnuts also make bold foliage trees, with large pinnate leaves, and an attractive furrowed bark—shiny gray in *Juglans regia*, dark brown or black in *Juglans nigra*. The timber is excellent, with a dark heartwood and a fine grain.

In gardens, walnuts can be planted only as specimen trees. They need plenty of space, and if given side shelter, will become lanky. The roots give off chemicals that are toxic to many other plants, thereby reducing competition for water and nutrients.

Pruning needs to be well timed. If large limbs are removed during the winter and spring, and to a lesser extent during the fall, the wound will bleed profusely. Apart from looking distressing, it can seriously weaken the tree, since the sap contains reserves of sugars. Pruning should be carried out during the summer, when the natural processes will stop bleeding.

Walnuts thrive on all normal, well-drained soils, but with a bias toward soils of a more alkaline nature. *Juglans regia* needs excellent drainage, but *Juglans nigra* requires a more moist soil.

Walnuts can be propagated by seed, which will germinate promptly in spring. Selected forms can be grafted, but it is important to prevent the rootstock bleeding and then drowning the scions.

soil	Happy in reasonable soils, whether acidic or alkaline in nature
site	Will perform at its best only if sited in a hot, sunny position
pruning	Carry out only during summer, otherwise there is a risk of heavy bleeding
general care	Does not associate with many other garden plants because of toxic substances produced by the roots
pests & diseases	Relatively trouble-free. Does not have any particular problems with pests and diseases

	SPRING	SUMMER	FALL	WINTER	height 5yrs (ft)	height 10yrs (ft)	spread 5yrs (ft)	spread 10yrs (ft)	color of blossom	
Juglans nigra	flowering		harvest		10	20	3	10		Yellow fall color, large hard nuts
J. regia	flowering		harvest		10	20	3	10		Good fruiting species, no fall color

flowering harvest

Koelreuteria

Pride of India

Koelreuteria carries its flowers like large yellow parasols held high above the foliage in a half-open or conical stance. The trusses consist of numerous rich yellow flowers each with four straplike petals, and en masse make the whole tree look yellow.

Koelreuteria paniculata

The fruits are inflated bladders, papery thin when ripe and containing three shiny black seeds. The leaves are large and have 9–15 pairs of leaflets, which turn yellow in fall; in spring they are a shade of pink or pale yellow-green.

Koelreuteria is useful as a specimen tree or as a part of a larger border. It can grow to 40–50ft (12–15m) but is more usually seen at 16–20ft (5–6m). It thrives on a wide range of well-drained soils. It can be propagated by root cuttings and by seed.

soil	Koelreuteria: dry and well-drained, including chalk. Laburnum: any garden soil
site	Koelreuteria: best in the sun. Laburnum: prefers sun to light shade
pruning	Koelreuteria: resents severe pruning; prune to remove defects. Laburnum: none
general care 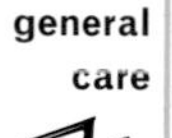	Koelreuteria: forms weak crotches with duplicate leaders. Laburnum: remove seed pods after flowering
pests & diseases 	Both are relatively trouble-free. Neither has any particular problem with pests and diseases

Laburnum

Another yellow-flowered tree, although this one flowers in late spring or early summer with pendulous racemes.

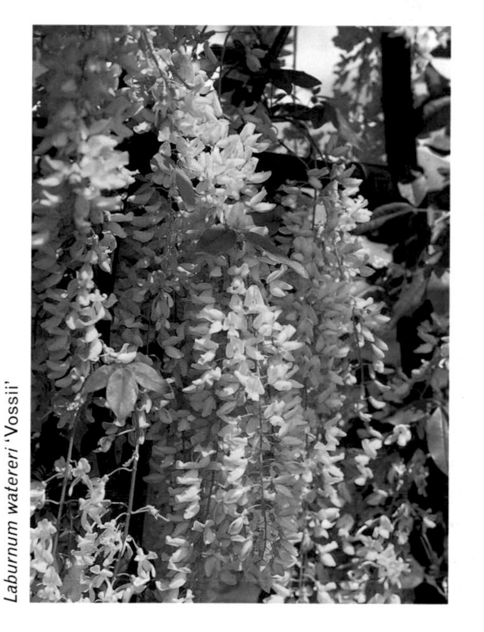

Laburnum watereri 'Vossii'

The flowers show its membership of the pea family, as does the fruit. Laburnum seeds are poisonous if eaten (as is the rest of the plant), although records of anyone being poisoned are extremely rare. The leaves are trifoliate, shiny green and may turn yellow in the fall. They make small trees, 16–26ft (5–8m) and as much in spread.

Use them as specimens trees, or as a larger item in a shrub or mixed bed. They can be trained over a pergola so that the flowers hang down below the structure.

Laburnum can be propagated by seeds, which will germinate more quickly if scarified (when the hard waxy seed coat is artificially breached so that the seed can absorb water and grow). Hardwood cuttings taken in late winter should also root, and they can be grafted onto seedling rootstocks.

	SPRING	SUMMER	FALL	WINTER	height 5yrs (ft)	height 10yrs (ft)	spread 5yrs (ft)	spread 10yrs (ft)	color of blossom	
Koelreuteria paniculata		flowering, flowering	harvest, harvest		10	16	6½	16		Late-flowering tree, unusual fruits
Laburnum alpinum 'Pendulum'		flowering			4	6½	4	6½		Stiffly weeping branches; flowers fragrant
L. anagyroides	flowering	flowering	harvest		10	16	6½	16		Short racemes to 8in
L. watereri 'Vossii'	flowering	flowering			10	16	6½	16		Very floriferous, with racemes to 2ft

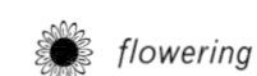 *flowering*  *harvest*

Laurus

Bay laurel

Bay laurel is used as a herb in cooking and has aromatic leaves. It is the true laurel that was used by the ancients as a mark of triumph and acclamation, and is the type of the laurel family. The English word "laurel" has been hijacked to mean an evergreen shrub, particularly the cherry laurel, *Prunus laurocerasus*. Laurus makes an evergreen tree to 33ft (10m) or more in sunny, hot, and fertile sites in mild climates.

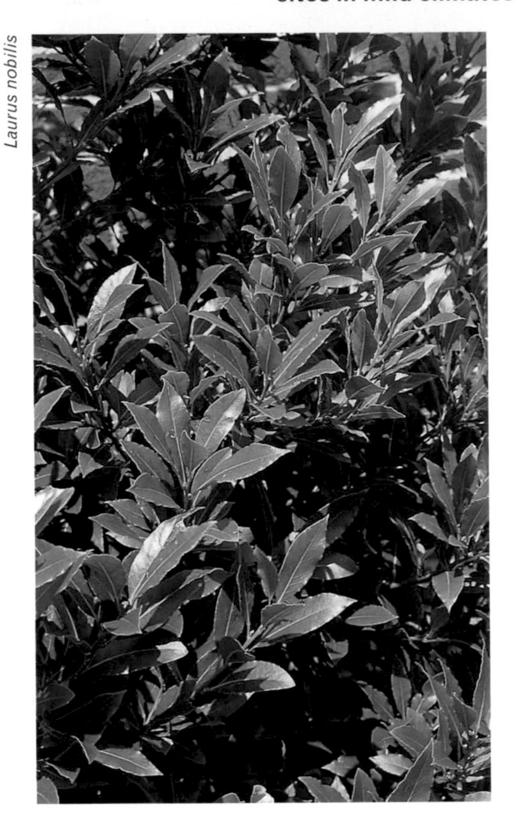

Laurus nobilis

In colder climes Laurus may be restricted to a shrub, and cut back to ground level in hard winters. However, it will normally regrow rapidly from the stump. The flowers are creamy yellow and carried in late spring. They add brightness to the bush but are not exactly colorful. They are followed by black berries.

In the garden, bay laurel is useful for its dense evergreen habit, especially at the back of a border, and as a trimmed shrub in the kitchen garden. It can also be used as a hedging plant in milder countries, and is excellent for this in coastal areas. Bay laurel grows well in pots and can be clipped as topiary. It thrives in full sun and on all well-drained soils, especially chalky sites.

It can be propagated by semi-ripe cuttings in summer or ripe shoots in mid- to late winter in a cold frame. Seed germinates readily and there are often seedlings around established fruiting plants.

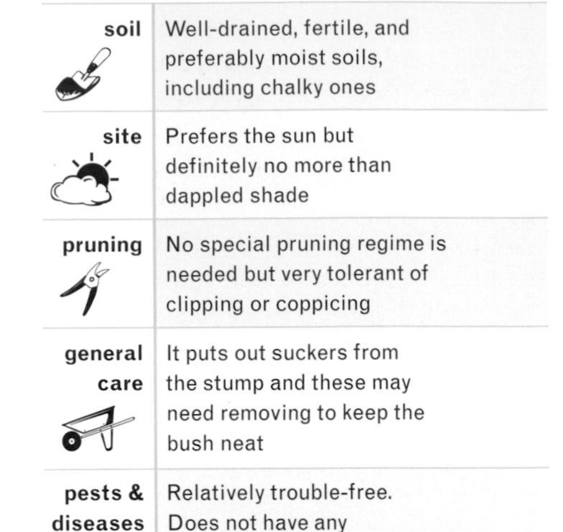

soil	Well-drained, fertile, and preferably moist soils, including chalky ones
site	Prefers the sun but definitely no more than dappled shade
pruning	No special pruning regime is needed but very tolerant of clipping or coppicing
general care	It puts out suckers from the stump and these may need removing to keep the bush neat
pests & diseases	Relatively trouble-free. Does not have any particular problem with pests and diseases

Laurus nobilis

	SPRING	SUMMER	FALL	WINTER	height 5yrs (ft)	height 10yrs (ft)	spread 5yrs (ft)	spread 10yrs (ft)	color of blossom	
Laurus nobilis	flowering		harvest		6½	11½	5	8		Evergreen, aromatic foliage used as kitchen herb
L. nobilis 'Aurea'	flowering		harvest		6½	11½	5	8		Golden yellow leaves, especially at tips
L. nobilis f. *angustifolia*	flowering		harvest		6½	11½	5	8		Willowlike leaves, hardier than most forms

flowering harvest

Ligustrum

Privet

Privets are usually encountered as hedges, for which they do an excellent, if uninspired, job (and are inclined to be fragile if clipped in a box shape and not with an "A"-shaped profile).

The forms of *Ligustrum ovalifolium* are particularly useful in the hedging role, where their semi-evergreen foliage provides density to the screen in winter. The flowers of this common privet are in conical terminal panicles in mid-summer; they contain a compound, trimethylamine, which can make them have a fishy odor to some people.

The Chinese privet, *Ligustrum lucidum*, is in a different class. This makes a small to medium tree, eventually reaching 33ft (10m) or so, and has large, glossy leaves. It is also valuable for flowering in early fall.

In the garden, *L. ovalifolium* is useful as a hedging and screening plant, or for the color variants of 'Argenteum' and 'Aureum', and *Ligustrum* 'Vicaryi'; the foliage is also a good food for stick insects. *L. lucidum* is a specimen tree, excellent when free standing and good when part of a taller screen or larger shrub border. 'Excelsum Superbum' contains one of the very best evergreen variegated forms.

They can be propagated by hardwood cuttings placed in a trench in winter (*L. ovalifolium* and *L.* 'Vicaryi') or by semi-ripe cuttings in summer, or else by seed.

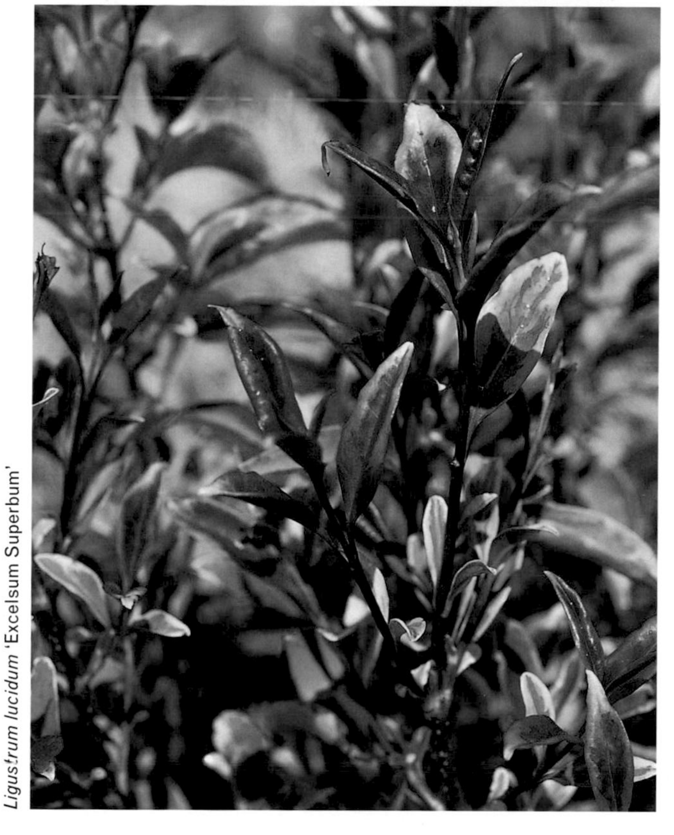

Ligustrum lucidum 'Excelsum Superbum'

soil	Well-drained to heavy soils, including chalks and clays, are the best
site	Tolerates a position ranging from the sun to moderate shade
pruning	Light clipping or coppicing; trim hedges of *L. ovalifolium* 2–3 times each year
general care	Easy to maintain and grow. Flowers, especially of *L. ovalifolium*, have a fishy scent
pests & diseases	Various insects can cause small leaf problems; more seriously, honey fungus can progressively kill a hedge

	SPRING	SUMMER	FALL	WINTER	height 5yrs (ft)	height 10yrs (ft)	spread 5yrs (ft)	spread 10yrs (ft)	flower color	
Ligustrum lucidum			flowering, harvest		5	10	3	6½		Glossy evergreen leaves
L. lucidum 'Excelsum Superbum'			flowering, harvest		5	10	3	6½		Bright green leaves with yellow margin
L. ovalifolium		flowering, flowering	harvest		6½	11½	5	6½		Semi-evergreen
L. ovalifolium 'Argenteum'		flowering, flowering	harvest		6½	11½	5	6½		Leaves with a creamy white margin
L. ovalifolium 'Aureum'		flowering, flowering	harvest		6½	11½	5	6½		Rich yellow leaves; golden privet
L. 'Vicaryi'		flowering, flowering	harvest		6½	11½	5	6½		Suffused yellow leaves in summer

 *flowering*  *harvest*

Liquidambar

Sweetgum

This small group of trees is the source of "liquid storax," which is a fragrant resin extracted from the bark and used in some medicinal compounds. In the garden, they are grown for the maplelike leaves, which turn wonderfully in the fall, giving displays of orange, scarlet, red, or crimson and lasting for two or more weeks.

The leaves are set alternately along the shoot and thus the trees can instantly be separated from maples (Acer). They are more closely related to the planes (Platanus), sharing with them the globular fruit that contains a number of separate fruits and are shaped like a medieval mace. The twigs have corky ridges or flanges.

Sweet gum makes a good specimen tree for garden or parkland settings wherever there is sufficient space to allow it to grow. If it reaches full maturity it may grow to 80ft (25m) in height with a high domed crown, but that would take a century or so.

It does not grow on shallow soils overlying chalk, where at best it is very chlorotic, but it will thrive in deeper soils. Care needs to be taken when transplanting trees since they can be slow to reform roots.

The species can be propagated by seeds, which germinate readily in spring after sowing in the fall (or a cold period in the refrigerator). Garden selections can be grafted onto seedling rootstocks. Softwood cuttings in summer may be successful.

Liquidambar styraciflua 'Silver Icing'

Liquidambar styraciflua 'Lane Roberts'

soil	Heavy wet sites and well-drained loams—not for low soils overlying chalk
site	This prefers a position in the sun, since it is a dominant tree
pruning	No special pruning regime required, except to restrict or reshape
general care	Fairly easy to cultivate and maintain. Can be propagated by seeds sown in the fall
pests & diseases	Relatively trouble-free. Does not have any particular problem with pests and diseases

	SPRING	SUMMER	FALL	WINTER	height 5yrs (ft)	height 10yrs (ft)	spread 5yrs (ft)	spread 10yrs (ft)	flower color	
Liquidambar formosana	flowering	harvest			6½	11½	3	6½		Generally cultivated as var. *monticola*
L. styraciflua 'Lane Roberts'	flowering	harvest			10	16	3	6½		Excellent form for fall color
L. styraciflua 'Silver Icing'	flowering	harvest			10	16	3	6½		Five-lobed leaves, fall color variable
L. styraciflua 'Variegata'	flowering	harvest			10	16	3	6½		Leaves stripped and mottled yellow

flowering · harvest

Liriodendron

Tulip tree

The flowers on Liriodendron are like upright tulips, with six green-white petals, which have an orange basal blotch. They are carried at the end of the leafy growths—formed from last summer's buds—on branchlets in the outer crown.

The fruit is a woody cluster of samaras, which persists over much of the winter as brown candles, before breaking apart to release the seeds. The flowers are attractive in their way but usually produced only on older trees out of sight of the ground. The leaves are more interesting—they have two side lobes but the tip is scalloped as if a giant caterpillar has removed a bite from the end. They also turn a beautiful golden yellow in the fall providing really excellent autumnal color. Tulip trees make tall-growing specimens, up to 80ft (25m) or so on good sites over a century or so. Young trees have narrow columnar-conic crowns; in older trees, the crowns are broad columnar or domed. They are specimen trees, having no other purpose in the garden or parkland setting. Locate where they can be viewed from a window if you want to enjoy the flowers fully, and where the fall color is best displayed.

The root system is fleshy and they do not transplant easily, requiring extra attention to make sure they form a new root system and do not dry out. They are most easily propagated by seed, which is sown in the fall or spring. Only about 10 percent of the seeds are viable. Garden forms are usually grafted onto seedling rootstocks. Layering and air layering can also be tried.

Liriodendron tulipferum

Liriodendron tulipiferum 'Aureomarginatum'

soil	Fertile, rich, well-drained to moist soils, including chalky ones
site	Locate in the sun as a specimen tree where they can be admired
pruning	No special pruning regime required, except to restrict or reshape
general care	Mulch and avoid sports or activities that may compact the soil around the tree
pests & diseases	Relatively trouble-free. Does not have any particular problem with pests and diseases

	SPRING	SUMMER	FALL	WINTER	height 5yrs (ft)	height 10yrs (ft)	spread 5yrs (ft)	spread 10yrs (ft)	flower color	
Liriodendron chinense		flowering	harvest harvest		10	16	5	10		Leaves glaucous beneath
L. tulipiferum		flowering	harvest harvest		13	23	6½	10		Leaves turn wonderful golden yellow in fall
L. tulipiferum 'Aureomarginatum'		flowering	harvest harvest		13	23	6½	10		Leaves with bright yellow border
L. tulipiferum 'Fastigiatum'		flowering	harvest harvest		13	23	6½	10		Upright branching structure, columnar crown

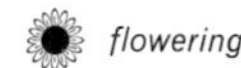 *flowering*  *harvest*

Luma

This evergreen tree is so amazing that it should be a good enough reason for moving to a mild region with high rainfall. The orange- or cinnamon-colored bark cracks to reveal white streaks in older trees and is quite stunning.

Luma apiculata

The newly exposed bark of Luma has a velvety texture. The leaves are small, shiny green with an apiculate (shortly pointed) tip and are aromatic if crushed. The flowers are carried singly in the leaf axils at the tips of the current year's growths in late summer or early fall, but the shoot tips tend to have a large number of short nodes, giving a more clustered appearance to the flowers. They have four white petals and very many stamens. The fruit is a globose fleshy berry, which is dark purple when ripe.

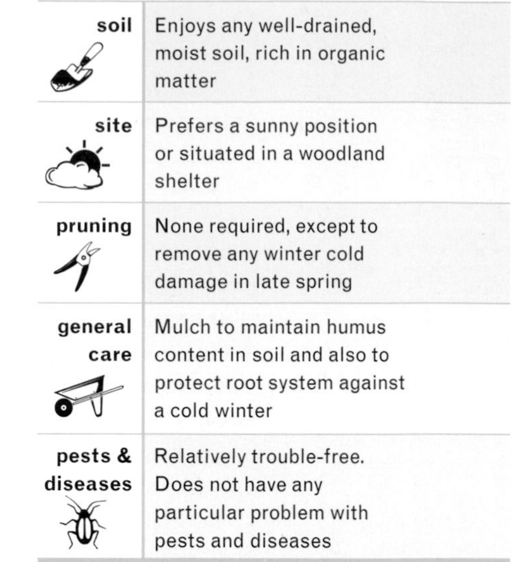

soil	Enjoys any well-drained, moist soil, rich in organic matter
site	Prefers a sunny position or situated in a woodland shelter
pruning	None required, except to remove any winter cold damage in late spring
general care	Mulch to maintain humus content in soil and also to protect root system against a cold winter
pests & diseases	Relatively trouble-free. Does not have any particular problem with pests and diseases

Unfortunately, this lovely tree is not winter-cold hardy in inland sites. Even with woodland shelter or when grown on the side of a house it is liable to be cut back by hard winters before attaining a size that displays the colorful bark. However, in milder areas, especially where it can be given woodland shelter, it is a really first-class, narrow-crowned tree or shrub. It can also be clipped to make hedges in mild gardens. Luma will thrive on all well-drained fertile soils. It will grow in full sun to moderate shade.

It is easily propagated by semi-ripe cuttings taken in summer or ripe cuttings taken with a heel of older wood over winter. The genus is often treated as part of Myrtus in many older books.

Luma apiculata

	SPRING	SUMMER	FALL	WINTER	height 5yrs (ft)	height 10yrs (ft)	spread 5yrs (ft)	spread 10yrs (ft)	color of blossom	
Luma apiculata		flowering	flowering, harvest		6½	13	3	6½		Stunning orange velvety bark
L. apiculata 'Glanleam Gold'		flowering	flowering, harvest		5	8	5	8		Leaves pink tinged when young

flowering · harvest

Trees & Shrubs

Magnolia

Cultivated Magnolia can be conveniently divided into two groups: those that flower on the bare shoots before the leaves and those that bear their flowers at the end of leafy shoots of the current year's growth.

Magnolia stellata

Magnolias need well-drained soils but are happy on either acidic sands or a good depth of topsoil overlying chalk. They will grow in shade, but scarcely flower. The roots are fleshy and need careful handling when planting them. They can be propagated by a variety of methods. The species will grow readily from seeds, which have a fleshy, oily orange aril that stinks as it rots down. Germination will often be better if the seeds are sown in the fall and kept in a cold frame.

Evergreen species like *Magnolia grandiflora* and *Magnolia delavayi* can be propagated by ripe cuttings in the fall in a cold frame; these should root over the next 12 months. Deciduous forms and most species can be struck from softwood or semi-ripe cuttings taken as soon as they are ripe. Wound on one side, treat with rooting powder, insert in an open potting mix, and keep moist by covering with thin clear polyethylene. Roots should form within a few weeks. They can also be propagated by grafting.

soil	Well-drained acidic/neutral; most will grow on deep soils overlying chalk or limestone
site	Prefers sun to light overhead shade and moderate side shade
pruning	None needed. If reshaping or restricting, prune after flowering
general care	Mulch and do not disturb soil under crown spread or you will damage the fleshy roots that are close to soil surface
pests & diseases	Relatively trouble-free. Does not have any particular problem with pests and diseases

Precocious flowering Magnolia

Precocious Magnolia are the Magnolia that flower on the bare boughs from large flower buds formed during the previous summer. The flowers are very conspicuous but are susceptible to frost damage. It is possible to reduce the incidence and frequency of frost damage by careful positioning. Avoid frost pockets and cold-facing aspects, since much of the damage caused by frost is a result of fast thawing.

The taller forms will carry their blooms way above one's head, so they are much more attractive if they can be seen from above. Precocious flowering Magnolia range in size from the small and relatively slow-growing *Magnolia stellata*, which may make 10ft (3m) by 13ft (4m) in 30 years, to *Magnolia campbellii* and its forms, which could reach as much as 100ft (30m), although not quite in 30 years (more like 50 to 80).

Magnolia loebneri and *Magnolia kewensis* are intermediates and well suited to modern gardens. They are shapely-looking trees and equally as interesting in flower as the best forms of *Magnolia soulangeana*.

Magnolia campbellii

Magnolia 'Iolanthe'

Later-flowering Magnolia

These Magnolia belong to quite separate groups but all flower on new leafy shoots. The most common species in cultivation is *M. grandiflora* and its forms. They bear enormous, fragrant white flowers from early summer until the fall frosts appear. The leaves are evergreen, glossy, and somewhat yellow-green in color with rufous hairy undersides. *M. delavayi* has even larger evergreen leaves, which are matt sea-green above. The flowers are more strongly fragrant and last for only a day but are carried in succession in late summer and early fall. Both these species are excellent for chalky soils.

Magnolia loebneri 'Leonard Messel'

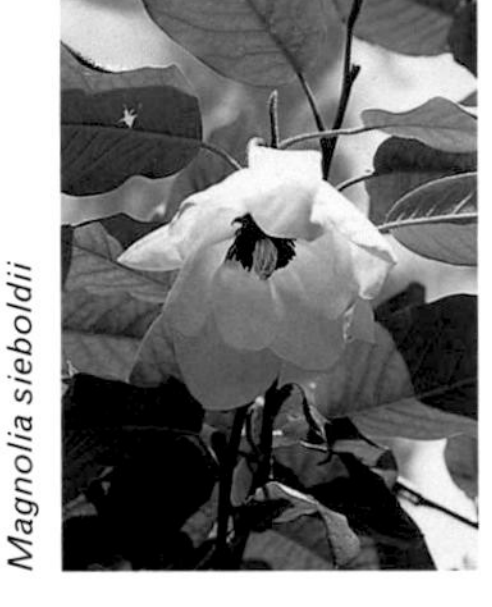

Magnolia sieboldii

Magnolia tripetala has deciduous leaves which can be 12–20in (30–50cm) in length by 7–10in (17–25cm) wide. The flowers are creamy colored and strongly scented, and followed by showy fruits. *M. sieboldii* and *M. wilsonii* are both deciduous large shrubs. The cup-shaped flowers are held facing out in *M. sieboldii* and hang down in *M. wilsonii*, and are followed by pendulous red cucumber-like fruits, which split to reveal two orange seeds in each carpel. *M. wilsonii* will take a certain amount of chalk in the soil.

	SPRING			SUMMER			FALL			WINTER			height 5yrs (ft)	height 10yrs (ft)	spread 5yrs (ft)	spread 10yrs (ft)	color of blossom	
[PRECOCIOUS] *Magnolia campbellii*	flowering	flowering					harvest						13	26	6½	13		Doesn't flower until 20+ years—worth the wait!
M. campbellii ssp. *mollicomata*	flowering	flowering					harvest						13	26	6½	13		Flowers within 12–15 years, good blooms
M. denudata		flowering	flowering										8	13	8	13		Goblet-shaped blooms
M. 'Galaxy'		flowering	flowering										8	16	6½	10		Goblet-shaped blooms
M. 'Iolanthe'		flowering	flowering										8	16	8	13		Cup-shaped flowers, large
M. kewensis 'Wada's Memory'		flowering											10	16	6½	10		Flowers fragrant
M. kobus		flowering					harvest						10	16	6½	10		Slightly fragrant flowers; blooms at 12–15 years
M. loebneri 'Leonard Messell'		flowering	flowering										8	13	6½	10		Flowers deeper in bud
M. loebneri 'Merrill'		flowering	flowering										8	13	6½	10		Fragrant flowers
M. soulangeana		flowering	flowering										8	13	8	13		Flowers frequently harmed by spring frosts
M. soulangeana 'Lennei'		flowering	flowering										8	13	8	13		Large goblet flowers; second flush in fall
M. soulangeana 'Rustica Rubra'		flowering	flowering										8	13	8	13		Cup-shaped flowers
M. stellata	flowering	flowering											5	8	6½	10		Slow-growing species, flowers fragrant
[LATER-FLOWERING] *M. delavayi*						flowering	flowering						6½	11½	6½	10		Large sea-green leaves, fragrant flowers
M. grandiflora				flowering	flowering	flowering	flowering	flowering					6½	11½	6½	10		Large, glossy evergreen leaves; flowers fragrant
M. grandiflora 'Exmouth'				flowering	flowering	flowering	flowering	flowering					6½	11½	6½	10		Fragrant flowers and carried on young trees
M. sieboldii			flowering	flowering	flowering	flowering	harvest						6½	11½	6½	10		Fragrant flowers; fruit showy; deciduous
M. tripetala			flowering	flowering			harvest	harvest					10	16	10	10		Large deciduous leaves
M. wilsonii			flowering	flowering			harvest						6½	11½	6½	10		Saucer-shaped flowers; best in light shade

flowering harvest

Mahonia

Mahonia have large pinnate leaves but, unlike their close cousins the Berberis, have no spines on the stems. That said, the leaves have a very stiff texture and the leaflets have sharp teeth! The larger-growing forms make excellent small flowering trees or large shrubs over 15 to 20 years.

The flowers are carried over the winter period and are set off by the evergreen foliage. Individually, the flowers are small but are carried in a cluster of long racemes. The fruit is a blue-black berry, which ripens in spring. The bark is deeply furrowed and has a pleasing texture.

Mahonia will grow in full sun or moderate shade. In the garden they are ideal as framework plants in a shrub or mixed border, or in a woodland garden for their winter flowering and as specimen shrubs. They can also be used to make thick hedges and screens.

They can be raised from seeds sown as soon as they are ripe (or the birds will eat them). The selected forms are usually propagated by cuttings. The best method is to use single nodes of a shoot in late winter. Cut the shoot both above and below a node, keeping the leaf (but reducing it to only two leaflets) and root in a cold frame. Each shoot will provide a number of cuttings. Growth will be made from the bud in the leaf axil.

soil	Is quite happy on any type of well-drained soil, including chalky ones
site	Prefers to be situated in the sun but will tolerate moderate shade
pruning	Pruning is needed only to restrict or reshape; will coppice freely
general care	Fairly easy to maintain and cultivate. Remove any winter damage to the foliage in spring
pests & diseases	Relatively trouble-free. Does not have any particular problem with pests and diseases

Mahonia japonica 'Bealei'

	SPRING			SUMMER			FALL			WINTER			height 5yrs (ft)	height 10yrs (ft)	spread 5yrs (ft)	spread 10yrs (ft)	color of blossom	
Mahonia japonica	flowering			harvest	harvest				flowering	flowering	flowering	flowering	5	8	3	6½		Evergreen, fragrant flowers
M. japonica 'Bealei'	flowering			harvest	harvest				flowering	flowering	flowering	flowering	5	8	3	6½		Flowers in shorter racemes, leaflets overlap
M. media 'Buckland'				harvest	harvest				flowering	flowering	flowering		5	8	3	6½		Evergreen; flowers in long spreading racemes
M. media 'Charity'				harvest	harvest				flowering	flowering	flowering		5	8	3	6½		Large leaves, up to 2ft in length
M. media 'Lionel Fortescue'				harvest	harvest				flowering	flowering	flowering		5	8	3	6½		Evergreen, fragrant flowers, upright racemes

 *flowering*  *harvest*

Malus

Crabapple

These relatives of the domestic apple are floriferous small trees. They are particularly effective in late spring when the massed flowers smother the new foliage. They are grown for their often fragrant flowers and for their attractive, edible fruits, although some of the varieties produce fruits that are unpalatable if uncooked.

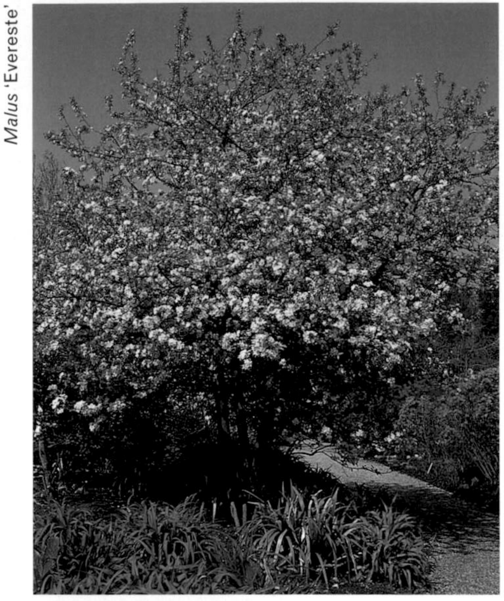

Malus 'Evereste'

The fruits are generally small and hard and only useful for their beauty, except in *Malus* 'John Downie' and *Malus robusta* 'Red Sentinel', where they are about 1–1¹/₄in (2.5–3cm) and can be used to make jelly. Some species can be effective for fall color, especially *Malus tschonoskii* whose leaves turn a mixture of golds and scarlets, and *Malus transitoria* whose leaves turn a warm yellow. The new foliage can also provide interest, mainly fresh green but coppery crimson in *Malus moerlandsii* 'Profusion'.

Crabapples provide features of interest in the garden for much of the year. They make excellent small specimen trees for lawns or the larger shrub beds. They can be trimmed to make flowering hedges. Malus thrive on a wide range of soils, provided they are not too moist or too dry in summer, and are excellent both for heavy clays and for chalky sites. They will tolerate light shade but flower, fruit, and fall color are all significantly better when grown in the full sun.

The species can be propagated by seed. All the species featured here are apomictic, which means they are genetically identical to the parent. However, the cultivars will not come from seed and these need to be propagated by cuttings (either semi-ripe in summer or hardwood cuttings after leaf fall), or by grafting onto a rootstock.

Malus 'Katherine'

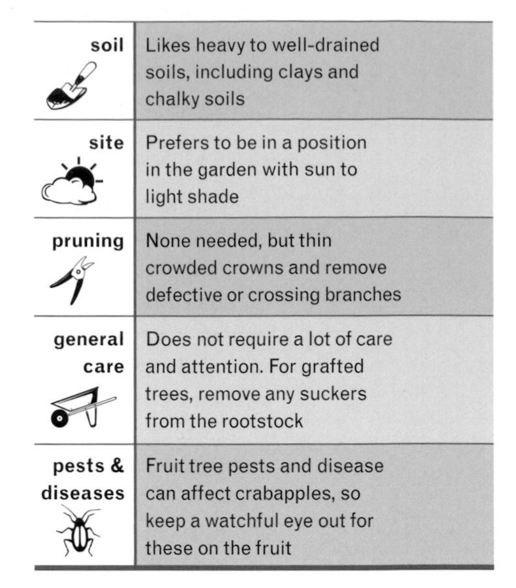

soil	Likes heavy to well-drained soils, including clays and chalky soils
site	Prefers to be in a position in the garden with sun to light shade
pruning	None needed, but thin crowded crowns and remove defective or crossing branches
general care	Does not require a lot of care and attention. For grafted trees, remove any suckers from the rootstock
pests & diseases	Fruit tree pests and disease can affect crabapples, so keep a watchful eye out for these on the fruit

	SPRING	SUMMER	FALL	WINTER	height 5yrs (ft)	height 10yrs (ft)	spread 5yrs (ft)	spread 10yrs (ft)	color of blossom	
Malus 'Evereste'	flowering, flowering		harvest		11½	16	10	16		Conical habit, orange to yellow-orange fruit
M. floribunda	flowering		harvest		11½	16	10	16		Floriferous, yellow fruit with a red face
M. hupehensis	flowering, flowering		harvest		13	20	10	20		Vigorous tree with a domed crown, to 22–33ft
M. 'John Downie'	flowering		harvest		11½	16	10	16		Conical fruit, orange/scarlet, useful for jellies
Malus 'Katherine'	flowering		harvest		11½	16	10	16		Habit dense and globular in shape
M. moerlandsii 'Profusion'	flowering		harvest		11½	16	10	16		Blood-red fruit; new leaves purplish
M. robusta 'Red Sentinel'	flowering		harvest, harvest	harvest	11½	16	10	16		Persistent fruit, red, glossy
M. transitoria	flowering		harvest		10	16	11½	16		Spreading habit, small, yellow fruit
M. tschonoskii	flowering		harvest		15	20	8	13		Conical habit; few flowers or fruits

flowering harvest

Mespilus

Medlar

The medlar is a small tree whose origins lie in central and eastern Europe. On short, leafy shoots it carries single white flowers 1–1½in (2.5–4cm) across. These look similar to some of the less common Crataegus and, as for this genus, it has short spines on the stronger shoots.

In flower it is quite attractive but not outstanding. The fruit, however, is unique. It is apple-shaped with a flat end, and has five large persistent stipules about 1in (2.5cm) long. The flesh is hard and inedible until it has been bletted. (This is a stage of incipient decay when the flesh becomes soft and sweet. Sounds horrid but the end result is very tasty.) The fruits are best left on the tree until mid-fall or even later (frost assists the bletting process). The cultivar 'Nottingham' has rather tasty fruits and is less thorny with larger leaves, flowers, and fruits. In the fall the leaves turn russet.

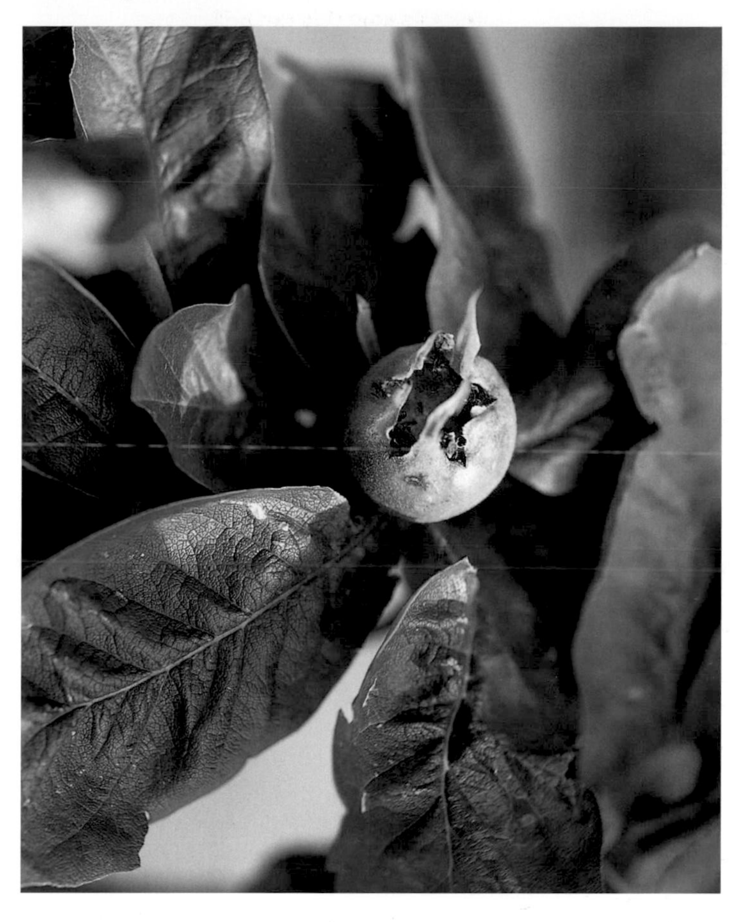

Mespilus germanica 'Nottingham'

soil	Does well on any type of well-drained soil, including clays and chalky soils
site 	Flowering and fruiting much better in full sun, although it does tolerate light shade
pruning 	No special pruning regime required, except to restrict or reshape
general care	Fairly easy to look after. Remove any suckers from the rootstock and beware of the thorns
pests & diseases	A leaf blotch fungus can cause flowers to become sterile; also mildew can affect the foliage

In the garden, medlar is useful as a small tree with a wide spreading habit. Apart from its use in the orchard, it makes an interesting specimen tree for a lawn area or wild garden, or in a shrub bed. It requires full sun but copes with moderate shade.

Mespilus thrives on a wide range of soil types, including clays and chalky soils. It can be propagated by seeds but is usually grafted on either a quince or pear rootstock.

	SPRING			SUMMER			FALL			WINTER			height 5yrs (ft)	height 10yrs (ft)	spread 5yrs (ft)	spread 10yrs (ft)	color of blossom	
Mespilus germanica			flowering	flowering				harvest					11½	16	10	16		Spreading small tree; fruit edible later on
M. germanica 'Nottingham'			flowering	flowering				harvest					11½	16	10	16		Larger flowers and fruits, especially tasty fruits

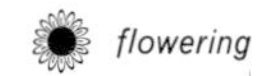 *flowering*  *harvest*

Morus
Mulberry

White mulberry (*Morus alba*) is important as the preferred food of the silkworm moth, whose caterpillar produces silk. The mulberry bushes are coppiced and the leaves stripped by hand and fed to the caterpillars.

When mature, the caterpillars spin their pupal case and the thin threads of silk are unwound from this. White mulberry has glossy green foliage and makes a neat tree, but apart from the silk industry, it is of limited horticultural value. Certainly the fruit, which is white or pink when ripe, is insipid.

The form 'Pendula' has the branches weeping, forming a small domed mound. Horticulturally, the black mulberry (*Morus nigra*) is very superior. It forms an attractive small tree, which quickly develops a stout trunk. It also has a wonderfully tasty but tart fruit. This ripens to purple-red (just edible at this stage) to dark purple-black (juicy and delectable) in mid- to late summer and into early fall.

soil	Will tolerate most well-drained soils, including chalky ones
site	This particular tree performs at its best in a sunny position in the garden
pruning	Avoid pruning unless really necessary as they may bleed
general care	Be careful when first establishing. They have brittle roots and need careful handling when planting
pests & diseases	Coral spot and mildew can cause occasional problems, but other than these they are fairly trouble-free

Morus alba 'Pendula'

Apart from their culinary use, mulberries make neat specimen trees. They are propagated either by layering or by hardwood cuttings using two-year-old shoots with a heel of older wood. These are taken in late fall or spring, and buried, except for the top 2in (5cm) in a cool shady spot.

Morus nigra

	SPRING	SUMMER	FALL	WINTER	height 5yrs (ft)	height 10yrs (ft)	spread 5yrs (ft)	spread 10yrs (ft)	color of blossom	
Morus alba	flowering	harvest, harvest			10	16	10			Glossy leaves, but thin; sweet but insipid fruit
M. alba 'Pendula'	flowering	harvest, harvest			10	13	10			Pendulous branches, forms mound-shaped tree
M. nigra	flowering	harvest, harvest	harvest		10	16	10			Leaves rough/thick in texture; sweet, tasty fruit

flowering   harvest

M

Trees & Shrubs

Nothofagus

Southern beech

Although these trees originate in the southern hemisphere, they are available worldwide and are similar to their northern counterparts. *Nothofagus dombeyi*, for instance, is evergreen, whereas all true beeches are deciduous. *N. dombeyi* is useful as a specimen tree, making a large and fast-growing evergreen, maybe 50ft (15m) in 30 to 40 years.

Nothofagus antarctica is a deciduous species, often forming a tanglewood of wiry stems. The new foliage is balsam scented, and in fall the leaves turn yellow. It forms a small tree, making 20–33ft (6–10m) in height. It is useful as a small specimen tree and is the only Nothofagus suitable for small gardens.

Nothofagus obliqua is a fast-growing tree, quickly making 50ft (15m) in almost as many years, and ultimately 80ft (25m) in 50 or so years. The bark is smooth and gray in young trees, becoming shaggy the longer it is around since it breaks into large scaly plates. It is used for timber and makes a majestic specimen tree. It can also be used for screening and shelter belts, as can *Nothofagus dombeyi*.

Nothofagus require full sun or at most dappled shade when young. They flourish in acidic to neutral soils, but are not suited either to really acidic peaty soils or to alkaline soils as found in overlying chalk. They can be propagated by semi-ripe cuttings in summer or by seed.

Nothofagus obliqua

soil 	Well-drained, acidic or neutral loams or soils; *N. antarctica* also grows on moist to boggy soils
site	This particular tree performs at its best in a sunny position in the garden
pruning	No pruning required, except to resize or reshape according to preference
general care	Shelter from cold winds. *N. dombeyi* needs care when transplanting as leaves will wither if drought-stressed
pests & diseases	Fairly trouble-free from pests and diseases, but could be susceptible to bark damage by squirrels

	SPRING	SUMMER	FALL	WINTER	height 5yrs (ft)	height 10yrs (ft)	spread 5yrs (ft)	spread 10yrs (ft)	color of blossom	
Nothofagus antarctica	flowering				8	16	6½	13		Balsam-scented leaves, glossy green
N. dombeyi	flowering				13	23	6½	13		Evergreen leaves, fast-growing dense crown
N. obliqua	flowering				16	26	6½	16		Fast-growing deciduous tree

 *flowering*

Nyssa

Tupelo

Rightly or wrongly, these trees are grown for just one particular period of the year, lasting two to three weeks. This is when the foliage turns scrumptious colors in the fall, with brilliant shades of deep bright red, gold, and scarlet. *Nyssa sylvatica* has glossy green foliage and makes a medium tree to 50ft (15m) or so in 40 years.

Nyssa sylvatica has a neat habit and is excellent beside water seen reflected in the surface. It is adapted to fairly wet conditions but best on well-drained but moist soil. The tree pictured is a fine, large example, perhaps better suited to more palatial gardens!

Nyssa sinensis has richer fall color and larger leaves but they are not glossy like *N. sylvatica*. The habit is rounded with usually several stems, rather than the single-stemmed tree of *N. sylvatica*. Apart from the even more superior fall color, the advantage that *N. sinensis* has in many garden situations is that it is a smaller tree. This makes it better suited to modern gardens, where it is likely to make a tree 26–33ft (8–10m) in height over 40 years. The flowers are greenish and insignificant, and are followed by blue-black berries—the main interest these have is to allow you to raise more!

Nyssa prefer either full sunlight or only light to dappled shade. In the garden they are specimen trees. They dislike alkaline soil conditions, being suited to acidic sands and neutral sites but not chalky ones.

They can be propagated by seed and by softwood and semi-ripe cuttings in summer.

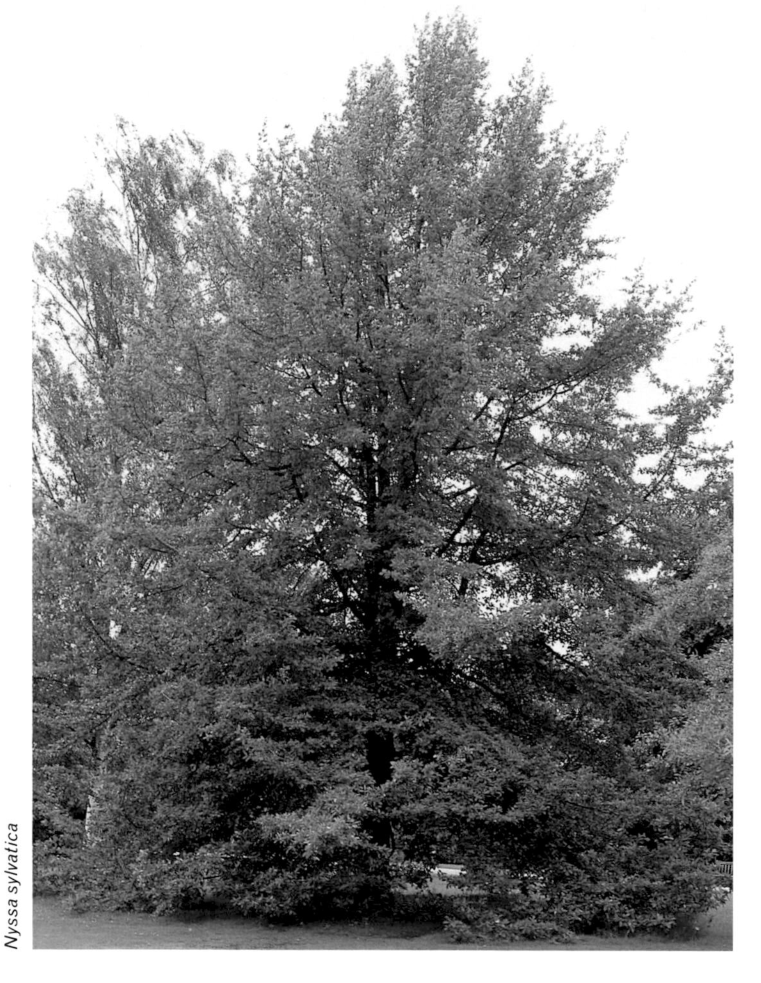

Nyssa sylvatica

soil	Performs best in acidic to neutral soils—avoid chalky ones
site	Does well in sun or dappled shade. Excellent beside water
pruning	None required except to resize or reshape according to preference
general care	Can be difficult to establish, so use pot-grown trees of around 12–20in (30–50cm) in height
pests & diseases	Relatively trouble-free. Does not have any particular problems with pests and diseases

	SPRING	SUMMER	FALL	WINTER	height 5yrs (ft)	height 10yrs (ft)	spread 5yrs (ft)	spread 10yrs (ft)	color of blossom	
Nyssa sinensis					6½	13	5	6½		Excellent fall color; small shrubby tree
N. sylvatica					8	16	6½	6½		Good fall color, medium-growing tree

flowering *harvest*

N

Trees & Shrubs

Olea
Olive

The olive must be the most characteristic tree of Mediterranean landscapes, and its fruits are the source of olive oil. The species is not reliably hardy and is not commonly cultivated in more temperate climates.

Olea europaea

Most olives seen in gardens are in pots but they can be grown in a bed outside in milder areas, especially if given the shelter of a wall. Olives have evergreen, gray-green leaves, which are glaucous beneath. The flowers are in axillary racemes in late summer. They are small, white, and fragrant. The fruit ripens from green to black over winter. They need full sun and a freely drained soil, either acidic or alkaline.

soil	Both trees prefer any type of soil, as long as it is well drained
site	These trees perform best if situated in a sunny position in the garden
pruning	Olea: prune to restrict size. Ostrya: no pruning needed, except to restrict or reshape
general care	No particular care regime is needed for Olea. Both tolerate hot dry sites in nature
pests & diseases	Olea: Scale insects and verticillium wilt can affect them. Ostrya: no particular problems

Ostrya
Hop hornbeam

This tree is related to Carpinus (hornbeam), differing in that the male catkins are exposed in the bud stage over winter and the seed is entirely enclosed in the papery bladder. It forms a broad conical to columnar tree, with a single stem and level branching.

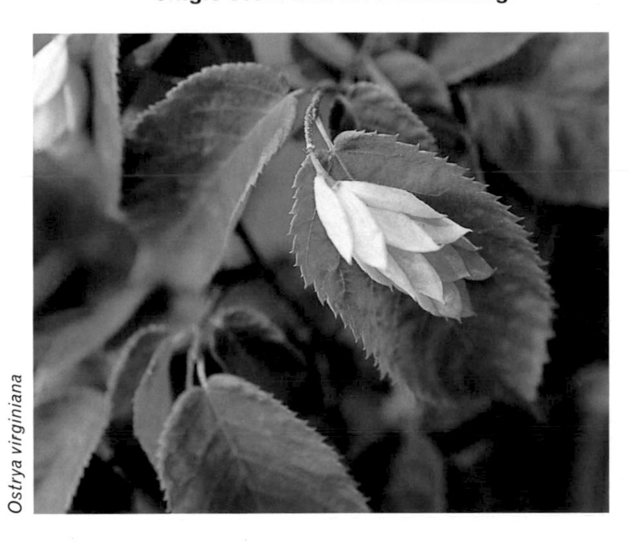
Ostrya virginiana

This particular shape of tree provides an excellent platform from which the yellow catkins are displayed. Ostrya makes attractive specimen trees for large gardens and parkland settings. The foliage looks especially attractive in the fall when it turns a lovely shade of yellow.

Ostrya requires full sun and will grow in both acidic sands and alkaline chalky sites, the main requirement being good drainage. It can be propagated by seed, which is best sown as soon as ripe in the fall. It can also be grafted, either on to its own seedlings or on to *Carpinus betulus* seedlings.

													height 5yrs (ft)	height 10yrs (ft)	spread 5yrs (ft)	spread 10yrs (ft)	color of blossom	
Olea europaea	harvest					flowering			harvest	harvest	harvest	harvest	5	10	4	8	☐	Evergreen tree, needs sheltered site
Ostrya carpinifolia		flowering				harvest	harvest	harvest					13	20	6½	13	☐	Neat leafy tree with excellent fall color
Ostrya virginiana		flowering		harvest	harvest	harvest							10	16	6½	13	☐	Good fall color but often very early

 *flowering*  *harvest*

Oxydendrum
Sorrel tree

This is a deciduous relative of the Pieris with white, fragrant, bell-shaped flowers. It is useful for its flowering in late summer or early fall, and the panicles, produced at the tips of the current season's growth, may be 6–10in (15–25cm) in length.

Oxydendrum arboreum

Sorrels produce small capsules containing many seeds but little beauty. The leaves turn lovely shades of red and scarlet in the fall, often while the flowers are still showing some "color." The common name, sorrel tree, is a reference to the taste of the leaves, which have a pleasant acid taste.

Sorrel trees thrive in full sun to moderate shade. They will not tolerate any lime in the soil but need acidic soils that are freely drained. Sorrels are capable of making a tree to 50ft (15m) or so after 50 to 80 years, but will do this only if grown in suitable woodland conditions.

Sorrels tend to be available only as small nursery plants and are relatively slow growing. Therefore, plan for them to grow to 16–26ft (5–8m) and enjoy the autumnal contribution to the garden while you wait. Best placed in a woodland garden setting or shrub bed, they are especially useful as taller plants in collections of rhododendrons and azaleas, where they add an interest after these have finished flowering.

Propagation can be by seeds sown on the surface of damp acidic seed starting mix or by softwood cuttings in summer.

soil	Oxydendrum: acidic, well-drained. Parrotia: well-drained, moisture-retentive
site	Oxydendrum: sun for best flower and fall color. Parrotia: sun to light shade
pruning	No specific pruning regime is necessary for either tree
general care	Oxydendrum: mulch to keep soil acidity and humus status. Parrotia: prune to give a clean stem
pests & diseases	Both Oxydendrum and Parrotia do not have any particular problems with pests and diseases

Parrotia
Persian ironwood

This tree flowers on the bare branches in late winter or early spring. They have no petals but are showy due to the numerous deep red stamens. At this time of the year, the bark, which peels like a plane tree to reveal pink-buff and yellow that darkens through gray-green to gray-brown, is also attractive.

Parrotia persica

The foliage is dense and glossy green, coming into its own in the fall when it turns red, orange, and crimson before falling, when it is a deep red. Parrotia is useful as a specimen tree, in shrub borders, or in screening plantings. It will grow in sun or light shade on all well-drained soils. It can be propagated by seed (which may not germinate until the second spring) or by softwood cuttings in summer.

	SPRING			SUMMER			FALL			WINTER			height 5yrs (ft)	height 10yrs (ft)	spread 5yrs (ft)	spread 10yrs (ft)	flower color	
Oxydendrum arboreum					flowering	flowering	flowering						5	10	3	6½		Glossy leaves turn red or scarlet in early fall
Parrotia persica	flowering										flowering	flowering	6	11½	6½	13		Wide-spreading tree, slow-growing

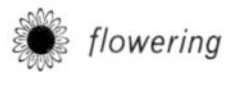
flowering

Paulownia

Foxglove tree *or* Empress tree

This tree has delicately lilac-scented flowers, which open in late spring. However, they are formed at the end of summer and are displayed as buds at the end of the stout shoots. The individual blooms are tubular in shape, like thimbles or foxglove blooms.

The flowers can be damaged by late spring frosts. The leaves are large, verging on the enormous; they can be up to 2ft (60cm) across on young or coppiced trees, but are more usually 6–14in (15–35cm) by 4–10in (10–25cm). They are ovate with sticky, glandular hairs on the underside, and are very thin and easily shredded by strong winds. They remain green until felled by the first strong frost. They cast only a light to moderate shade and are late coming into leaf. This makes *Paulownia tomentosa* the most useful species for the garden as an overstory tree above spring-flowering shrubs. (See page 14 for a habit picture of a mature Paulownia.)

In the garden they are best as specimen trees; locate Paulownia so that you can get your nose close to the blooms by planting beside steps or on a balcony, or where you can look down on the blooms from above. The other way is to grow it as a foliage plant. Cut back an established plant growing in a well-manured spot to ground level in late winter and thin the new growth to a single stem.

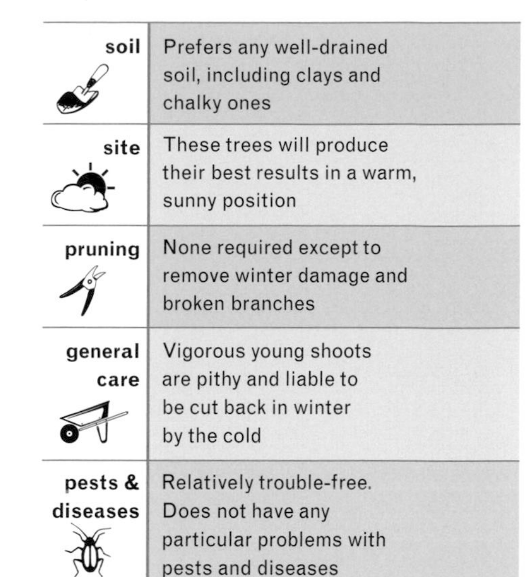

soil	Prefers any well-drained soil, including clays and chalky ones
site	These trees will produce their best results in a warm, sunny position
pruning	None required except to remove winter damage and broken branches
general care	Vigorous young shoots are pithy and liable to be cut back in winter by the cold
pests & diseases	Relatively trouble-free. Does not have any particular problems with pests and diseases

This will make 8ft (2.5m) by the fall and will have leaves individually to 2ft (60cm) across. It thrives on all well-drained soils, including chalky ones.

Propagate from seeds sown thinly on the surface of a pot, or root from softwood cuttings in summer and from root cuttings.

Paulownia tomentosa (coppiced)

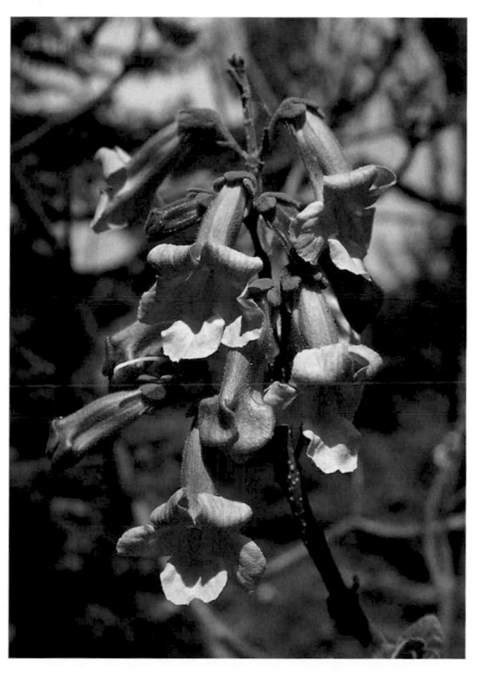

Paulownia tomentosa (flowers)

Phellodendron

Cork tree

This tree is of interest for the pinnate leaves and the bark, which is corky in old trees. The leaves are aromatic and turn clear yellow in early fall.

The flowers are yellow-green and carried in early summer in large terminal panicles. On female trees, they are followed by the pea-sized black fruits that may persist well into winter, depending on the mildness of the season. The fruits have a strong, citrus scent. Old trees develop an open branching habit and make picturesque specimen trees for large lawns.

Phellodendron thrives on any well-drained soil, being especially good on chalky soils.

They can be propagated from seed, from softwood or semi-ripe cuttings in summer, and from root cuttings in winter.

Phellodendron amurense

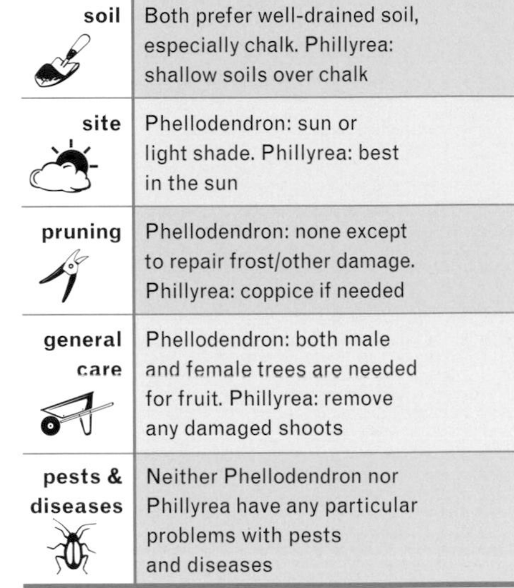

soil	Both prefer well-drained soil, especially chalk. Phillyrea: shallow soils over chalk
site	Phellodendron: sun or light shade. Phillyrea: best in the sun
pruning	Phellodendron: none except to repair frost/other damage. Phillyrea: coppice if needed
general care	Phellodendron: both male and female trees are needed for fruit. Phillyrea: remove any damaged shoots
pests & diseases	Neither Phellodendron nor Phillyrea have any particular problems with pests and diseases

Phillyrea

This makes an evergreen shrub with a rounded domed crown with narrow dark green leaves, giving a dense leafy crown.

The flowers are creamy white and fragrant, and carried in late spring and early summer from buds on last summer's growth. The fruit ripens in late summer and is blue-black, although only reliably produced in regions with fairly warm climates.

Phillyrea is an excellent small evergreen for the front garden where something reliable but unusual is desired. It can also be clipped as a hedge. It requires full sunlight but will thrive on all well-drained soils, being especially good on shallow chalky sites. It is propagated by semi-ripe cuttings in late summer.

Phillyrea decora

	SPRING			SUMMER			FALL			WINTER			height 5yrs (ft)	height 10yrs (ft)	spread 5yrs (ft)	spread 10yrs (ft)	color of blossom	
Phellodendron amurense				flowering			harvest	harvest	harvest	harvest			13	20	6½	13		Pinnate leaves have a citrus scent
Phillyrea decora			flowering	flowering		harvest							5	10	4	8		Good evergreen with fragrant flowers

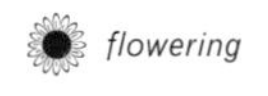 *flowering*  *harvest*

Trees & Shrubs

P

Photinia

This genus is noted for the large corymbs of white hawthorn-like flowers and the small berries, like miniature apples. Most of the species are evergreen but they contain some of the most colorful of foliages. In *Photinia davidiana* (sometimes listed as *Stranvaesia davidiana*) the leaves are matte green, and most persist through the winter.

A few leaves of *Photinia davidiana* do drop in the fall, displaying red or orange colors. A few more do the same over winter and most of the others follow in spring. So, while it does not have outstanding fall color, it does provide a protracted display. 'Palette' has blotched leaves that are streaked with creamy white and that have a pinkish tinge when new. *Photinia fraseri* 'Red Robin' has foliage that flushes brilliant red, contrasting with the dark glossy green of last year's foliage. The color of the new foliage is as good as that of Pieris, but Photinia has the advantage of being able to grow on chalk and other alkaline sites, as well as on neutral and acidic soils. *Photinia serrulatifolia* (*Photinia serrulata*) can make a large tree with time, and is a high-quality evergreen. It is slightly tender when young. The new foliage is often bronze or red for an extended period, during which it contrasts effectively with the glossy older leaves. The bark is gray-brown, exfoliating to reveal red-brown beneath. *Photinia davidiana* and *Photinia fraseri* 'Red Robin' are good in shrub beds and can be used as hedges—'Red Robin' is excellent for hedging. *Photinia serrulatifolia* has to be positioned as a specimen tree.

All Photinia like full sun to light shade and tolerate a wide range of soils, including chalk, provided there is good drainage. Photinia can be grown from seed or from semi-ripe cuttings in summer.

Photinia davidiana 'Palette'

soil	Grows well in any soil that is well drained, including clays and chalky soils
site	Prefers a sunny position but is quite happy to tolerate light shade
pruning	No special pruning regime is required except to restrict or reshape
general care	*P. serrulatifolia* can be damaged by spring frosts so give winter protection when young, or plant by a wall
pests & diseases	These trees are fairly trouble-free from pests and diseases but can be susceptible to fire blight

	SPRING	SUMMER	FALL	WINTER	height 5yrs (ft)	height 10yrs (ft)	spread 5yrs (ft)	spread 10yrs (ft)	color of blossom	
Photinia davidiana	flowering	flowering	harvest harvest harvest		6½	13	6½	13		Evergreen, but some leaves color in fall
P. davidiana 'Palette'	flowering	flowering	harvest harvest harvest		6½	13	6½	13		Leaves blotched and streaked, creamy white
P. fraseri 'Red Robin'	flowering		harvest harvest harvest		6½	13	6½	13		Bronze-red new foliage, evergreen
P. serrulatifolia	flowering flowering	flowering	harvest harvest harvest		8	16	8	13		Evergreen tree to 50ft in 50–80 years

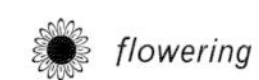 *flowering*  *harvest*

P

Trees & Shrubs

Pittosporum

This genus is distributed worldwide. The plants in this group are all evergreen shrubs and trees. In colder climates they can be damaged by hard winters but are excellent for coastal sites. *Pittosporum tenuifolium*, originating from New Zealand, is the main species in cultivation but a Chinese species, *Pittosporum tobira*, is also common.

Other more tender species are occasionally available but they may be lost in the next hard winter, except in milder gardens. The chief attractions are in the fragrant flowers and the foliage. The flowers are chocolate-purple in *Pittosporum tenuifolium* but creamy white in *Pittosporum tobira*. *Pittosporum tenuifolium*, in particular, has given a number of forms with attractive foliage, ranging from bronze-purple in 'Purpureum', to variegated foliage, which may be creamy white as in 'Irene Paterson', to gold in 'Warnham Gold'. There are also a number of slow-growing selections, of which 'Tom Thumb' is perhaps the smallest.

In the garden, the smaller forms are excellent as part of shrub beds, with the larger ones at the back. They can be sited beside house walls, especially in colder areas, and make good hedges. The species can be propagated by seeds sown in the spring. The colored forms are propagated by semi-ripe cuttings in summer, or by layering.

Pittosporum tenuifolium 'Tom Thumb'

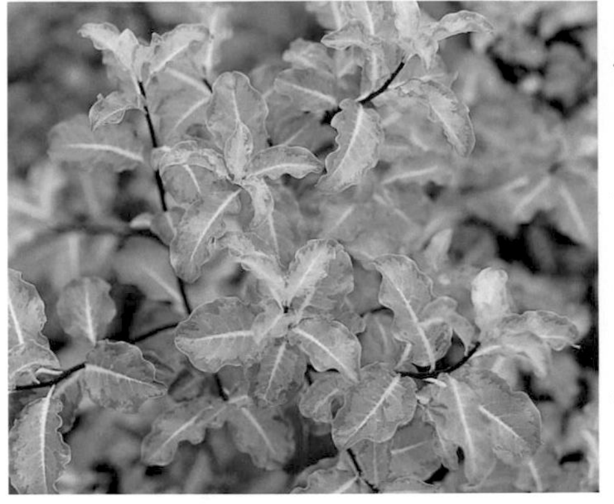

Pittosporum tenuifolium 'Abbotsbury Gold'

soil	Well-drained and preferably fertile soils, both acidic and alkaline
site	Grows well in full sun and tolerates a moderate amount of shade
pruning	No special pruning regime required except to restrict or reshape
general care	In colder gardens, your Pittosporum will benefit from side or wall shelter
pests & diseases	Mildew and tar spot fungi can be occasionally problematic but are not usually serious

	SPRING	SUMMER	FALL	WINTER	height 5yrs (ft)	height 10yrs (ft)	spread 5yrs (ft)	spread 10yrs (ft)	color of blossom	
Pittosporum 'Garnetii'	flowering	flowering			5	10	3	6½		Erect habit when young, later arching out
P. tenuifolium	flowering	flowering			5	10	3	6½		Columnar when young, later broader
P. tenuifolium 'Abbotsbury Gold'	flowering	flowering			5	10	3	5		New yellow leaves with irregular green margin
P. tenuifolium 'Irene Paterson'	flowering	flowering			3	6½	3	6½		Slow-growing; creamy white leaves in spring
P. tenuifolium 'Silver Queen'	flowering	flowering			3	6½	3	6½		Gray-green leaves with irregular white margin
P. tenuifolium 'Tom Thumb'	flowering	flowering			1½	3	1	2		Bronze-purple foliage
P. tenuifolium 'Warnham Gold'	flowering	flowering			3	6½	3	6½		New leaves greenish-yellow
P. tobira	flowering	flowering			3	6½	3	6½		Leathery leaves; flowers in large clusters
P. tobira 'Variegatum'	flowering	flowering			3	6½	3	6½		Gray-green leaves with creamy white margin

flowering

Platanus
Plane

Planes are large trees, characteristic of major open spaces in many cities. As free-growing trees, they will make 80ft (25m) or more in a century, with correspondingly enormous boles, and can live for several hundred years.

Platanus hispanica

These are suitable only for the largest gardens as trees. However, they can have a role to play. The trees can be pleached, where the branches are woven to create a framework; the growths are cut back to this framework each winter. Vigorous regrowth quickly forms a dense canopy of foliage, giving good shade from early summer onward. Planes require full sunlight.

They can be propagated by seed or by hardwood cuttings taken in early winter.

soil	Both like well-drained— Platanus: gravel, sand, clay; Poncirus: acidic or alkaline
site 	Platanus: grows well in full sun. Poncirus: likes sun or dappled shade
pruning 	Platanus: hard, or pollarded in winter. Poncirus: trim after flowering or fruiting
general care	Platanus: the fine hairs can cause dermatitis in some people. Poncirus: beware of the spines!
pests & diseases 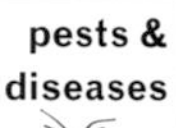	Platanus: Anthracnose can cause death of new foliage in wet springs, but later growth is unaffected

Poncirus
Hardy orange

This makes a small shrub. The main attraction is in the large white and strongly fragrant flowers that are carried in spring. The fruit ripens in the fall and is a small, globose orange.

Poncirus trifoliata

The fruit is extremely bitter in taste. The leaves are trifoliate but are set on green stems, which are provided with stout spines. In the garden it is useful for the fragrant flowers and the all-year attraction of the green stems. Its spiny nature means it can be used to form barriers. As a hardy orange tree it is also used as a rootstock for grafting true oranges and lemons (*Citrus* sp). It thrives on a wide range of soils and requires full sunlight. It can be propagated by seeds sown in the spring or by semi-ripe cuttings in late summer, rooted with some bottom heat.

	SPRING	SUMMER	FALL	WINTER	height 5yrs (ft)	height 10yrs (ft)	spread 5yrs (ft)	spread 10yrs (ft)	color of blossom	
Platanus hispanica	flowering		harvest		13	23	10	16		Large palmate leaves, bark exfoliates late summer
P. orientalis	flowering		harvest		10	20	6½	13		Leaves more deeply lobed
Poncirus trifoliata	flowering	flowering	harvest		5	8	3	6½		Brilliant red fall color and scarlet fruits

 *flowering*  *harvest*

Populus
Poplar

The poplars are a genus of large trees. They grow vigorously on a wide range of soils, except shallow chalky ones where growth is less satisfactory. They are useful for their attractive foliage, be it the foliage of the European aspen (*Populus tremula*), which rustles in the wind due to a flattened petiole; the silvery undersides of the various forms of white poplar (*Populus alba*); or the large heart-shaped leaves of the Chinese necklace poplar (*Populus lasiocarpa*).

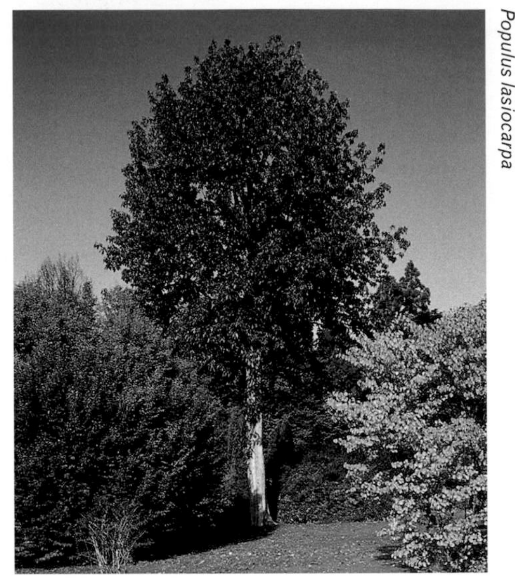

Populus lasiocarpa

Poplars like plenty of soil moisture, although they are not trees for really boggy conditions. However, their fast growth rate, coupled with a profligate use of water, can cause problems on shrinkable soils where foundations are inadequate. The problem is that certain soils, primarily clays, shrink or expand depending upon their moisture content. If a house is built upon inadequate foundations, the shrinkage can lead to subsidence, wreaking havoc on the structure, and damage drains.

This is not just a problem for poplars; other trees and shrubs can cause subsidence, but poplars have acquired a reputation for doing so. Generally, if you are on a shrinkable clay soil—one that cracks deeply in dry summers—keep large trees like poplars at least their height away from buildings, which includes garages. However, if you are not on a clay soil, but on a sand or loam, you are unlikely to have a problem.

White poplar and aspen can be propagated by root cuttings in winter. *Populus lasiocarpa* is best raised from seed, which ripens in early summer and must be sown onto a damp surface immediately. The other poplars will root from cuttings—10in (25cm) hardwood cuttings in late winter, inserted with just the top bud showing, should root quickly.

soil	Performs well in any soil type, except extremely wet and boggy soils
site	Loves to be in a warm spot where it can get lots of full sunshine
pruning	No special regime required but they are very tolerant of pruning
general care	Easy to cultivate and maintain. Branches are brittle and can be broken by strong winds
pests & diseases	Cankers cause stem lesions on *P. jackii* 'Aurora'; fungi and insects attack them but without causing real harm

	SPRING	SUMMER	FALL	WINTER	height 5yrs (ft)	height 10yrs (ft)	spread 5yrs (ft)	spread 10yrs (ft)	color of blossom	
Populus alba	flowering				13	23	6½	13		Silvery leaves, hairy beneath; ultimately 65ft+
P. alba 'Raket'	flowering				13	23	3	6½		Narrow columnar to conical crown
P. alba 'Richardii'	flowering				13	23	6½	13		Golden yellow foliage above, silvery beneath
P. 'Balsam Spire'	flowering				20	36	8	16		Fast-growing hybrid, foliage balsam scented
P. jackii 'Aurora'	flowering				13	20	6½	13		Very liable to canker
P. lasiocarpa	flowering	harvest			13	20	6½	13		Makes a large tree, to 65ft on warm sites
P. nigra 'Italica'	flowering				13	23	3	6½		Lombardy poplar, with narrow crown
P. tremula	flowering				13	20	5	10		Also known as the European aspen

flowering 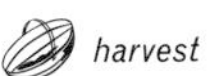 harvest

Prunus

Cherry, plum

Prunus is a large genus, ranging from tropical rain forest trees to the cool temperate species found in gardens. The genus is diverse and often split into several genera. The cherries belong to the Cerasus group and are considered first. The other species are members of the plum group, which retains the generic name Prunus; the bird cherry group, or Padus; the almonds, or Amygdalus; and the cherry laurel group, Laurocerasus.

The unifying feature of this genus is that the fruit is a drupe—a fruit in which the seed is enclosed by a hard stony layer surrounded by a fleshy layer. Most Prunus leaves have one to three glands toward the end of the petiole, or at the base of the leaf blade; these secrete sugars to feed ants, which the tree encourages to ward off aphids and caterpillars. The species can be propagated by seed, which usually will not germinate until the second spring. Traditionally they have been propagated by grafting or budding. Most of the smaller hybrids and species can be propagated by semi-ripe cuttings in early summer.

Prunus avium

Prunus lusitanica

soil	Any well-drained soil types, but best on deep heavy loams
site 	Tolerates positions in both the sun as well as light shade
pruning 	Best carried out in mid-summer, reduces risk of silver leaf infections
general care	On chalky soils, can become chlorotic; improve leaf color by watering with Epsom salts for extra magnesium
pests & diseases	Silver leaf disease can kill cherries; various leaf/petal fungi can kill leaves; aphids (blackfly) are also a problem

Cerasus

The true cherries (Cerasus) are trees and shrubs with the flowers single or in umbels. They are mainly grown for the beauty of the flowers in spring, and often for the color of their foliage in the fall. The best autumnal color, in early fall, is provided by *P. sargentii*. The Tibetan cherry, *P. serrula*, is grown for the smooth polished mahogany bark. *P. subhirtella* 'Autumnalis' flowers at any time from mid-fall to late winter, depending on temperature; not all the flowers open at once, so although the display is not strong, it is valuable for the length of time it is in bloom.

This group also includes the Japanese cherries. These make some of the most floriferous of all trees, such as the purple-pink 'Kanzan', the white 'Shirotae', the great-sized 'Taihaku', or the haunting yellow-green 'Ukon'.

Other groups

This group includes the almond (*Prunus dulcis*) with its pink flowers carried on the bare boughs in early spring. The kernel of the fruits is edible in the sweet almonds but the bitter almonds contain a high concentration of prussic acid and can be lethal if too many are eaten.

Prunus lusitanica 'Variegata'

This acid is also found in the foliage and fruits of the cherry laurel (*P. laurocerasus*). This evergreen shrub can make a medium-sized tree. It becomes chlorotic on thin soils over chalk. The Portugal laurel, *P. lusitanica*, is also evergreen, although usually only a small tree, and is tolerant of thin soils over chalk, as well as richer sites. The cherry plum, *P. cerasifera*, is one of the earliest flowering. The flowers can open at any time from mid-winter to mid-spring, depending upon the prevailing weather conditions. Fruits are occasionally set. *P. cerasifera* is used as an informal hedging plant.

The bird cherries have racemes of flowers carried at the end of leafy shoots in spring. A good form is *P. padus* 'Watereri', but 'Colorata' is unusual for the dark purple shoots, purple new foliage, and pale flowers.

		SPRING			SUMMER			FALL			WINTER			height 5yrs (ft)	height 10yrs (ft)	spread 5yrs (ft)	spread 10yrs (ft)	color of blossom	
[CERASUS]	*Prunus* 'Amanogawa'		flowering	flowering										13	20	3	10		Narrow upright habit, opening with age
	P. avium		flowering	flowering		harvest								16	23	13	20		Color fair in fall; single flowers
	P. 'Kanzan'		flowering	flowering										13	20	10	16		Habit upright when young, good fall color
	P. 'Okame'	flowering	flowering											10	16	10	16		Good fall color; single flowers
	P. 'Pink Perfection'		flowering	flowering										13	20	10	16		New leaves bronze, double flowers
	P. sargentii	flowering	flowering		harvest									13	20	13	20		Brilliant color in early fall
	P. serrula		flowering		harvest	harvest								13	20	10	16		Bark mahogany colored; small, white flowers
	P. 'Shirotae'		flowering	flowering										13	20	13	20		Large, single or semi-double flowers
	P. 'Shogestsu'		flowering	flowering										13	20	13	20		Double flowers, new leaves green
	P. 'Spire'		flowering		harvest									13	20	8	13		Upright habit and single flowers
	P. subhirtella 'Autumnalis'	flowering							flowering	flowering	flowering	flowering	flowering	13	20	10	16		Flowers may open before the leaves fall
	P. 'Ukon'		flowering	flowering										13	20	10	16		Stunningly odd flower color, semi-double
	P. yedoensis	flowering	flowering		harvest									13	20	13	20		Flowers profusely; fragrant
[OTHER GROUPS]	*P. cerasifera*	flowering	flowering			harvest						flowering	flowering	13	20	10	16		Early white flowers, mistaken for blackthorn
	P. cerasifera 'Pissardii'	flowering	flowering			harvest						flowering	flowering	13	20	10	16		Dark red leaves when new, later dull purple
	P. dulcis		flowering	flowering			harvest	harvest						13	20	10	16		Common almond
	P. laurocerasus			flowering					harvest					10	16	6½	13		Large evergreen leaves
	P. lusitanica				flowering			harvest						8	13	8	13		Fragrant flowers; a tough evergreen
	P. lusitanica 'Variegata'				flowering									6½	10	6½	10		Variegated leaves
	P. padus			flowering		harvest	harvest							16	23	13	20		Also known as European bird cherry

flowering harvest

Ptelea

Hop tree

These are small shrubby trees, rarely making more than 26ft (8m) and usually only 20ft (6m) over 30 years. They belong to the Rutaceae, the same family as oranges and lemons, along with Phellodendron (see page 98).

All members of this family have small translucent glands in the foliage, which make it aromatic if crushed. Ptelea are deciduous with trifoliate leaves. The flowers are greenish-white and are usually strongly scented. They are followed by the flattened winged fruits, which are similar to those of elm. These are bitter and have been used as substitute hops for flavoring beer.

Ptelea thrive on all well-drained soils, preferring fertile loams but will tolerate less fertile sites. They are trees for open sites in the garden and make attractive shrubs that will slowly translate into small trees. They can be sited in a shrub border, but are better as a specimen in a lawn or rough grass area. The form 'Aurea' has leaves of a soft yellow and is rather effective if used to contrast with dull purple foliage (especially shrubs with bright new foliage that soon "matures" to a dank purple-green, since Ptelea tends to be late before it is in full leaf). They can be propagated by seeds, sown when ripe in the fall or the following spring. They can also be propagated by softwood or semi-ripe cuttings in early summer.

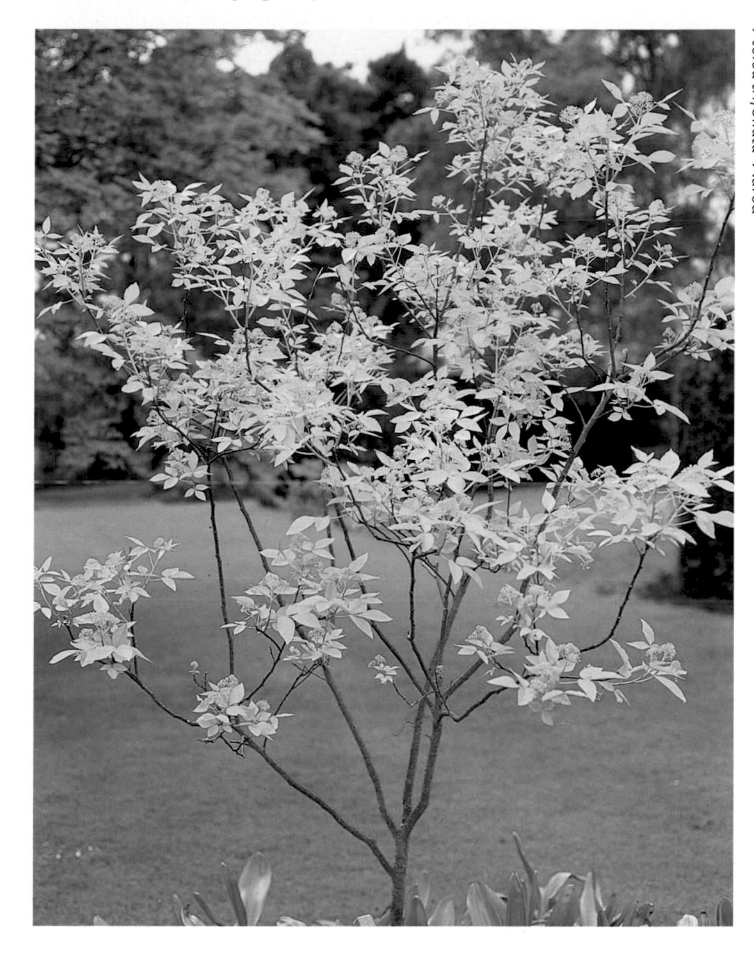

Ptelea trifoliata 'Aurea'

soil	Likes any well-drained type of soil, including sands and chalky ones
site	Enjoys being sited in a position that has lots of sun in the garden
pruning	No special pruning regime required except to restrict or reshape
general care	An extremely easy tree to cultivate and manage, tolerating both fertile and poor rocky soils
pests & diseases	Relatively trouble-free. Does not have any particular problems with pests and diseases

	SPRING	SUMMER	FALL	WINTER	height 5yrs (ft)	height 10yrs (ft)	spread 5yrs (ft)	spread 10yrs (ft)	color of blossom	
Ptelea trifoliata		flowering, harvest	harvest		6½	11½	5	8		Aromatic leaves if crushed; flowers scented
P. trifoliata 'Aurea'		flowering, harvest	harvest		6½	11½	5	8		Soft yellow leaves

 *flowering* 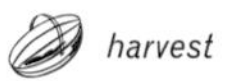 *harvest*

Pterocarya
Wingnut

These relatives of Juglans (walnut) and Carya (hickory) make fast-growing trees with pinnate leaves. The fruit is a small nut, too small to be edible but with two wings, hence the common name. They make bold foliage trees, but are also attractive for the long fruiting catkins. These may be 20in (50cm) in length and hang beneath the boughs.

They thrive on a wide range of soils, including rather damp sites. *Pterocarya fraxinifolia* suckers freely from the roots, forming thickets where these are allowed to develop. *P. stenoptera* does not sucker, but has longer, erect wings on the fruit. These are trees for parks and larger gardens, especially beside lakes and rivers, where they can be indulged with a permanently moist soil.

Pterocarya fraxinifolia

They can be raised from seed, or from semi-ripe cuttings but *P. fraxinifolia* is most easily propagated from root cuttings or by removing suckers.

soil	Pterocarya: damp to well-drained. Pterostryax: well-drained soils, not over chalk
site	Both Pterocarya and Pterostryax prefer sun or light shade
pruning	No pruning required for either, except to reshape or restrict
general care	Pterocarya: tend to have low spreading crowns unless trained to give a clear stem. Pterostryax: easy to manage
pests & diseases	Both are relatively trouble-free and do not have any particular problems with pests and diseases

Pterostyrax

This genus is related to Styrax and Halesia. It differs in its smaller flowers, which are much less showy than in the above genera, but make up for it by being carried in larger clusters; they are also fragrant.

Pterostyrax make attractive trees either for lawns in the full sun, larger shrub beds, or in light woodland settings, and will grow on all well-drained soils, except shallow ones overlying chalk.

Pterostyrax can be grown from seed sown in the fall, where it should germinate next spring. If sown in spring, germination of the seeds will be delayed and is unlikely to occur before the following spring. They can also be grown from semi-ripe cuttings in early summer.

Pterostyrax hispida

	SPRING			SUMMER			FALL			WINTER			height 5yrs (ft)	height 10yrs (ft)	spread 5yrs (ft)	spread 10yrs (ft)	flower color	
Pterocarya fraxinifolia			flowering			harvest	harvest						13	23	10	16		Large suckering tree
P. stenoptera			flowering			harvest	harvest						13	20	10	13		Doesn't sucker, unless grafted onto *P. fraxinifolia*
Pterostyrax corymbosa			flowering	flowering									6½	13	3	6½		Large shrub/small tree, with fragrant flowers
P. hispida				flowering	flowering								6½	13	3	6½		Large shrub/small tree, to 26–33ft

flowering · harvest

Pyracantha

Firethorn

Pyracantha are often grown as wall shrubs, a task for which they are very well suited, but they can also be grown as free-standing shrubs or in shrub beds. They have two main seasons of display—early summer and fall.

In the early summer, the branches of Pyracantha are smothered by clusters of white hawthornlike flowers. These are followed in the fall by the berries, which are small applelike fruits and indicate the relationship of Pyracantha with other members of the apple family. The fruits ripen to red, orange, or golden yellow. In some forms they last well into the winter.

Pyracantha will withstand clipping and can be used to form topiaries across the front of dwellings or as hedges. They are very tolerant of soil conditions, whether acidic sands or chalky soils, although they will perform at their best on fertile loams.

They are evergreens and can get damaged by cold dry winds in winter, so shelter from such weather is beneficial.

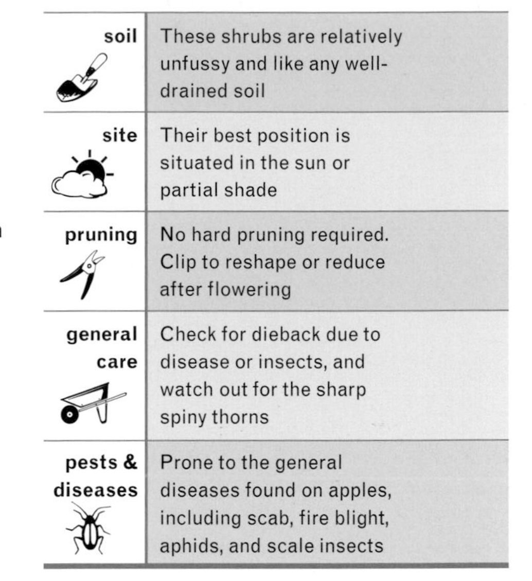

soil	These shrubs are relatively unfussy and like any well-drained soil
site	Their best position is situated in the sun or partial shade
pruning	No hard pruning required. Clip to reshape or reduce after flowering
general care	Check for dieback due to disease or insects, and watch out for the sharp spiny thorns
pests & diseases	Prone to the general diseases found on apples, including scab, fire blight, aphids, and scale insects

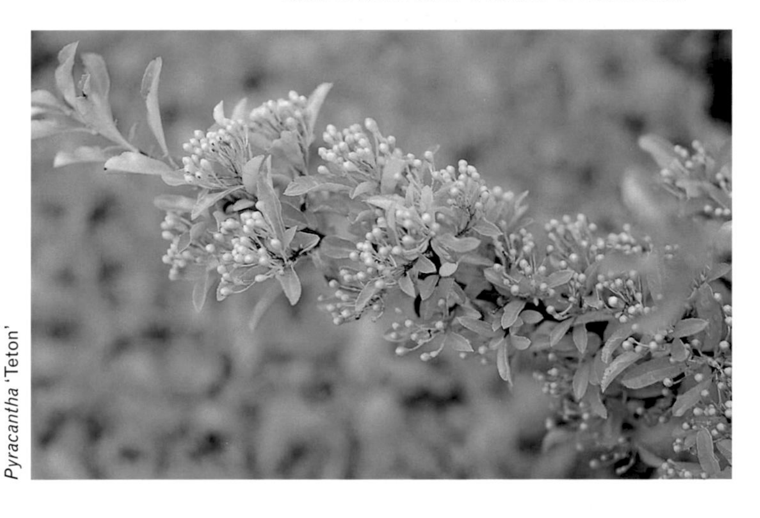

Pyracantha 'Teton'

They are also liable to the usual diseases of apples, such as scab and fire blight, plus ubiquitous pests like scale insects and aphids.

They can be raised from seed, but this will often give hybrids of lesser value than the parents. They are easily propagated from cuttings. Traditionally, these cuttings would be taken during the early summer, but they can be rooted into the fall.

Cuttings that are about 12in (30cm) taken in early fall will flower the next spring and make larger plants by the fall, rather than smaller cuttings taken early in the summer.

	SPRING	SUMMER	FALL	WINTER	height 5yrs (ft)	height 10yrs (ft)	spread 5yrs (ft)	spread 10yrs (ft)	color of blossom	
Pyracantha coccinea 'Red Column'		flowering	harvest harvest harvest	harvest	6½	13	3	6½		Scarlet fruits, ripening early; glossy leaves
P. 'Golden Charmer'		flowering	harvest harvest harvest	harvest	6½	13	5	10		Orange-yellow fruits, ripening early
P. 'Mohave'		flowering	harvest harvest harvest	harvest	6½	13	5	10		Bright orange-red berries ripen early
P. 'Orange Charmer'		flowering	harvest harvest harvest	harvest	6½	13	5	10		Deep orange fruits, flattened, long lasting
P. 'Orange Glow'		flowering	harvest harvest harvest	harvest	6½	13	5	10		Orange-red fruits, long lasting
P. rogersiana		flowering	harvest harvest harvest	harvest	6½	13	5	10		Reddish-orange fruits
P. rogersiana 'Flava'		flowering	harvest harvest harvest	harvest	6½	13	5	10		Bright yellow fruits
P. 'Teton'		flowering	harvest harvest harvest	harvest	6½	13	5	10		Resistant to fire blight, yellow-orange fruits

 flowering  harvest

Pyrus

Pear

Pears are most often found in the orchard or as espaliers along the fence of the kitchen garden, where they are grown for their fruit. However, they are very attractive in flower and include species well worth growing in the garden. The common pear is *Pyrus communis*, of which over 1,000 fruiting cultivars are recorded, ranging from dessert varieties to those intended for perry production (cider with pears).

The variety 'Beech Hill' is a form of common pear with small fruits about 1in (3cm) across; the branches are erect, giving a narrow crowned tree, and the glossy green leaves turn a bright orange-yellow in the fall. *Pyrus calleryana* 'Chanticleer' is also narrow crowned with an upright habit. The glossy green leaves last long into the fall—in mild winters they may not display their fall tints until early winter and may still have some leaves in mid-winter. The flowers are white and carried in early spring. This tree is widely used as a street tree, but the same characteristics of a tough constitution, narrow ovoid habit, and colorful flowers make it desirable for smaller gardens.

Pyrus calleryana 'Chanticleer'

The most common amenity pear is the weeping form of *Pyrus salicifolia*, 'Pendula'. The narrow leaves are silvery-gray and the pendent branch habit makes a small, neat tree. It has white flowers, but these are rather lost against the foliage.

Pears thrive on a wide range of soils, including clays and chalks, provided they have reasonable drainage. They are usually propagated by grafting onto rootstocks—most commercial pears are grafted onto a quince rootstock. The species can be raised from seed.

soil	Well-drained or moist but not wet. Preferably fertile soils including chalk and clay
site	Enjoys being sited in a position that has lots of sun in the garden
pruning	None, except to restrict or reshape; remove damaged and crossing branches
general care	Fairly easy to cultivate and look after. Be careful to remove suckers from the root stocks
pests & diseases	They can get scab and fire blight, and other diseases of fruit trees, but are generally healthy

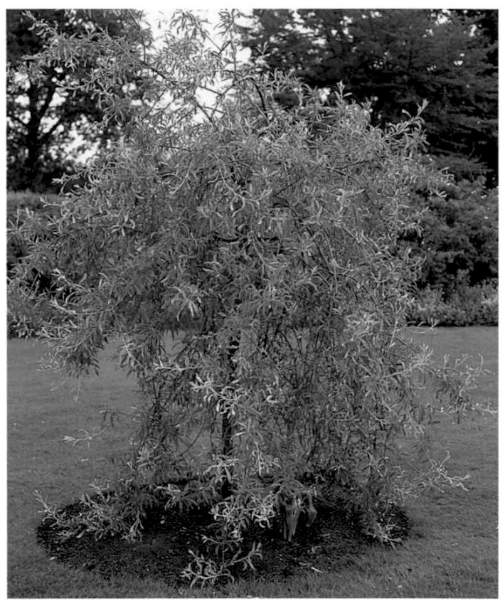

Pyrus salicifolia 'Pendula'

	SPRING	SUMMER	FALL	WINTER	height 5yrs (ft)	height 10yrs (ft)	spread 5yrs (ft)	spread 10yrs (ft)	color of blossom	
Pyrus calleryana 'Chanticleer'	flowering, flowering		harvest		13	23	3	8		Upright ovoid crown, can make 33–40ft+
P. communis	flowering		harvest, harvest		13	23	6½	13		Orchard pear, fall color often poor
P. communis 'Beech Hill'	flowering		harvest		13	23	6½	10		Long upright branches, good fall color
P. salicifolia 'Pendula'	flowering		harvest		10	16	6½	16		Silvery gray foliage and pendulous branches

flowering harvest

Quercus

Oak

Oaks are mainly large-growing trees and few are suitable for small gardens. The genus comprises several hundred different species, a few of which make shrubs only 3ft (1m) in height, such as *Quercus sadleriana*, but these are not common in cultivation.

The smallest-growing oaks in general cultivation are two forms of the English oak, *Quercus robur*: *Q. robur* 'Concordia' and *Q. robur* 'Fastigiata'. *Q. robur* 'Concordia' has leaves that are suffused a golden green during spring and summer. It is slow growing, but will make 33ft (10m) in 50 years or more. *Q. robur* 'Fastigiata' has erect branches and makes a narrow crown tree, although it is potentially as tall as any other form of *Q. robur*.

Other oaks featured here are all capable of making tall trees. This is especially true with Turkey oak (*Q. cerris*), scarlet oak (*Q. coccinea*), Hungarian oak (*Q. frainetto*), pin oak (*Q. palustris*), durmast oak (*Q. petraea*), English oak (*Q. robur*), and northern red oak (*Q. rubra*).

Oaks need full sun for the best development. They are excellent on heavy clay soils, but watch out for subsidence risk. Oaks are usually propagated from acorns, which must not be allowed to dry out; it is best to sow them as soon as ripe in deep pots. Forms like the *Q. robur* are grafted in late summer.

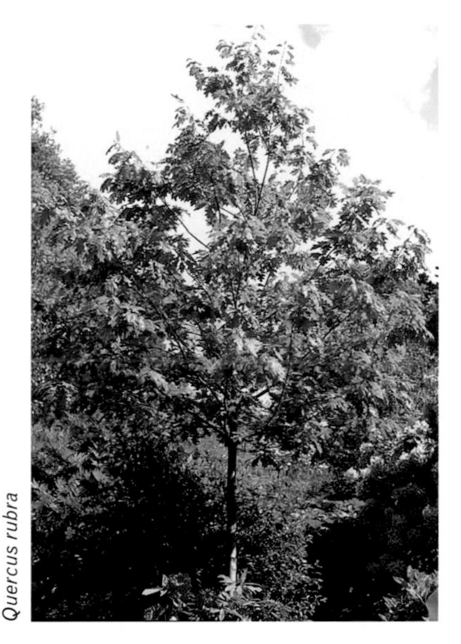

Quercus rubra

soil	These particular trees perform best in heavy to well-drained soils
site	Enjoys being sited in a position that has lots of sun in the garden
pruning	None, except to restrict or reshape; remove damaged and crossing branches
general care	Easy to care for. Large-growing trees, which are efficient in extracting water from clay soils
pests & diseases	Mildew can cause foliage loss but only serious in shade; various insects eat the foliage—rarely cause harm

	SPRING	SUMMER	FALL	WINTER	height 5yrs (ft)	height 10yrs (ft)	spread 5yrs (ft)	spread 10yrs (ft)	color of blossom	
Quercus cerris	flowering		harvest		13	23	6½	10		Narrow crowned as a young tree
Q. cerris 'Argenteomarginata'	flowering				6½	10	3	6½		Usually available only as a small shrub
Q. coccinea	flowering				13	20	10	13		Leaves turn scarlet in fall—can be variable
Q. coccinea 'Splendens'	flowering				13	20	10	13		Best form for fall color
Q. frainetto	flowering		harvest		13	23	10	13		Bold foliage turns russet colors in fall
Q. hispanica 'Lucombeana'	flowering				13	20	10	13		Semi-evergreen, thick and corky bark
Q. ilex		flowering	harvest		6½	11½	3	6½		Evergreen; new growth/flowers early summer
Q. palustris	flowering				13	20	10	13		Neater habit than scarlet oak, foliage as good
Q. petraea	flowering		harvest		13	20	10	13		Grows on better-drained sites
Q. phellos	flowering				8	13	5	8		A few leaves often retained into winter
Q. robur	flowering		harvest		13	20	10	13		Not as slow-growing, if weed control is good
Q. robur 'Concordia'	flowering				5	8	3	6½		Soft, yellow-green foliage; slow-growing
Q. robur 'Fastigiata'	flowering				13	20	3	6½		Upright growth habit with erect branches
Q. rubra	flowering				13	20	10	13		Select best forms when in fall color
Q. rubra 'Aurea'	flowering				13	20	6½	10		Needs sheltered site, liable to scorch in full sun
Q. suber	flowering				5	8	3	6½		Evergreen, with thick corky bark

 *flowering*  *harvest*

Rehderodendron

Rehderodendron belongs to the Storax family, having white funnel-shaped flowers that hang down from branches in late spring like Styrax and Halesia.

Rehderodendron macrocarpum

The fruit, however, is a large woody structure, to 3in (8cm). Rehderodendron makes a small tree and is useful for its attractive flowers. It likes full sunlight but will take partial shade and is well suited to a woodland garden. It thrives on a wide range of soils, preferably acidic or neutral and well drained. It is not suitable for exposed sites, preferring shelter from cold winds. The best method of propagation is semi-ripe cuttings in early summer. It can also be raised from seed, but the fruit is slow to break down to release the seeds; some I collected in northern Vietnam in 1992 didn't germinate until 1999, whereupon they were promptly eaten by slugs!

soil	Rehderodendron and Rhododendron: acidic, well-drained but moist. Rhus: any
site	Rehderodendron and Rhododendron: sun/light shade. Rhus: prefers full sun
pruning	Rhododendron: benefit from removal of spent flowers. Rehderodendron/Rhus: none
general care	Rehderodendron: avoid exposed sites. Rhododendron: mulch with leaf mold or peat. Rhus: sap may give allergy
pests & diseases	All are relatively trouble-free and do not have any particular problems with pests and diseases

Rhododendron

This genus contains a wealth of attractive shrubs and trees, perhaps 800 species and innumerable hybrids.

The plants range from codominant trees in the rainforest to low shrubs in alpine moorland. The Rhododendron discussed here are all capable of making large, evergreen shrubs or small trees, upward of 13–18ft (4–5m) in height. They all require an acidic soil.

Some of the species, such as *R. falconeri* and *R. fulvum*, have beautiful red-brown hairs on the underside of the leaves, and *R. falconeri* also has an attractive peeling bark. These require the shelter of a light woodland setting, but *R. makinoi*, with narrow leaves that have a white or tawny-white underside, will take full sun. Also liking shelter are the 'Loderi' group of hybrids. These make large shrubs and have bold fragrant flowers, of white or pale pink, in late spring or early summer. 'Polar Bear' is rather similar, but flowers in mid- to late summer.

The old "Hardy Hybrids" are tougher and will take full sun. They combine several species in their parentage and were first developed in the 19th century. 'Gomer Waterer' has white flowers, which are flushed mauve around the edges of the petals. 'Loder's White' has white petals edged pink. 'Mrs G.W. Leak' has rosy pink flowers. 'Pink Pearl', with its conical trusses of deep lilac-pink, is very attractive, if somewhat garish, and fades as the flowers mature. 'Purple Splendour' has rich

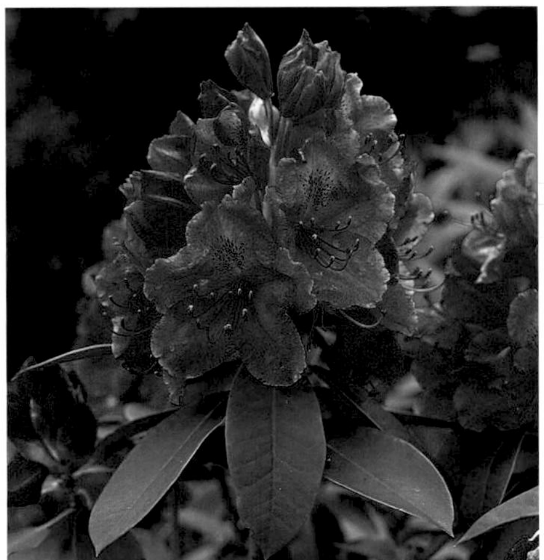
Rhododendron 'Pink Pearl'

purplish-blue flowers and in 'Susan' they are bluish-mauve.

The alpine rose group of Rhododendron are generally smaller plants but two commonly available ones have sufficient stature to be included here. *R. augustinii* has masses of blue flowers and makes an excellent woodland shrub. 'Lady Alice Fitzwilliam' has strongly scented, white flowers flushed with pink; the plant requires a sheltered woodland setting.

Although these plants will make large shrubs or small trees, they will do so only at a modest rate, roughly 8–12in (20–30cm) a year or less. They can be propagated by cuttings and by layering. Generally, the larger the leaves, the longer it takes for cuttings to root, and the large-leaved species like *R. falconeri* are best layered!

	SPRING			SUMMER			FALL			WINTER			height 5yrs (ft)	height 10yrs (ft)	spread 5yrs (ft)	spread 10yrs (ft)	flower color	
Rhododendron falconeri			flowering										4	6½	3	6½		Leaves are reddish-brown beneath, bark flaky
R. fulvum	flowering	flowering											4	6½	3	6½		Leaves with a cinnamon underside
R. 'Gomer Waterer'			flowering	flowering									4	6½	3	6½		Tolerant of dry sites
R. 'Lady Alice Fitzwilliam'			flowering	flowering									4	6½	3	6½		Tender, fragrant flowers
R. 'Loder's White'				flowering	flowering								4	6½	3	6½		Not the same as 'Loderi' group of hybrids
R. makinoi				flowering									4	6½	3	6½		Narrow leaves, densely white or fawn
R. 'Mrs G.W. Leak'			flowering	flowering									4	6½	3	6½		Rose-pink, compact
R. 'Pink Pearl'			flowering	flowering									4	6½	3	6½		Old plants tend to become bare at the base
R. 'Polar Bear'					flowering	flowering							5	8	4	6½		Excellent for its late flowering, fragrant
R. ponticum				flowering									4	6½	3	6½		Makes good hedges on acidic soils
R. 'Purple Splendour'			flowering	flowering									4	6½	3	6½		Very strong-colored hybrid
R. 'Susan'		flowering	flowering										4	6½	3	6½		Mauve-blue flowers, vigorous

Rhus
Sumac

This genus of trees and large shrubs is renowned for its fall color, which is usually red and yellow or orange.

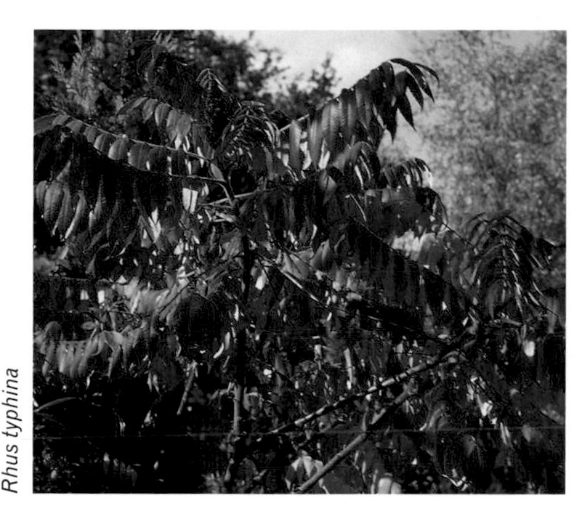
Rhus typhina

The common staghorn sumac (*Rhus typhina*)—so called as the furry coat on the shoots resembles the velvet on a stag's new antlers—is interesting for the large red flower heads that are carried on separate male and female trees. Other sumacs are less commonly grown, but make bigger trees, including the varnish tree, *Rhus verniciflua*, from which lacquer is obtained.

All sumacs have a thick sap, which is an irritant and poisonous in contact with the skin. This is more of a problem with *R. verniciflua*, but some people also find the sap of *R. typhina* causes allergic reactions. Another problem, particularly of *R. typhina*, is that they sucker. Not a problem if you leave the tree alone, but get rid of one and you find a score of suckers challenging to take over. In the garden they are useful in shrub beds, where they can be set toward the back, or as specimen trees. They are most easily raised from root cuttings, or by lifting a sucker.

	SPRING			SUMMER			FALL			WINTER			height 5yrs (ft)	height 10yrs (ft)	spread 5yrs (ft)	spread 10yrs (ft)	color of blossom	
Rhus typhina				flowering			harvest						7	16	8	16		Brilliant fall color on stout, furry shoots
R. typhina 'Dissectum'				flowering			harvest						7	16	8	16		Deeply divided leaflets; female only

 flowering  harvest

R

Trees & Shrubs

Robinia

This is a genus of trees or large shrubs with pinnate leaves and showy, pealike flowers. These are usually white but in *Robinia hispida* they are a deep rose color. The shoots usually have two recurved spines, one on either side of the bud or leaf.

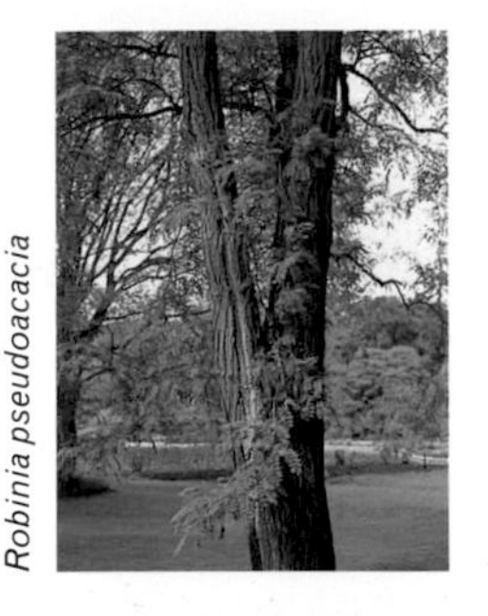

Robinia pseudoacacia

Robinia are excellent for dry and sandy sites, and are used to stabilize such soils. They can spread by root suckers, which is useful where soil stabilization is required, but not so in the garden. They are tolerant of urban conditions, with *R. pseudoacacia* quickly forming a medium-sized tree with a gnarled trunk, looking much older than its years. The leaves drop without adopting any color in the fall.

Robinia pseudoacacia 'Lace Lady'

Another drawback is that the branches are very brittle. Young trees are inclined to grow too dense and heavy too soon, only to fall apart in strong winds in late summer and early fall. It is worth pruning young trees in late summer to remove or shorten any branches that start at narrow forks, and generally lighten the crown density.

In the garden, the bright foliage of *R. pseudoacacia* 'Frisia' makes an excellent golden yellow tree. It does flower, but the white blooms do not show against the foliage. Other forms of *R. pseudoacacia* are excellent both for their flowers and the light open crowns, and make good specimen trees. The rose acacia, *R. hispida*, is attractive both for the deep rose flowers and for the bristly stems.

The species can be propagated either by seed or by suckers. The forms have to be grafted onto a seedling rootstock.

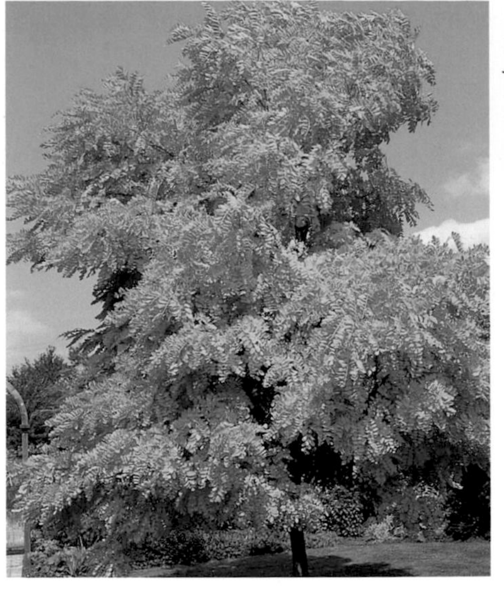

Robinia pseudoacacia 'Frisia'

soil	Any well-drained soil—not good for shallow chalk soils but excellent on sandy ones
site	This tree is a sun-lover and does not appreciate any shade
pruning	No special pruning is required but can be trimmed to restrict growth
general care	The stems are quite brittle and liable to snap during windy periods when in full leaf
pests & diseases	Relatively trouble-free. Does not have any particular problems with pests and diseases

	SPRING			SUMMER			FALL			WINTER			height 5yrs (ft)	height 10yrs (ft)	spread 5yrs (ft)	spread 10yrs (ft)	flower color	
Robinia hispida			flowering	flowering									6½	11½	6½	11½		Shrub with interesting bristly shoots
R. pseudoacacia				flowering									13	23	6½	16		Flowers fragrant; vigorous suckering tree
R. pseudoacacia 'Frisia'				flowering									13	23	6½	16		Golden yellow foliage
R. pseudoacacia 'Lace Lady'				flowering									3	6½	3	6½		Twisted habit
R. pseudoacacia 'Tortuosa'				flowering									8	13	5	10		Slow-growing form with contorted branches
R. slavinii 'Hillieri'				flowering									10	16	6½	13		Small-growing tree

flowering

R

Trees & Shrubs

Salix

Willow

The genus Salix is widely distributed, from moors to thicket and forest, with species ranging from less than 1in (3cm) in height to 100ft (30m) or more. They are often associated with water, and the weeping willow, *Salix sepulcralis* 'Chrysocoma', is really good when reflected in a large lake.

Salix need only damp conditions to germinate seeds, and can grow quite happily in normal or even dry soils. They are extremely tolerant of being cut back. This is useful when keeping a large weeping willow in too small a garden or bringing out the best twig color in *Salix alba* ssp. *vitellina* 'Britzensis'; the one-year shoots only develop the full bright orange-scarlet color in mid-winter.

Trees can be pollarded at 10–13ft (3–4m) or coppiced near ground level to maximize

S. alba ssp. *vitellina* 'Britzensis'

Salix gracillistyla 'Melanostachys'

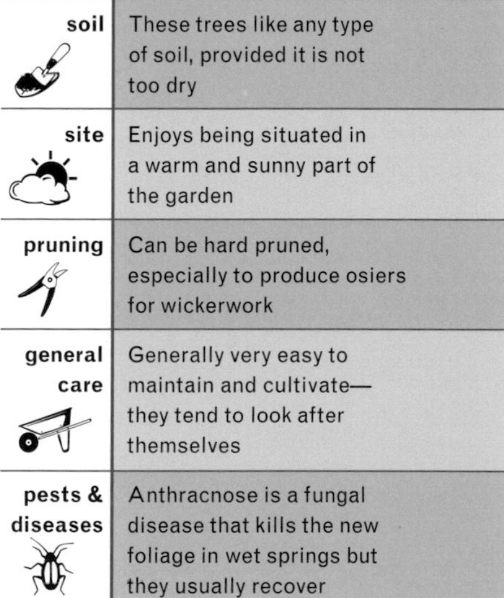

soil	These trees like any type of soil, provided it is not too dry
site	Enjoys being situated in a warm and sunny part of the garden
pruning	Can be hard pruned, especially to produce osiers for wickerwork
general care	Generally very easy to maintain and cultivate—they tend to look after themselves
pests & diseases	Anthracnose is a fungal disease that kills the new foliage in wet springs but they usually recover

the production of colorful shoots, whether annually or better still on a two- or three-year cycle. The catkins can be attractive but the two sexes occur on different trees; the male ones with their pollen-bearing anthers are generally more showy, especially at the silky hairy stage, than the green female catkins. The catkins of *Salix gracillistyla* 'Melanostachys' are almost black with brick-red anthers and yellow pollen. The smaller-growing species can be very attractive for their foliage, especially *Salix fargesii* and *Salix magnifica*.

Willows have a high water demand and can cause problems on shrinkable clay subsoils if put too near inadequately founded structures. Willows are extremely easy to propagate from hardwood cuttings, best taken in late winter. They can be rooted in a glass jar of water on the kitchen window sill. This ability to grow in water can cause the occasional problem with drains—if there is a leak in the drainage system, the roots can penetrate the leak in the structure to get to the supply of water.

Salix fargessii

	SPRING			SUMMER	FALL	WINTER	height 5yrs (ft)	height 10yrs (ft)	spread 5yrs (ft)	spread 10yrs (ft)	catkin color	
Salix acutifolia 'Blue Streak'	flowering						13	23	6½	13		Blackish-purple stems, waxy covering
S. alba ssp. *vitellina* 'Britzensis'		flowering					16	30	13	20		Grown for the orange-scarlet twig color
S. alba var. *sericea*		flowering					13	26	13	20		Leaves with a silky covering of hairs
S. caprea	flowering	flowering					13	20	13	20		Males provide pussy willow catkins
S. daphnoides	flowering	flowering					16	26	13	20		Purple-violet shoots have waxy white bloom
S. elaeagnos		flowering	flowering				13	20	10	16		Excellent for waterside plantings
S. exigua		flowering	flowering				10	13	10	16		Catkins with the gray-green new leaves
S. fargesii			flowering				10	13	10	13		Glossy green leaves on stout red-brown shoots
S. gracillistyla 'Melanostachys'	flowering	flowering					13	20	10	16	■	Attractive for the color of the catkins
S. magnifica			flowering				10	13	10	16		Large leaves like a magnolia
S. sepulcralis 'Chrysocoma'		flowering					16	30	13	20		Golden yellow twigs, weeping on older trees

 *flowering*

Sambucus

Elder

The elders are valuable for their flowers and fruit. Both can be used to make cordials, although if using the flowers, make sure there are no blackfly or other aphids.

The flowers are carried in large, usually flat-topped trusses and are white or ivory-colored. The fruits may be purple or red; they (like other parts of the plant) can be an irritant but cooking removes this blemish. The foliage is pinnate, but drops without giving any color in the fall. However, there are a number of selections with golden yellow foliage that are among the best of their class; these include *Sambucus nigra* 'Aurea', *Sambucus racemosa* 'Plumosa Aurea', and *Sambucus racemosa* 'Sutherland Gold'. *Sambucus nigra* 'Guincho Purple' and *Sambucus nigra* 'Black Beauty' have blackish-purple leaves and pinkish flowers.

soil	Any well-drained soil, whether acidic sands or shallow chalky ones
site	Prefers the sun but is also happy in moderately dense shade
pruning	No specific requirement. Can be hard pruned to restrict spread
general care	Easy to maintain. Colored foliage forms the best when it is situated in dappled shade
pests & diseases	Relatively trouble-free. Does not have any particular problems with pests and diseases

Sambucus racemosa 'Plumosa Aurea'

Sambucus racemosa 'Sutherland Gold'

Sambucus nigra 'Black Beauty'

The species of Sambucus are extremely tough, flourishing on barren sites whether acidic or derived from a shallow layer of topsoil over chalk. They make medium to large shrubs, up to small trees. The vigorous current year's shoots have a very thick and soft pith but later wood is dense and hard.

In the garden they can be used in shrub borders or as specimen trees. They can withstand shade and the golden foliage forms can enliven dank corners. They can be raised from seed, from hardwood cuttings, and from softwood cuttings in summer.

	SPRING	SUMMER	FALL	WINTER	height 5yrs (ft)	height 10yrs (ft)	spread 5yrs (ft)	spread 10yrs (ft)	color of blossom	
Sambucus nigra 'Aurea'		flowering, flowering	harvest		10	16	10	16	white	Golden yellow leaves
S. nigra 'Black Beauty'		flowering, flowering	harvest		10	16	10	16	pink	Blackish-purple leaves; fragrant flowers
S. nigra 'Guincho Purple'		flowering, flowering	harvest		10	16	10	16	pink	Leaves open green then blackish-purple to red
S. nigra forma *laciniata*		flowering, flowering	harvest		10	16	10	16	white	Deeply divided leaflets
S. racemosa 'Plumosa Aurea'	flowering, flowering		harvest		10	16	10	16	white	Leaves deeply cut, golden yellow
S. racemosa 'Sutherland Gold'		flowering, flowering	harvest		10	16	10	16	white	Leaves coarser than 'Plumosa Aurea'
S. racemosa 'Tenuifolia'		flowering, flowering			4	6½	4	6½	white	Makes a small shrub like a Japanese maple

flowering harvest

Sassafras

Sassafras albidum makes a small to medium-sized tree with an upright ovoid crown and is the best species for a woodland or fairly large garden. The leaves are ovate or obovate; most are entire but some have one or two deep rounded sinuses and conspicuous lobes, often on the same shoot.

Sassafras albidum

The leaves turn a rich yellow, orange, or red in the fall. If crushed, they are strongly aromatic, as are the green shoots, and if chewed, have a spicy flavor, which numbs the mouth. The flowers are carried in spring with the new foliage; they are yellow and discretely showy. Fruits are formed only where separate male and female trees are grown; these fruits are dark blue and set on a red stalk.

Sassafras has several medicinal uses. The bark of the root is used to make a beverage and also to flavor beers. The trees are usually surrounded by some suckers from the root system.

Sassafras albidum

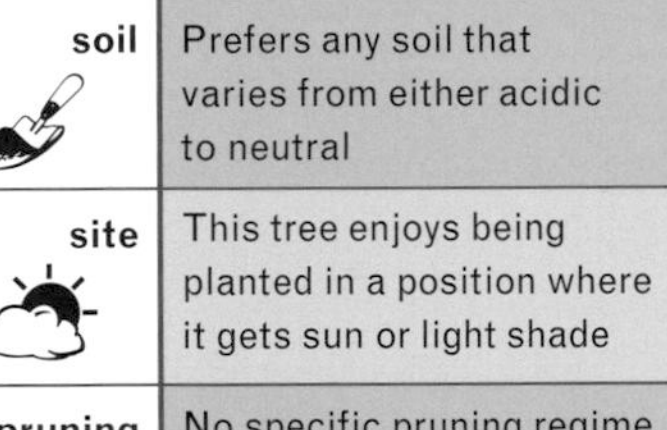

soil	Prefers any soil that varies from either acidic to neutral
site	This tree enjoys being planted in a position where it gets sun or light shade
pruning	No specific pruning regime is required, except to resize or reshape
general care	Reasonably easy to cultivate and maintain. It would benefit from some side shelter
pests & diseases	Relatively trouble-free. Does not have any particular problems with pests and diseases

In the garden, *S. albidum* is useful as a specimen tree or planted in a woodland area. It is best with some shelter and requires a lime-free soil, of moderate fertility and drainage. The species is easily sown from seeds won in spring. It can also be raised from root cuttings taken in winter. Suckers can also be separated and grown on with care.

Sophora

Pagoda tree

This is a large genus of mainly woody plants. The ones in cultivation include two species from the southern hemisphere—*Sophora microphylla* and *Sophora tetraptera*—and one from eastern Asia, *Sophora japonica*. This latter species is now commonly placed in a segregate genus, Styphnolobium.

Sophora microphylla and *Sophora tetraptera* both have small, evergreen leaves composed of many small leaflets, from 10 to 40 pairs. They have yellow flowers in small clusters, carried in late winter or spring. They make shrubs or small trees, to 20ft (6m). *Sophora japonica* is a much taller-growing tree, capable of making 75ft (23m) in height and spread under the best conditions. The leaves are dark green with eight pairs of leaflets; the base of the leaf stalk hides the bud for next year's shoot until the leaves turn yellow and drop in the fall. The flowers are fragrant, white, and carried in late summer or early fall at the ends of the current year's growths.

Sophora microphylla and *Sophora tetraptera* are useful grown in shrub beds, or as specimen shrubs; they can also be used as wall shrubs. *Sophora japonica* is a specimen tree, for a large lawn or spacious area.

Sophora microphylla and *Sophora tetraptera* can be propagated by semi-ripe cuttings in summer or fall. *Sophora japonica* is better raised from seed, although cuttings are worth trying. Selected forms can be grafted onto a seedling rootstock.

Sophora microphylla

soil	Grows well in any type of well-drained soil, including sandy ones
site	This plant enjoys being situated in a position where it gets lots of sun
pruning	No special pruning regime is required, except to reshape or restrain
general care	As members of the Legume family, they can make fertilizer using atmospheric nitrogen
pests & diseases	Relatively trouble-free. Does not have any particular problems with pests and diseases

	SPRING			SUMMER			FALL			WINTER			height 5yrs (ft)	height 10yrs (ft)	spread 5yrs (ft)	spread 10yrs (ft)	flower color	
Sophora japonica						●	●						10	16	3	8		Known as the Japanese pagoda
S. microphylla	●	●										●	8	16	8	16		Spreading small tree or shrub
S. microphylla 'Sun King'	●	●										●	8	16	8	16		Selected form, from Chile
S. tetraptera		●										●	8	16	8	16		Best in southwest and with wall shelter

 *flowering*

S

Trees & Shrubs

Sorbaria

The Latin name of this genus combines two elements of Sorbus and Aria. The pinnate leaves resemble those of the rowans (Sorbus) but it is actually more closely related to Spiraea. Sorbaria is valuable in the garden for its large panicles of small white flowers. Each bloom has five starlike petals.

The panicles terminate the current season's growth in mid- to late summer after the spring flowers have finished and the trusses may be 1ft (30cm) or so in length. Like many white-flowered plants, the spent blooms turn a less attractive brown but these can be removed as part of the pruning regime.

Sorbaria are vigorous shrubs, throwing shoots 3–6ft (1–1.8m) in a year, and some forms can make 13–20ft (4–6m) in height. They thrive on slightly acidic to slightly alkaline soils, preferring good fertility and good drainage. In the wild they are found in light woodland or along river banks in full sun.

As garden plants they fit into the shrub border, where they can provide bulk and late flowering at the rear. They also fit in a woodland garden setting and in a wild garden. Their size also makes them useful as screens that will not grow too tall, provided you can allow some width to the planting.

The genus suckers, and these suckers can be removed to make new plants. The seeds are small and should be sown in spring onto a moist seed starting mix. They can also be propagated from semi-ripe cuttings in summer.

soil	A slightly acidic to a slightly alkaline soil is preferable
site	This genus thrives in a position where there is sun to moderate shade
pruning	Remove older shoots to keep vigorous shoots, after flowering or in spring
general care	A fairly vigorous-growing shrub but reasonably easy to cultivate and look after
pests & diseases	Relatively trouble-free. Does not have any particular problems with pests and diseases

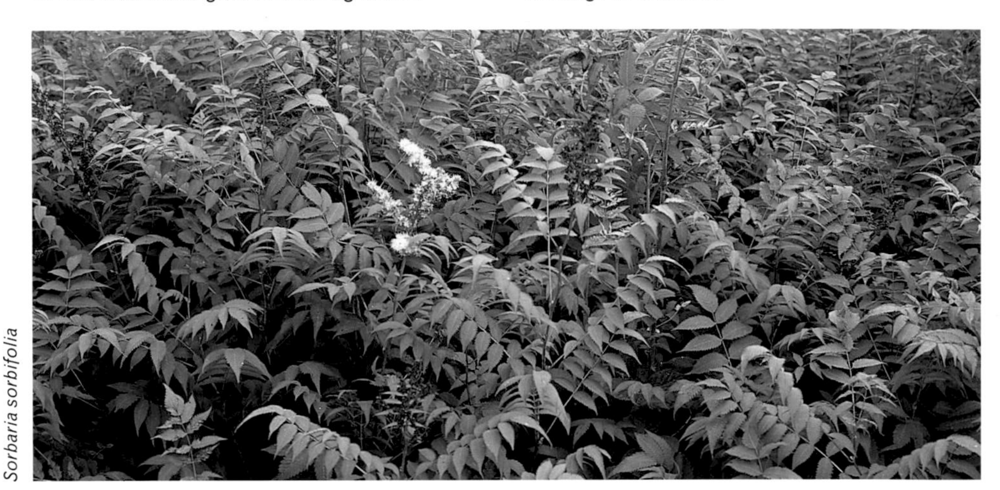
Sorbaria sorbifolia

	SPRING			SUMMER			FALL			WINTER			height 5yrs (ft)	height 10yrs (ft)	spread 5yrs (ft)	spread 10yrs (ft)	flower color	
Sorbaria sorbifolia		flowering	flowering	flowering									5	6½	5	8		Suckering shrub
S. tomentosa var. *angustifolia*		flowering	flowering	flowering									6	10	6	10		Suckering shrub; typical *S. tomentosa* is larger

flowering

Sorbus

Rowan and Whitebeam

Rowans and whitebeams form part of the apple group of the Rose family (Rosaceae). They are usually treated as the same genus—Sorbus—but botanically this is an artificial genus, comprising several genera, which are not closely related.

In the strict sense, the generic name Sorbus belongs to the rowans. The other major group are the whitebeams. These are more closely related to the apples (Malus) than they are to the rowans. Several smaller groups are also commonly included in Sorbus, particularly *Sorbus domestica* and *Sorbus torminalis*. If these groups kept themselves to themselves, it would be simple to recognize the separate genera. However, apart from *S. domestica*, they hybridize. So it has been common practice to call them all Sorbus.

The genus can be characterized by the large clusters of small flowers from which develop small fruits. The species have three main horticultural attributes: the flowers are showy, mainly in late spring or early summer; in most species the fruits ripen to attractive colors and are impressive; and most give good color in the fall. They can be raised from seed, which may not germinate until the second spring. They are often grafted or budded. A related rootstock should be used—rowan scions onto rowans and whitebeams onto whitebeams. Be careful about suckers with grafted stock. Some rowans will also root from semi-ripe cuttings in early summer; *S. torminalis* can be propagated from root cuttings.

soil 	Well-drained. Rowans do best on acidic to neutral; whitebeams thrive on chalk
site 	These all prefer to be situated where there is sun or dappled shade at most
pruning 	No specific pruning regime is needed, except to restrict or reshape
general care 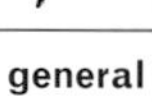	Fairly easy to maintain. If grafted, be careful to remove suckers from the root system
pests & diseases  	Fire blight can cause damage, as can other common diseases but not greatly troubled by pests

Rowan

Rowans (*S. aucuparia*) have red fruits that ripen in mid-summer and in mild regions are often devoured by the local birds before the fall. The fall color can be yellow but is not outstanding, and often the leaves drop without assuming spectacular colors. The cultivar 'Fructu Luteo' has orange-yellow fruits that are not so attractive to birds and last later into the fall.

Sorbus aucuparia

Better fall color is provided by *Sorbus commixta* and its form 'Embley', which turn through yellow or purple to brilliant scarlet. They have orange-red fruits but these are not regularly carried in quantity. *Sorbus* 'Joseph Rock' combines an upright habit with amber berries, which last long after the leaves have turned through crimson and purple and fallen. It can be afflicted by fire blight but is a good tree for restricted space. The rowans with white fruits provide much longer-lasting fruits, since the birds are slower to eat them. Some may last until well into the new year, depending on the local bird population. The best of these will be found in garden centers as *Sorbus hupehensis*, although this name

Sorbus cashmiriana

rightly belongs to another species; it may also be encountered as *Sorbus glabrescens* or *S. oligodonta*, which are better names. The leaves are bluish-green and the fruits hard and white. It makes a small to medium tree roughly 26ft (8m). *Sorbus forrestii* is similar, with slightly larger white fruits but is a smaller tree, while *Sorbus cashmiriana* is little more than a large shrub. It has the largest fruits, about ½in (1cm), but it is not as attractive as the former two trees.

Very different in many respects is *Sorbus domestica*; this has a scaly bark and larger pear- or apple-shaped fruits to just over 1in (2.5–3cm), which ripen to russet or green with a red tinge. It is better for heavier clay soils than the true rowans.

Whitebeam

The whitebeams are so called because they have silvery white undersides to the leaves, and beam is from the Old English word for a tree. The tree that best fits this description is *Sorbus aria*. This makes a dense crowned tree that is attractive for the silvery new foliage, particularly in the form 'Lutescens', and for the red fruits. It is particularly happy on chalky and other alkaline sites but content on acidic ones.

Even better for foliage is *Sorbus thibetica* 'John Mitchell'; this has large leaves and makes a medium tree with a spreading crown. The upper surface of the leaves turn russet colors in the fall while the underside remains silver, and it can look especially effective in winter sunlight if the leaves are not collected. The Swedish whitebeam, *Sorbus intermedia*, has grayish hairy leaves. Its best attribute is that it is remarkably tough, tolerating poor soils and coastal exposure. *Sorbus torminalis*, has attractively lobed leaves but these are green and quickly hairless. The fruits are russet colored, as is the fall color. It suckers and can be raised from root cuttings.

	SPRING			SUMMER			FALL			WINTER			height 5yrs (ft)	height 10yrs (ft)	spread 5yrs (ft)	spread 10yrs (ft)	color of blossom	
[ROWANS] *Sorbus aucuparia*			✿		H	H	H						11½	16	6½	10	□	Red fruit, needs moist site for best growth
S. aucuparia 'Asplenifolia'			✿		H	H	H						11½	16	6½	10	□	Red fruit, leaves give a fernlike aspect
S. aucuparia 'Fructu Luteo'			✿		H	H	H						11½	16	6½	10	□	Orange-yellow fruit, longer lasting than red forms
S. cashmiriana			✿	✿					H	H	H		10	13	5	8	■	White fruit, lasts into winter
S. commixta				✿				H	H				13	20	6½	10	□	Good fall color, variable fruiting
S. commixta 'Embley'				✿				H	H				13	20	6½	10	□	Excellent fall color, few orange-red fruits
S. domestica			✿	✿				H					13	20	6½	10	□	Will make a large tree, fall color poor
S. forrestii			✿					H	H	H			10	16	6½	10	□	White fruit, may persist into winter
S. hupehensis			✿			H	H	H					11½	16	6½	10	□	White fruit, bluish-green leaves
S. 'Joseph Rock'			✿		H	H	H						13	20	6½	10	□	Amber berries and excellent fall color
[WHITEBEAMS] *S. aria*			✿	✿			H	H	H				13	20	10	16	□	Leaves silvery beneath; fall color russet
S. aria 'Lutescens'			✿	✿			H	H	H				13	20	10	16	□	New leaves particularly silvery
S. aria 'Magnifica'			✿	✿			H	H	H				13	20	10	16	□	Larger leaves, to 6in by 3½in
S. intermedia			✿	✿			H	H	H				13	20	6½	13	□	Leaves gray-green beneath, fruit red
S. thibetica 'John Mitchell'			✿	✿			H	H	H				13	20	10	16	□	Large leaves, to 10in by 6in
S. torminalis			✿	✿			H	H	H				11½	16	8	13	□	Lobed, green leaves; fruit russet; suckering tree

✿ flowering  H harvest

Spartium
Spanish broom

Spanish broom is a large shrub to 10–16ft (3–5m), almost, but not quite, a small tree. Like most brooms, it has only small and transient leaves, and photosynthesis is carried on through the green shoots.

Spartium makes an excellent flowering plant, carrying masses of yellow pealike and fragrant flowers on the new shoots in mid- to late summer. It tolerates a wide range of conditions, but is especially good for coastal situations and dry chalk soils. In the garden, use it in shrub beds and in hot sunny sites. It can be restricted by pruning in early spring but, as with most brooms, it is important to cut only into green shoots and not so hard that the cuts are made into old wood or it is likely to fail. It is easily propagated from seed sown either in spring or fall.

Spartium junceum

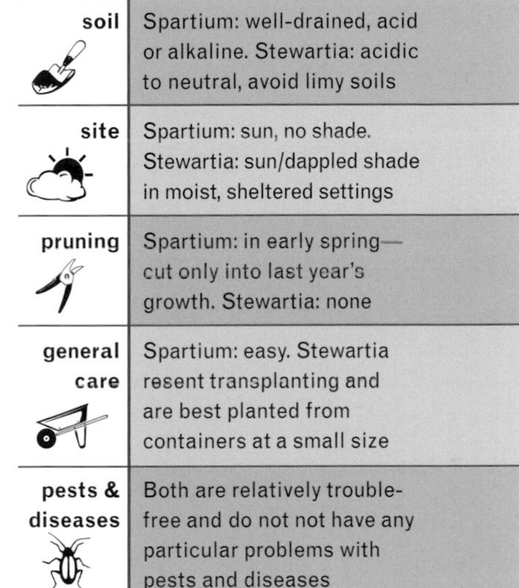

soil	Spartium: well-drained, acid or alkaline. Stewartia: acidic to neutral, avoid limy soils
site	Spartium: sun, no shade. Stewartia: sun/dappled shade in moist, sheltered settings
pruning	Spartium: in early spring—cut only into last year's growth. Stewartia: none
general care	Spartium: easy. Stewartia resent transplanting and are best planted from containers at a small size
pests & diseases	Both are relatively trouble-free and do not not have any particular problems with pests and diseases

Stewartia
Stuartia

Expect to find this plant in books and nurseries under either Stewartia or Stuartia because the name may have been historically altered.

Stewartia malacodendron

The genus is related to the Camellia. The flowers are white or cream up to 3in (8cm) across and carried on short shoots of the current season's growth. Individually the flowers are short lived but borne in a succession that makes the tree (large shrub) attractive for several weeks over the summer. Fall color is also good, mainly yellow or red.

The species also have interesting barks, with the bark of *S. sinensis* particularly outstanding; it is smooth, pink to gray or creamy orange, and peels into small translucent coiled strips. Stewartia should be planted in a moist, light woodland setting or with side shelter. They can be propagated by seed sown in the fall, layering, or by softwood or semi-ripe cuttings in summer.

	SPRING			SUMMER			FALL			WINTER			height 5yrs (ft)	height 10yrs (ft)	spread 5yrs (ft)	spread 10yrs (ft)	flower color	
Spartium junceum					flowering	flowering							6½	13	5	11½		Shoots green; flowers fragrant
Stewartia malacodendron				flowering	flowering	flowering							6½	11½	5	10		Floriferous shrub to 16ft with time
S. pseudocamellia				flowering	flowering	flowering							6½	13	6½	10		Grows into a small to medium tree; bark flaking
S. sinensis				flowering	flowering	flowering							6½	13	6½	10		Almost unbelievably good bark

 *flowering*

S

Trees & Shrubs

Styrax

Storax

This is a large genus of mainly small to medium trees, although some uncommon species, like *Styrax wilsonii*, are only shrubs. They are valuable for their massed, medium-sized, bell-shaped flowers, which are carried on leafy shoots on last summer's twigs.

soil	Acid to neutral, moist but well-drained—not for chalk or lime soils
site	For the best results position in dappled shade or full sun with side shelter
pruning	No special pruning regime required, except to remove defective branches
general care	Plant beside paths where the blooms can be seen both from below and from the side
pests & diseases	Both are relatively trouble-free and do not not have any particular problems with pests and diseases

The flowers are white with yellow anthers—some forms of *Styrax japonicus* have pink flowers. In *S. japonicus* the flowers hang down from the shoots in mid-summer and are best seen from beneath, against a background of fresh green foliage. It makes a beautiful small tree. *Styrax obassia* and *Styrax hemsleyana* have the flowers in large racemes and much larger leaves. They are also taller growing and are among the best medium-sized summer-flowering trees. Small plants, at least of *S. obassia*, are tasty to slugs.

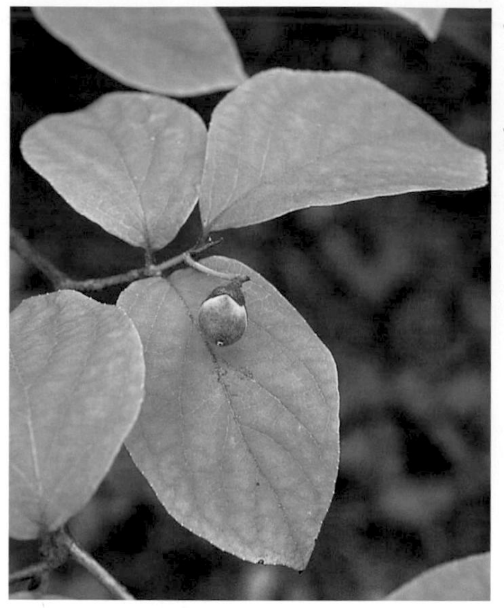
Styrax hemsleyana

These trees are best when given light woodland conditions, with some shelter and a moist soil, but will take full sun, provided the site is not dry. Unfortunately, their display in the fall is rather mediocre.

They can be raised from the seeds; their fruit is a green drupe containing a hard, light brown seed. Germination requires three warm months to break down the hard stony seed coat, followed by three cold months to break dormancy. This can be given in a warm closet (mix the seeds with damp peat substitute or leaf mold) and then the salad crisper in the refrigerator, or by sowing in the spring and waiting for the next spring. They can also be propagated from softwood or semi-ripe cuttings in summer.

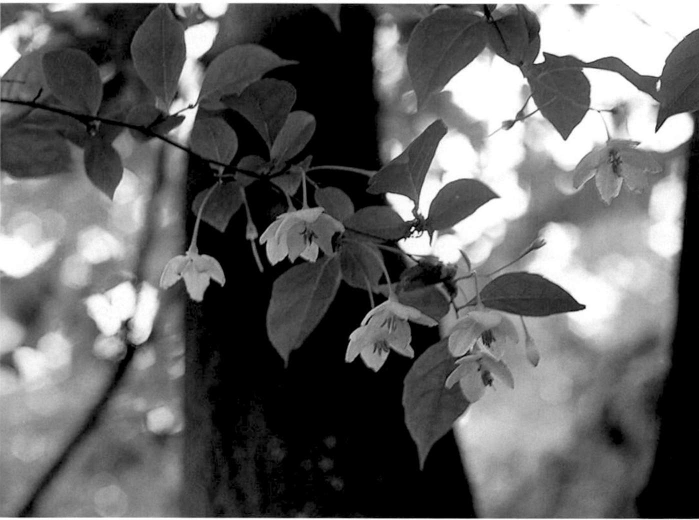
Styrax japonicus

	SPRING			SUMMER			FALL			WINTER			height 5yrs (ft)	height 10yrs (ft)	spread 5yrs (ft)	spread 10yrs (ft)	flower color	
Styrax hemsleyana				✿	✿								10	16	6½	13	white	Flowers in long lax racemes
S. japonicus				✿	✿								11½	16	6½	13	white	Flowers—small clusters, close to green leaves
S. obassia				✿	✿								10	16	6½	13	white	Flowers in long lax racemes, fragrant

 *flowering*

Syringa
Lilac

The lilacs are useful for their fragrant flowers in late spring or early summer. The flowers are carried on new growth made from buds laid down last summer, mainly from the terminal bud.

There are about 20 species but many hybrids, including both single- and double-flowered forms. The common name of the genus is the natural flower color of *Syringa vulgaris*, but a host of other colors have been bred since then, especially whites and purples. Out of flower, they are green and leafy but with no specific beauty and no significant color in the fall. This can be addressed by using them as supports for summer climbers, such as some Clematis and *Eccremocarpus scaber*, which will not cast too dense shade. They can also be underplanted with spring bulbs.

Lilacs are especially well suited to chalky sites. Frost pockets should be avoided, since late spring frosts can destroy the terminal flower buds. They are usually placed in shrub beds, or as specimen shrubs or small trees. They can be used to make informal hedges, provided they are trimmed after flowering.

They can be rooted from softwood cuttings in early summer. However, those that are difficult to root are often grafted. They can be layered.

Syringa vulgaris

soil	Well-drained, especially chalky soils but good on acidic ones
site	Sun or light shade; will not flower satisfactorily in dense shade
pruning	Remove older wood after flowering. Can be hard pruned to rejuvenate
general care	Avoid spring frost pockets and do not allow suckers from a grafted plant to suppress the desired variety
pests & diseases	Lilac blight can affect them, in addition to common problems, such as honey fungus

	SPRING			SUMMER			FALL			WINTER			height 5yrs (ft)	height 10yrs (ft)	spread 5yrs (ft)	spread 10yrs (ft)	flower color	
Syringa josiflexa 'Bellicent'			✿	✿									6	10	5	8		Fragrant flowers, in large loose panicles
S. meyeri var. *spontanea* 'Palibin'			✿	✿									3	5	3	5		Small-growing lilac, eventually to 8ft
S. pubescens ssp. *microphylla*				✿			✿						4	5	4	5		Small-leaved shrub, fragrant flowers
S. pubescens ssp. *patula* 'Miss Kim'			✿	✿									4	6	5	6½		Fragrant; leaves with wavy margins
S. vulgaris 'Andenken an Ludwig Späth'			✿										6	10	5	8		Single flowers
S. vulgaris 'Charles Joly'				✿									6	10	5	8		Double, late flowers
S. vulgaris 'Katherine Havemeyer'			✿	✿									6	10	5	8		Double-flowered

✿ *flowering*

Tamarix

Tamarisk

These shrubs are most often seen in temperate coastal areas, where they really thrive in the windswept, salt-laden climate.

The genus is suitable for wider cultivation than restricted to the coast. The merits are in the small, almost cypress-like foliage in vigorous sprays and the equally small but prolifically carried small flowers. Individually you almost need a magnifying glass to see the flowers, but they are carried in such numbers that they create a plumose spray at the ends of the branches. Flower color is always some form of pink. In the garden they are excellent in shrub borders or as specimen shrubs. They can also be used to make hedges. Apart from their tolerance of exposure, they also thrive on poor soils and tolerate salt in the ground. If you have a problem from salt spray off a highway in winter, try a hedge of Tamarix instead of the usual cypresses. The only soil in which they do not appear to thrive is a shallow soil overlying chalk.

Some species, including *Tamarix ramosissima*, flower in late summer on the current season's shoots; these can be hard pruned in spring. Other species, such as *Tamarix tetrandra*, flower in spring on short leafy shoots on last summer's growths; these should be pruned after flowering. Unpruned, they tend to become rather straggly. They can be propagated from hardwood cuttings taken in winter or from semi-ripe cuttings in summer. They can also be raised from seed sown as soon as it is ripe.

Tamarix ramosissima

Tamarix gallica

soil	Well-drained, especially sands, not good on shallow soils over chalk
site	This shrub thrives where there is plenty of sun; excellent in coastal areas
pruning	Summer/fall flowerers—Group 2; spring flowerers—after flowering (Group 1)
general care	Easy shrubs to cultivate. In inland situations, they need side shelter from cold, dry winds
pests & diseases	Relatively trouble-free. Does not have any particular problems with pests and diseases

	SPRING	SUMMER	FALL	WINTER	height 5yrs (ft)	height 10yrs (ft)	spread 5yrs (ft)	spread 10yrs (ft)	flower color	
Tamarix ramosissima		flowering (late)	flowering (early)		6	10	5	8		Branches reddish-brown; pruning Group 2
T. ramosissima 'Pink Cascade'		flowering (late)	flowering (early)		6½	10	6½	10		Vigorous grower
T. ramosissima 'Rubra'		flowering (late)	flowering (early)		6	10	5	8		Very floriferous
T. tetrandra	flowering (late)	flowering (early)			6	10	5	8		Open-growing shrub; pruning Group 1

flowering

Tilia

Linden

Lindens make large trees. As natural trees, they need large spaces, and most can make 50–80ft (15–25m) in height. There are a few smaller ones, especially the rare *Tilia kiusiana*, which is only a large shrub or small tree to about 20ft (6m).

The Mongolian linden, *Tilia mongolica*, is a small tree, usually to around 26ft (8m), and both this and *T. kiusiana* are useful where space is limited. The value of lindens lies in their fragrant flowers, which scent the air in mid-summer.

There is an aphid problem with some lindens, especially *Tilia europaea,* which is far too large for the garden—up to 120ft (35m) in height. It produces copious quantities of honeydew at times in the summer. *Tilia* 'Euchlora' is an alternative, with glossy upper sides to the leaves, but as it ages, it becomes ugly with an untidy mass of lower branches in winter. Far superior are the silver lindens (so called because of the silvery white undersides to their foliage); *Tilia* 'Petiolaris' with its pendent habit is the best of these.

Lindens like pruning and can be kept restricted by annual or biennial pollarding. Pleaching is a variant of this, where the tree is cut back to a framework of branches to produce a dense leafy shade in summer. Lindens will grow on almost any well-drained soil. They can be raised from seed, which will usually germinate in the second spring. The varieties are usually grafted onto seedling rootstocks; they can also be layered.

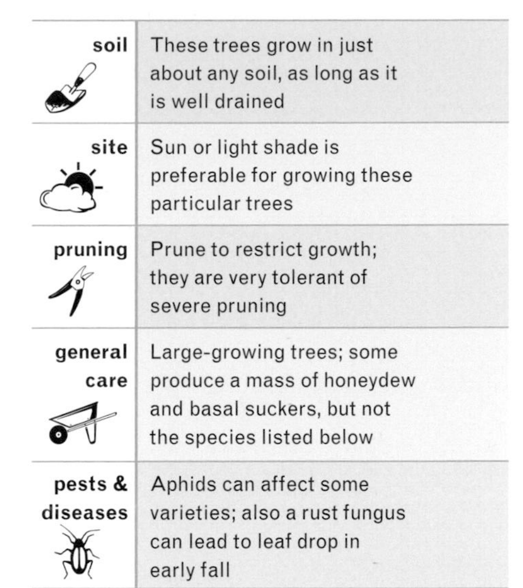

soil	These trees grow in just about any soil, as long as it is well drained
site	Sun or light shade is preferable for growing these particular trees
pruning	Prune to restrict growth; they are very tolerant of severe pruning
general care	Large-growing trees; some produce a mass of honeydew and basal suckers, but not the species listed below
pests & diseases	Aphids can affect some varieties; also a rust fungus can lead to leaf drop in early fall

Tilia mongolica

Tilia 'Petiolaris'

	SPRING	SUMMER	FALL	WINTER	height 5yrs (ft)	height 10yrs (ft)	spread 5yrs (ft)	spread 10yrs (ft)	color of blossom	
Tilia cordata		flowering			13	23	8	13		Large tree, to 80ft; limited honeydew
T. 'Euchlora'		flowering			13	23	8	13		Medium tree, untidy habit as it ages
T. henryana		flowering			10	16	6½	10		Silvery leaves with long cusps
T. mongolica		flowering			11½	20	6½	10		Leaves with jagged teeth; small tree, few aphids
T. 'Petiolaris'		flowering			13	23	8	13		Upright tree with pendent branches; no aphids
T. platyphyllos		flowering			13	23	8	13		Large-growing tree with large leaves
T. platyphyllos 'Rubra'		flowering			13	23	8	13		Has red twigs after one year in winter
T. tomentosa		flowering			13	20	8	13		Leaves strongly silver beneath; upright habit

flowering

Toona

This genus is represented in cultivation by *Toona sinensis*, which is called *Cedrela sinensis* in some older references. The foliage is large and pinnate, giving a bold appearance. The terminal leaflet is often missing, meaning that the leaf has an even number of leaflets.

The new foliage ofToona is edible and has an oniony flavor. In Beijing it is grown for this purpose, rather than for the fragrant white flowers, which are produced in mid-summer, or the yellow fall color. In the garden, *Toona sinensis* 'Flamingo' is especially attractive in early summer with its brilliant pink new foliage. Use it as a specimen tree. The genus can be propagated from root cuttings, division of suckers, or by seed, if available.

Toona sinensis 'Flamingo'

soil 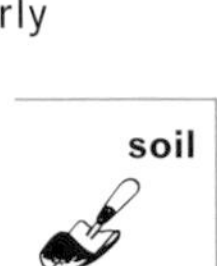	Toona: fertile, well-drained. Trochodendron: acidic to neutral, not over chalk
site	Toona: prefers full sun. Trochodendron: enjoys sun to moderate shade
pruning 	None required for both Toona and Trochodendron, except to reshape or restrict
general care	Toona: 'Flamingo' best with sun shining through foliage. Trochodendron thrives with side shelter
pests & diseases	Both are relatively trouble-free and do not not have any particular problems with pests and diseases

Trochodendron

This genus contains only a single species. It is a broad-leaved tree or large shrub with wood characteristics of a conifer.

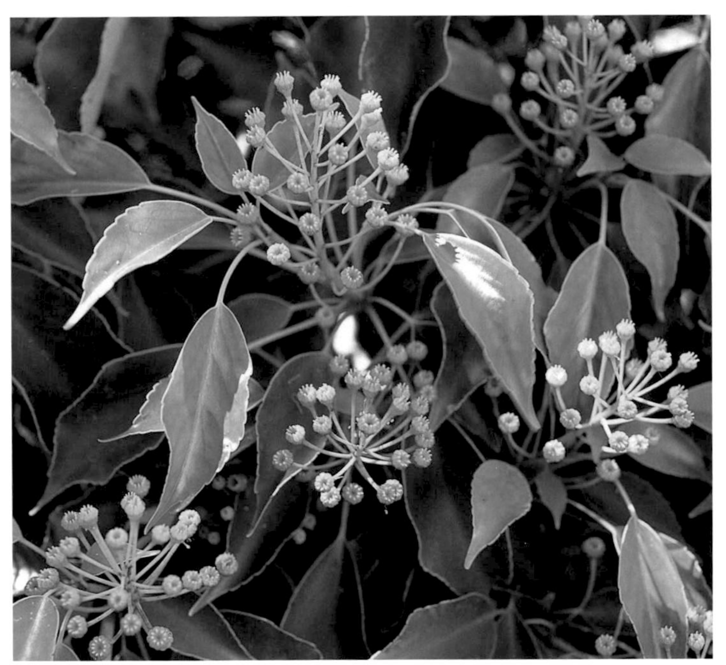

Trochodendron aralioides

The foliage looks a little like ivy (Hedera). It makes a slow-growing, evergreen bush, although with time it can make a tree. The flowers are vivid green, very distinctive, and useful for flower arrangements. It appears tender but is actually very tough, especially if given some side shelter.

In the garden it is useful as an evergreen shrub in a border or in a woodland garden area. It can be raised from seed or semi-ripe cuttings in summer.

	SPRING			SUMMER			FALL			WINTER			height 5yrs (ft)	height 10yrs (ft)	spread 5yrs (ft)	spread 10yrs (ft)	flower color	
Toona sinensis					flowering	flowering							10	16	3	6½		Large bold foliage
T. sinensis 'Flamingo'						flowering							10	16	3	6½		New foliage stunning pink in spring
Trochodendron aralioides			flowering	flowering									5	8	4	6½		Evergreen shrub, leathery apple-green

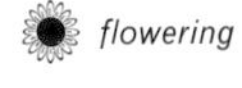 *flowering*

Ulmus

Elm

The advent in the late 1960s of the aggressive strain of Dutch elm disease (so named because of the research carried out by Dutch scientists in the early 20th century) has reduced the appearance of elms significantly.

Elms are excellent trees, tolerant of salt spray and exposure, and a wide range of soil types. Some modern hybrids are not affected by the disease but these are not widely planted. Wych elm (*Ulmus glabra*) is still frequently planted, as is the smooth-leaf elm (*Ulmus minor*).

But the majestic trees of *Ulmus procera* (English elm) are now replaced by short-lived suckers, making perhaps 40ft (12m) before succumbing to infection (the disease is caused by a fungus, but spread by a bark beetle).

Elms can be propagated by semi-ripe cuttings in summer or by grafting. Most will grow from root cuttings, but not *U. glabra*, the only species easily raised from seed sown as soon as ripe in early summer.

Ulmus minor 'Dampieri Aurea'

Ulmus minor 'Jaqueline Hillier'

 **soil**	Both well-drained. Ulmus: well-drained to heavy soils, acidic to alkaline
 **site**	Both Ulmus and Umbellularia prefer sun to light shade
 **pruning**	Ulmus and Umbellularia: none required but both tolerant of heavy pruning
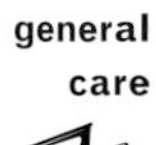 **general care**	Ulmus: susceptible to Dutch elm disease. Umbellularia: resist smelling aromatic foliage (see text)
pests & diseases	Ulmus: prone to Dutch elm disease. Umbellularia: fairly trouble-free from pests and diseases

Umbellularia

California *or* Oregon laurel

The common name depends upon whether you are in California or Oregon! This relative of the bay laurel (*see* page 82) makes an attractive evergreen tree. The yellow flowers are followed by the purple fruits, which contain a single seed.

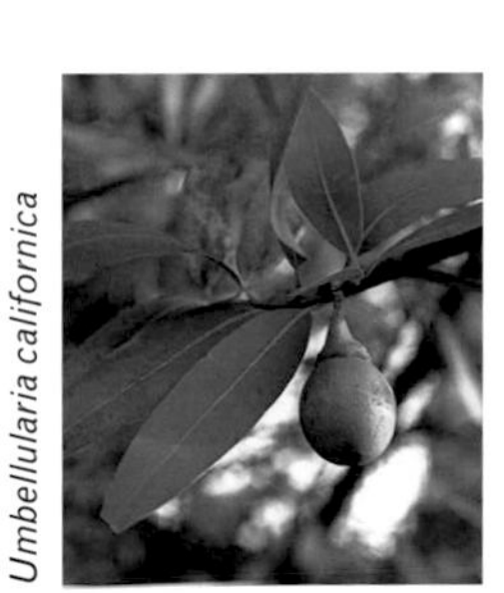

Umbellularia californica

The foliage is strongly and attractively fragrant; resist sniffing for too long because the volatile component will give a splitting headache half an hour or so later—an alternative name is California headache tree. The volatile oil in the foliage is also reported to have given some people dermatitis. In the garden it makes an attractive evergreen, which is colorful in spring. It can be propagated from fresh seed sown in the fall or from semi-ripe cuttings in summer.

	SPRING			SUMMER			FALL			WINTER			height 5yrs (ft)	height 10yrs (ft)	spread 5yrs (ft)	spread 10yrs (ft)	color of blossom	
Ulmus glabra	flowering	flowering		harvest									10	20	3	10	■	Only elm to reproduce by seed
U. glabra 'Camperdownii'	flowering	flowering		harvest									10	13	6½	13	■	Excellent weeping tree
U. minor 'Dampieri Aurea'	flowering	flowering		harvest									6½	13	3	6½	■	Leaves golden yellow, crowded; habit upright
U. minor 'Jacqueline Hillier'													3	6½	3	6½		Small shrub
Umbellularia californica	flowering	flowering					harvest					flowering	8	13	5	8	□	Attractive evergreen tree with thin brown bark

 *flowering*  *harvest*

U

Trees & Shrubs

Wisteria

This genus is naturally a climber, quick growing and capable of making 20ft (6m) in a year. It is excellent for growing into and through tall trees.

Wisteria floribunda

Since Wisteria can grow into a 65ft (20m) tree, forget pruning at that height and just enjoy the flowers! It is only the current season's growth that is flexible and wandlike. It can easily be trained to form a free-standing shrub. The first stage is to get woody stems 6½ft (2m) or so high (or however big fits the space available). Use a stake or stout cane and stop further growth once this framework is covered.

The next phase is regular pruning, both to keep it within the space and also to encourage flower set. Shorten the vigorous growths to about 6in (15cm) from the old wood in mid- to late summer and further shorten them in mid-winter, removing the small flattened vegetative buds but keeping the plum and rounded flower buds (which are nearer the base). Wisteria can be raised from seed but such plants are slow and erratic to flower. A much better idea is either grafted plants (grafted in winter) or to to layer a long shoot. Basal cuttings in early summer should also root.

soil	Both Wisteria and Zelkova grow in well-drained soils, both acidic and alkaline
site 	Wisteria: full sun, best on south and west walls. Zelkova: sun to light shade
pruning 	Wisteria: shorten long shoots mid- to late summer to 6in. Zelkova: none needed
general care	Wisteria: to grow into tree, plant at edge of crown; use rope/chain to let it grow into crown. Zelkova: very easy
pests & diseases	Wisteria: no particular problems. Zelkova: can get Dutch elm disease but only in an epidemic

Zelkova

Zelkova serrata

This genus is related to the elms but is much less at risk of Dutch elm disease and has a small drupe instead of the winged fruit found in elms.

The leaves are small and turn good colors in the fall; unlike the leaves of elms, they are symmetrical at the base without the oblique base of an elm. The bark is smooth and gray, but small flakes exfoliate to reveal an orange inner bark. In the garden, they make imposing specimen trees, although they can be trimmed to keep them small. They tolerate a wide range of soils, from acidic sands to alkaline chalks and limestones, provided they have reasonable drainage. They can be propagated by grafting onto a seedling rootstock, or from semi-ripe cuttings in early summer.

	SPRING	SUMMER	FALL	WINTER	height 5yrs (ft)	height 10yrs (ft)	spread 5yrs (ft)	spread 10yrs (ft)	colors	
Wisteria brachybotrys 'Shiro-kapitan'	flowering				10	10	13	13		Fragrant flowers
W. floribunda 'Alba'	flowering				10	10	13	13		Flower trusses to 2ft
W. floribunda 'Multijuga'	flowering				10	10	13	13		Flowers to 3ft; also called 'Macrobotrys'
W. sinensis 'Alba'	flowering				10	10	13	13		Fragrant flowers in racemes to 1ft
W. sinensis 'Prolific'	flowering				10	10	13	13		Fragrant flowers in racemes to 1ft
Zelkova carpinifolia					10	16	6½	11½		Upright habit with several erect stems
Z. serrata					10	16	10	16		Squat tree; also known as Japanese zelkova

flowering

Bamboos

Bamboos are primitive woody grasses and are totally unlike anything else featured in *Trees & Shrubs.* They have no beauty of flower or fruit, but incomparable elegance. The stems or culms (canes) grow from the rhizome system which is below ground. They make all their height and diameter growth in a few weeks during the summer. Below ground the rhizome can be one of two different types—leptomorph or pachymorph. In the leptomorph species, the rhizome runs and the culms are formed from side branches. Leptomorph species can be invasive; *Pseudosasa japonica* is in this group and of limited beauty. In the pachymorph species, the end of the rhizome is a culm and there are usually two side buds. When the side buds grow, they have a neck that takes the next culm away from the last one. *Architectural Plants* in this series features a wider variety of bamboos.

Bamboos give a wonderful exotic look to a garden. The foliage can be damaged by cold periods, making some look a little dull until new foliage is made in late spring. The first-year culms are generally erect but splay out under the weight of the foliage in the second year, making graceful arching mounds of foliage. They make excellent screens. Since they do not grow too tall, you can select a bamboo to grow more or less to the height of screen needed—unlike Leyland cypress, which has to be constantly clipped to keep it within bounds—and the wall of culms makes a dense, impenetrable screen. One of the best Bamboos for this purpose is *Semiarundinaria fastuosa.* This has closely spaced erect culms, which do not arch over. It grows to a maximum of 26ft (8m) in height and the culms can be over 1in (4cm) in diameter. It is also good in exposed gardens.

Chimonobambusa

This genus is leptomorph and can run. It is worth growing for the unusual culms in the two species featured here, although it should probably be kept in a large container rather than in the open ground. In *Chimonobambusa quadrangularis* the culms have four sides, rather square in section. The nodes are prominent and on the lower ones there are thornlike aerial roots (gloves are advised).

Chimonobambusa tumidissinoda

This species grows well in deep shade, as long as it is suitably provided with moisture, and the culms can make 23ft (7m) with diameters of over 1in (3cm). *Chimonobambusa tumidissinoda* (also called *Qiongzhuea tumidissinoda*) does not have thorns on the culm nodes; instead, the nodes are greatly expanded, about twice the diameter of the culm. It grows to 20ft (6m) with culms to 1in (3cm). It is a very vigorous grower and is perhaps best restricted to a large container. They can be divided by taking a length of the rhizome with at least two buds and a culm.

soil	Chimonobambusa: moist but not wet soil. Chusquea: moist but well-drained
site	Chimonobambusa: light to moderate shade. Chusquea: sun but only light shade
pruning	Chimonobambusa: remove older stems when 3–4 years old. Chusquea: none needed
general care	Chimonobambusa: can be invasive; thorns on culms of *C. quadrangularis*. Chusquea: keep moist during growth
pests & diseases	Both are relatively trouble-free and do not have any particular problems with pests and diseases

Chusquea

This is a genus of clump-forming bamboos from South America. They are characterized by the solid culms and the way in which branches form from the nodes on the culms.

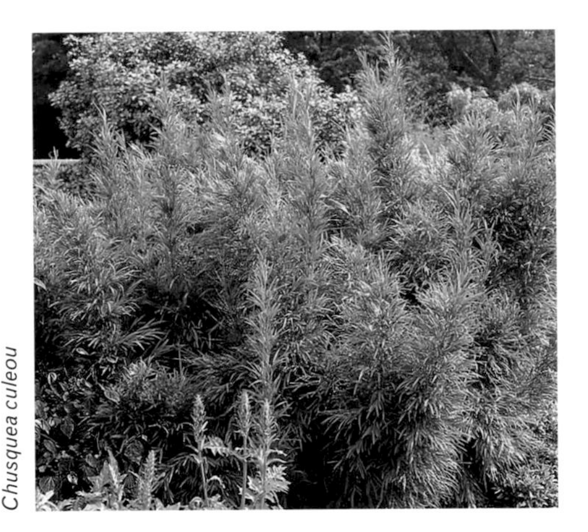
Chusquea culeou

Only *Chusquea culeou* is in general cultivation, but *C. gigantea* with its much larger culms is worth finding. In cool maritime conditions, they tolerate exposure, but are less well adapted to regions with high summer temperatures. Like all bamboos, they are native to areas where most, or at least sufficient, rain falls during the summer growing season and do not like droughts. Chusquea are propagated by division, but this can be difficult. Take divisions in the fall and keep them cool and moist, perhaps in a shaded greenhouse, until they have rooted.

	SPRING	SUMMER	FALL	WINTER	height 5yrs (ft)	height 10yrs (ft)	spread 5yrs (ft)	spread 10yrs (ft)	color of blossom	
Chimonobambusa quadrangularis					16	23	16	33+		New culm growth made in the fall
C. tumidissinoda					16	20	16	33+		New culm growth late spring/early summer
Chusquea culeou					10	16	6½	13		Can grow to 20ft, with culms to 1in diameter
C. gigantea					16	26	6½	13		Upright habit to 50ft; also called *C. breviglumis*

Fargesia

This genus contains some of the best clump-forming or pachymorph bamboos. The species in cultivation make reliably hardy and very attractive plants. They will form clumps with initially erect culms that later arch over with pendulous foliage.

Fargesia nitida

Over 50 years or so, a clump may extend to more than 6ft (2m) in diameter, containing hundreds of culms, but they are always well behaved and never run amuck. Fargesia will also make effective screens where there is sufficient width, but if space is restricted, choose *Semiarundinara fastuosa*.

Fargesia murieliae

The species of Fargesia have been ascribed to several genera, especially Arundinaria, Sinarundinaria, and Thamnocalamus, and may be found in catalogs under these names. Also, some species often listed as Fargesia actually belong to the related genus Borinda (most easily distinguished by the finely grooved culms), although these are not as yet common in cultivation. Fargesia may lose their leaves in severe winters or strong gales but are quick to form bright new leaves in the spring. The culms are slender, scarcely ½in (1cm) in diameter and round in section. They have 4–5 branches at each node, at least in the first year, and this separates them from Chusquea, with far more branches, and Phyllostachys, which only has two branches. New culms are often glaucous.

They can be easily propagated by division, although dividing a part of the clump can require considerable effort, especially in an old clump where there is no clear gap between the culms! Spring, when they are making new growth, is probably the best time to do this but, provided they are kept moist and planted before they dry out, any time should work.

soil 	Well-drained soils, whether acidic or chalky, but must be moist and water retentive
site 	The most preferable site would be in full sun to moderate shade
pruning 	None needed; older canes can be harvested after their second summer
general care	This forms tight clumps. Important to keep well watered during summer growing season
pests & diseases	Relatively trouble-free. Does not have any particular problems with pests and diseases

	SPRING	SUMMER	FALL	WINTER	height 5yrs (ft)	height 10yrs (ft)	spread 5yrs (ft)	spread 10yrs (ft)	color of blossom	
Fargesia dracocephala					13	16	10	16		Hardy with tough leaves and upright culms
F. murieliae					13	13	10	13		Hardy, graceful; culms to 13ft by ⅝in diameter
F. murieliae 'Simba'					6½	6½	3	6½		Modern cultivar with culms only to 6½ft
F. nitida					13	13	10	13		Leaves half the size of other *Fargesia*, to 2in
F. robusta					13	13	6½	13		Upright habit; culms to 13ft and ⅝in diameter

Phyllostachys

This genus is easily recognized by the culms, which have only two (very rarely three) branches at each node, but with branches growing off other branches, along with a groove (sulcus) in the culm above the bud.

Semiarundinara is the only other genus with a groove above the buds, but in this the groove is small and short, and there are several branches at each node.

Phyllostachys has a leptomorph rhizome. In colder climates, it rarely runs amuck but in warm ones, the rhizomes can spread widely. The spaced culms make very effective plantings, especially if the older culms are harvested. The culms can be a variety of colors, with most developing the full color in the second year. *P. aurea* has stout green culms, which turn a soft yellow in strong light. *P. aureosulcata* has green culms but the groove is yellow. *P. nigra* has culms aging to black, but in the common form 'Boryana' the culms are green with dark brown spots in the second year. *P. viridi-glaucescens* has mid-green culms, whereas in *P. vivax* 'Aureocaulis' they are rich yellow with a few green stripes. Phyllostachys can be propagated by division of the rhizome, selecting a piece with at least two buds and a culm.

soil	Enjoys any type of well-drained but moisture-retentive soils
site	Prefers to be situated where there is plenty of sun to light shade
pruning	None needed but canes can be harvested in the second year
general care	Can run amuck in warmer climates so may need to be cut back hard to prevent it spreading too far
pests & diseases	Aphids can affect some species, but fairly trouble-free from most pests and diseases

Phyllostachys viridi-glaucescens

	SPRING	SUMMER	FALL	WINTER	height 5yrs (ft)	height 10yrs (ft)	spread 5yrs (ft)	spread 10yrs (ft)	color of blossom	
Phyllostachys aurea					16	26	6½	13		Culms to 1½in in diameter, green at first
P. aureosulcata					16	26	6½	13		Culms to 1¼in; large leaves, to 7¼in
P. nigra					16	26	6½	13		Culms green at first, aging to black
P. nigra 'Boryana'					20	30	6½	13		New culms in spring edible
P. viridi-glaucescens					16	26	6½	13		Mid-green culms to 2in diameter
P. vivax 'Aureocaulis'					16	26	6½	13		Culms can make 50ft by 4in diameter

Tree ferns & Palms

This page covers a small selection of tree ferns and palms that are both hardy and will make trees. They tend to be slow growing, with the tree fern *Dicksonia antarctica* growing perhaps 1in (2–3cm) a year and the palms growing less than 8in (20cm) a year. However, they can be purchased as sizeable plants, and for this reason fit well in this book. They have very bold foliage, making a rosette of large leaves at the end of a long stem. This foliage gives them architectural qualities, and they are more fully treated in the *Architectural Plants* book in this series.

Trachycarpus fortunei

The palms are monocotyledons, which means that they cannot make secondary thickening. The thickness of the stem is determined by the growing conditions at the time it is formed, and if these improve, the stem may become thicker further up! They also cannot make secondary roots, so the roots are relatively small and radiate out from the base of the trunk. This allows them to be easily moved, unlike broad-leaved trees and conifers where the roots grow larger with time.

Dicksonia antarctica

Although not related, Dicksonia has a similar stem and root system. The one difference is that the roots in Dicksonia originate from just below the leaves and grow down the fibrous trunk. If a tree fern becomes too tall (or is snapped in half), cut it off cleanly, bury the base in the soil, and it will resume growth. *Dicksonia antarctica* needs protecting from wet periods in winter in colder gardens. Fold the old leaves over the crown to make a tent. The palms can be propagated from seeds sown in spring, but germinating fern spores requires scattering them onto a damp surface; do this by sitting a pot in a shallow bowl of water and covering it with a polyethylene bag.

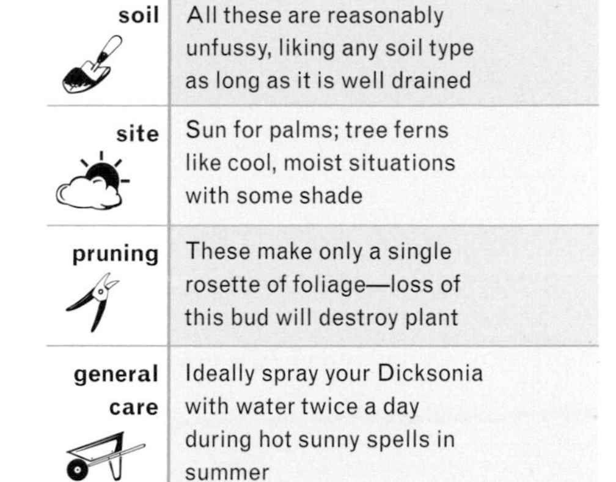

soil	All these are reasonably unfussy, liking any soil type as long as it is well drained
site	Sun for palms; tree ferns like cool, moist situations with some shade
pruning	These make only a single rosette of foliage—loss of this bud will destroy plant
general care	Ideally spray your Dicksonia with water twice a day during hot sunny spells in summer
pests & diseases	All are relatively trouble-free and do not have any particular problems with pests and diseases

Trachycarpus fortunei

	SPRING	SUMMER	FALL	WINTER	height 5yrs (ft)	height 10yrs (ft)	spread 5yrs (ft)	spread 10yrs (ft)	color of blossom	
Dicksonia antarctica					5	6	13	13		Fibrous trunk; can grow to 6in
Phoenix canariensis		flowering	harvest		5	8	16	20		Leaves can be 20ft in length, pinnate
Trachycarpus fortunei		flowering	harvest		5	8	8	10		Palmate leaves, to 4ft across; fruit bluish

flowering *harvest*

Conifers

Conifers evoke emotions, whether it is the neighbor's Leyland cypress blocking out the light or serried ranks of Sitka spruce covering upland areas. Like all plants we grow, they have their place and, if misused or overplanted, become an eyesore. However, I think a rounded landscape needs something like 10–40 percent of evergreens; any less and it is bare in winter, any more and it is dark in summer. And conifers make some of the best evergreens. The tight crown of a cypress or the tiered branching of a pine provide shape and scale to any planting, while the range of foliage colors, from golden through silvery grays to bright blues and silvers, provide characteristics no other group can offer, let alone surpass.

The flowers—yes, flowers—and fruits include some outstanding features. The brick-red male flowers of *Picea orientalis* are the best flowers, but those of common *Chamaecyparis lawsoniana* run them a close second. The mature fruits of *Abies koreana* and *Abies procera* are the best in this category. Conifer foliage is either in linear leaves, usually called needles as they are often sharp, or scale leaves. Most, but not all, are evergreen. Conifers include some of the very best deciduous trees. The bright green foliage of larch in early spring, before most other trees come into leaf, make a good harbinger of spring, while the golden fall color of Ginkgo and Pseudolarix, or the pink to red-brown fall color of Metasequoia, is as good as any broad-leaved tree. Conifers also tolerate a wide range of soils and sites, from dry acidic sands (*Tsuga heterophylla* does wonders in such sites) to thin soils over chalk (Cedrus, Cupressus, some Pinus, and Taxus thrive here). Metasequoia and Taxodium will grow happily in 6in (15cm) of water.

Conifers also provide plants with a range of growth rates, from extremely fast, such as *Abies grandis*, *Cupressus leylandii*, *Pinus radiata*, *Sequoia sempervirens*, and *Sequoiadendron giganteum*—each of which can exceed 60ft (18m) in 16–18 years, to slow-growing beauties, such as *Juniperus recurva* var. *coxii*, Pseudolarix, or Thujopsis. (There are also dwarf and slow-growing conifers but these are not considered in this book.) Generally, expect to plant conifers as container-grown plants 2–3ft (60–90cm) in height. Larger conifers can be moved but require substantial rootballs and are therefore extremely heavy.

Abies
Silver fir

Silver firs are so named due to the silvery white bands on the underside of the needles. They are evergreen conifers with regular whorls of branches and, usually, soft foliage. The female, or seed, cones are carried erect on the top side of the upper branches.

soil	Well-drained, moderately fertile to fertile, including chalk soils (except *A. procera*)
site	Performs best when situated where there is sun to moderate shade
pruning	No special pruning regime is required for this group of trees
general care	More or less look after themselves. They are shade tolerant, especially when young
pests & diseases	Aphids can cause some problems; also honey fungus is troublesome and can kill young trees

The seed cones range from violet-purple in *Abies fraseri* and *A. koreana* (and even brighter colors in some less common species such as *A. forrestii*), to green or violet in *A. concolor* and *A. grandis*, to green and brown in *A. nordmanniana* and *A. procera*, which both have very prominent bracts. The male cones hang down from the lower branches and are designed to catch the wind and take the pollen onto nearby trees.

In the garden, silver firs fit into a number of roles. *A. fraseri* and *A. koreana* are small trees with colorful cones and silvery foliage; they make excellent specimen plants for a lawn where there is not much space. *A. grandis* is a fast-growing large tree and makes a good specimen tree for a large garden or where it can be seen at the end of a vista. *A. nordmanniana*, *A. concolor*, and *A. procera* are slower and smaller than *A. grandis*, but also make moderately large trees within a short space of time. *A. concolor* has bluish or grayish foliage, while the foliage of *A. procera* is a bright glaucous blue.

They all make good Christmas trees, with *A. nordmanniana* probably the best of all. Their immense advantage is that they drop few or no needles. *A. concolor* and *A. nordmanniana* will grow on relatively dry sites, including soils derived from chalk, but *A. procera* must have an acidic soil. They are best propagated from seed, sown in spring.

Abies koreana

	SPRING			SUMMER			FALL			WINTER			height 5yrs (ft)	height 10yrs (ft)	spread 5yrs (ft)	spread 10yrs (ft)	color of blossom	
Abies concolor			flowering			harvest	harvest	harvest					5	10	5	8		Blue/gray-green foliage, open habit; to 50–80ft
A. fraseri			flowering			harvest	harvest	harvest					6½	16	3	6½		Fast-growing, short-lived (less than 40 years), to 50ft
A. grandis			flowering			harvest	harvest	harvest					8	23	5	10		Fast-growing, does not flower until 40 years old
A. koreana			flowering			harvest	harvest	harvest					5	8	3	6½		Slow-growing; produces cones often profusely
A. nordmanniana			flowering			harvest	harvest	harvest					5	13	5	8		Dense habit, makes best Christmas tree
A. procera			flowering			harvest	harvest	harvest					5	13	3	8		Bright glaucous blue foliage; needs acidic site

flowering *harvest*

Araucaria

Monkey puzzle

The common name refers to the viciously sharp foliage that makes climbing them tricky. As the genus was around at the time of the dinosaurs, the foliage probably evolved to stop them eating it.

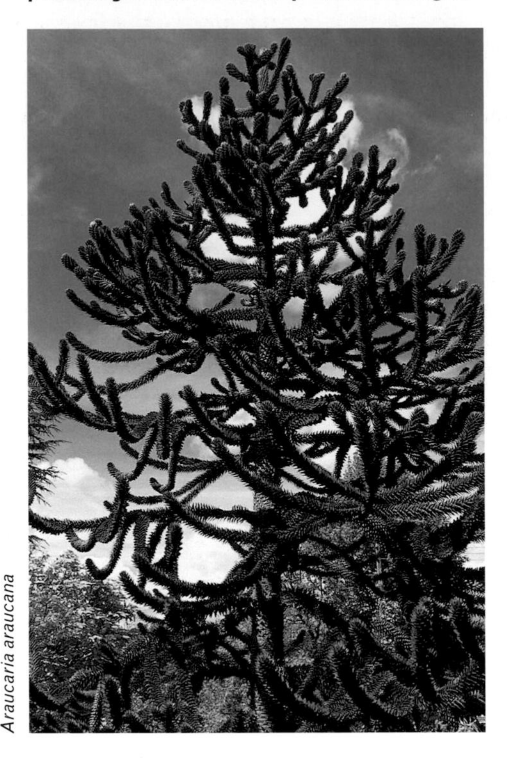

Araucaria araucana

Araucaria araucana makes a medium-sized evergreen tree with an open, whorled crown. At its best, the foliage descends to ground level, setting off the trunk, which is gray and wrinkled like an elephant's hide. The fruits are on large rounded cones, 6–8in (15–20cm) across, which are carried at the tips of the branches but only on female trees. They ripen in the second year and split apart to release the large and very tasty seeds. The cones are only full when there is a male tree close by.

In the garden the tree is excellent as a specimen, but it does need space. It is less happy in small front gardens, but is very tolerant of coastal exposure. Monkey puzzles can be propagated by seed.

soil	Araucaria: well-drained, acidic or alkaline. Calocedrus: likewise, even sands or chalk
site	Both Araucaria and Calocedrus enjoy a position in the full sun
pruning	Araucaria: none required. Calocedrus: likewise, but can be clipped
general care	Araucaria: plant in groups. Calocedrus: good on soils where honey fungus and Phytophthora are problematic
pests & diseases	Araucaria: can be killed by honey fungus. Calocedrus: fairly trouble-free from pests and diseases

Calocedrus

Incense cedar

The incense cedar makes a tight, columnar, evergreen tree in cultivation, although in its native haunts it has a wider-spreading crown.

Calocedrus decurrens

It has flat sprays of foliage, which are glossy, dark green in color. In some ways it resembles the narrow-crowned forms of Lawson cypress (*Chamaecyparis lawsoniana*) but has two distinct advantages over these: it is not susceptible to either honey fungus or phytophthora root rot, which makes it an excellent choice for places where this has been a problem. It will grow on a wide range of soils, provided it is given good drainage. It can be propagated from seed, sown in spring, or from semi-ripe cuttings taken in late summer or early fall. The wood is fragrant and can be cut in any direction, making it the timber of choice for pencils.

	SPRING			SUMMER			FALL			WINTER			height 5yrs (ft)	height 10yrs (ft)	spread 5yrs (ft)	spread 10yrs (ft)	color of blossom	
Araucaria araucana						flowering	harvest						5	8	3	6½		Slow- but steady-growing, to around 50ft
Calocedrus decurrens		flowering							harvest				6	10	2	3		Narrow upright habit, can make 50ft

flowering  harvest

Cedrus

Cedar

The cedars are some of the most stately of evergreen trees originating from areas in the western Himalayas and the Mediterranean. With their large, spreading branches, cedars are extremely majestic-looking trees. Because of the potential size of some species, make sure you have a garden that can provide ample space, if they are to reach their full growth potential.

The best way to deal with the species is to treat the cedar of Lebanon, *Cedrus libani*, with a subspecies in southwest Turkey (ssp. *stenocoma*), and have the other three as separate species—the Cyprus cedar (*Cedrus brevifolia*), the Atlas cedar (*Cedrus atlantica*) and the Deodar cedar (*Cedrus deodara*). Another way is to have the Mediterranean species as forms of *Cedrus libani* and keep *Cedrus deodara* as distinct, but this halfway house approach is less satisfactory.

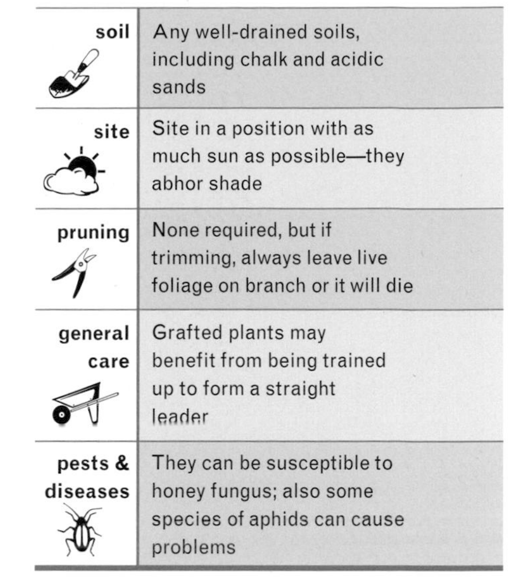

soil	Any well-drained soils, including chalk and acidic sands
site	Site in a position with as much sun as possible—they abhor shade
pruning	None required, but if trimming, always leave live foliage on branch or it will die
general care	Grafted plants may benefit from being trained up to form a straight leader
pests & diseases	They can be susceptible to honey fungus; also some species of aphids can cause problems

Cedars need light. They are used to hot, dry sunny sites, and don't mind whether the soil is acidic or alkaline, provided it is well drained. But if they are shaded, they either look miserable or lose all the lower foliage, looking like a pole with a tuft of leaves on top.

Cedrus atlantica (male cones)

Cedrus deodara

Your time span and available space should dictate which species to choose. *C. deodara* is the most attractive as a small tree, until about 33ft (10m) in height, with a dense crown of level branches with weeping tips. After it has grown this big, it often becomes thin and less attractive. For a small garden, it is the best species and should be chopped down and replaced every 15 to 20 years.

C. atlantica looks beautiful from age 10 onward. It is ideal for moderate spaces, especially for the silvery blue new foliage. *C. libani* is wonderful from around 100 years—assuming you can wait that long!—by which time it has developed its level branching habit. It needs a large and long-term site.

Cedars can be raised from seed sown in spring or by grafting onto seedling rootstocks. The male cones emerge above the branches in the fall, and the female cones expand during the next summer and ripen in late summer, falling apart sometime over the winter/spring period.

	SPRING	SUMMER	FALL	WINTER	height 5yrs (ft)	height 10yrs (ft)	spread 5yrs (ft)	spread 10yrs (ft)	color of blossom	
Cedrus atlantica			flowering, flowering, harvest	harvest, harvest, harvest	6½	11½	3	8		Blue foliage, silvery when young; to 50–80ft
C. deodara			flowering, flowering, harvest	harvest, harvest, harvest	6½	15	3	10		Drooping branch tips; to 65–80ft
C. libani			flowering, flowering, harvest	harvest, harvest, harvest	6½	11½	3	8		Gray-green foliage; to 50–80ft

flowering harvest

Chamaecyparis

Cypress

Chamaecyparis, literally false cypress, is a small, evergreen genus but one that has had a major impact upon horticulture.

C

Conifers

The main species is Lawson cypress, *Chamaecyparis lawsoniana*, from northwest America. This has produced hundreds of different forms, many of which are dwarf or slow growing. The tree forms range from the golden yellow foliage of 'Stewartii' to the narrow habit of 'Columnaris' with pale, blue-gray foliage or 'Kilmacurragh' with green foliage, and the bright blue-gray foliage in pendulous sprays of 'Pembury Blue'. Other tree-growing species are *C. pisifera* and *C. obtusa* but they are mainly represented as small or dwarf forms rather than trees.

soil	Any type of well-drained soils, both acidic and alkaline
site	These will do well if positioned in either the sun or a light shade
pruning	Can be clipped provided there is live (green) foliage left on the shoot
general care	Avoid depressions where water may sit, since trees in these sites are liable to phytophthora root rot
pests & diseases	Honey fungus and phytophthora root rot can kill trees, so keep a watchful eye out for these diseases

Chamaecyparis lawsoniana 'Columnaris'

In the garden, Lawson cypress makes an excellent specimen tree with its narrow habit and dense foliage. Older trees tend to lose the tight habit and develop crowns with some short spreading branches with pendulous tips. Lawson cypress makes excellent hedges. Like most other conifers, it can only be clipped into live foliage but the growth rate is not too fast. Unpruned trees can also be used to make effective high screens. One drawback as a hedge or screen is that they are susceptible to honey fungus and phytophthora root rot, both of which can kill lines of trees.

The cultivars can be raised from semi-ripe cuttings in late summer, whereas the species can be grown from seed sown in spring.

	SPRING	SUMMER	FALL	WINTER	height 5yrs (ft)	height 10yrs (ft)	spread 5yrs (ft)	spread 10yrs (ft)	colors	
Chamaecyparis lawsoniana	flowering		harvest		5	10	2½	4		Male cones showy; branch tips pendulous
C. lawsoniana 'Columnaris'	flowering		harvest		5	10	2½	4		Narrow upright habit with blue-gray foliage
C. lawsoniana 'Kilmacurragh'	flowering		harvest		5	10	2½	4		Narrow upright habit with green foliage; to 50ft
C. lawsoniana 'Intertexta'	flowering		harvest		5	10	2½	4		Gray-green foliage in lax pendulous sprays
C. lawsoniana 'Pembury Blue'	flowering		harvest		5	10	2½	4		Broadly conical tree, bright blue-gray foliage
C. lawsoniana 'Stewartii'	flowering		harvest		4	8	2½	4		Foliage in golden fernlike sprays

flowering *harvest*

Cryptomeria

Japanese cedar

***Cryptomeria japonica* makes a vigorous, evergreen, upright tree with a columnar-conic habit. It is one of the few conifers that will coppice if cut down.**

Cryptomeria has given rise to a large number of forms, including many dwarfs. 'Sekkan-sugi', with creamy yellow foliage that turns white in winter, is one of the most effective cultivars; it makes a small tree of moderate growth. There is a stabilized juvenile form, forma *elegans*, with long soft foliage, which will breed true. This makes a medium tree, but is best as a bush—periodically cut it back to keep it within bounds. However, the normal form is much better as a tree, with a fairly fast growth rate and a developing stout trunk. The crown is open and rather billowing, set against the stringy red-brown bark, which peels off to reveal orange below. In the garden, use the tree form as a specimen tree, with ornate cultivars like 'Sekkan-sugi' and *elegans* as shrubs for smaller spaces. Cryptomeria can be propagated by seeds or by cuttings at almost any time of the year.

Cryptomeria japonica forma *elegans*

soil 	Both well-drained. Cryptomeria: moist, acidic/alkaline. Cunninghamia: deep and fertile
site 	Both Cryptomeria and Cunninghamia: sun to light shade
pruning 	Cryptomeria: can be coppiced. Cunninghamia: tolerates coppicing and clipping
general care	Cryptomeria: can be cut back. Cunninghamia: shelter from cold winds and keep the soil moist during dry periods
pests & diseases	Both are relatively trouble-free and do not have major problems from pests and diseases

Cunninghamia

China fir

The foliage is similar to the Monkey puzzle tree, but not as sharp or hard.

Cunninghamia lanceolata

The genus coppices, and trees are often surrounded by a cluster of suckers at the base of the trunk. At its best it makes a very attractive and interesting tree. It likes a moist site with good ground water and, if allowed to dry out during the summer, the older foliage tends to turn brown and fall. It is perfectly hardy. It can be propagated either from seed sown in spring or from cuttings taken in late summer.

	SPRING	SUMMER	FALL	WINTER	height 5yrs (ft)	height 10yrs (ft)	spread 5yrs (ft)	spread 10yrs (ft)	color of blossom	
Cryptomeria japonica	flowering		harvest		6½	13	4	6½	■	Male cones in clusters at tips of shoots; 50–80ft
C. japonica forma *elegans*					6½	13	4	6½		Form with soft greenish juvenile foliage; to 50ft
C. japonica 'Sekkan-sugi'	flowering		harvest		5	8	3	4	■	Slow-growing form, creamy-white foliage; 33ft+
Cunninghamia lanceolata	flowering		harvest		5	10	2½	4	■	Upright habit, fresh green foliage; to 50ft
C. lanceolata 'Glauca'	flowering		harvest		5	10	2½	4	■	Foliage glaucous green, waxy bloom; to 33–50ft

flowering · harvest

Cupressus

Cypress

Tolerance of drought and chalky soils characterize some of the true cypresses, especially *Cupressus glabra* (*C. arizonica* var. *glabra*). This makes a small to medium tree with a dense conical habit and blue-gray foliage. The reddish-purple and smooth bark peels to reveal pale patches beneath.

Cupressus sempervirens 'Stricta'

Like all the true cypresses, the cones take two years to ripen. *Cupressus sempervirens* is mainly grown as the narrow crowned form so typical of the Mediterranean landscape. *C. macrocarpa* can make a large tree and looks very similar to a Cedar of Lebanon when over 100 years old. However, it is much faster growing and in the past was widely used as a hedging plant; old hedges are still seen but it is not very suitable for this task since it requires regular and careful trimming. 'Goldcrest' and 'Golden Pillar' are two foliage forms. The hardiest cypress is *C. nootkatensis*; this is often called *Chamaecyparis nootkatensis* but the cones ripen in the second year and have more seeds per scale. It occurs in areas with high winter snowfall and tolerates wet soils. The cultivar 'Pendula' has a wonderfully gaunt habit with pendulous branching, best described as the "Afghan hound cypress." Leyland cypress is a hybrid between *C. macrocarpa* and *C. nootkatensis*; it is usually called *Cupressocyparis leylandii.*

Cupressus macrocarpa 'Goldcrest'

Cypresses all make good specimen evergreen trees. They can all be grown from cuttings, most easily if taken in late summer. They should be planted out as small trees and grown in pots, since the root systems are wide ranging and they do not transplant well.

soil	Well-drained, acidic to alkaline; can get chlorotic on shallow chalk soils
site	Much prefers a sunnier site—not suitable for shady positions
pruning	Will not regrow unless there is live (green) foliage, so do not clip into brown branches
general care	When transplanting, best grown in pots and plant out small as coarse root system does not establish freely
pests & diseases	Corynium canker can weaken, even kill, entire trees; also honey fungus and phytophthora root rot

	SPRING			SUMMER			FALL			WINTER			height 5yrs (ft)	height 10yrs (ft)	spread 5yrs (ft)	spread 10yrs (ft)	flower color	
Cupressus glabra	✹	✹										✹	6	10	2½	5		Gray-green or blue-gray foliage; conical habit
C. glabra 'Blue Ice'	✹	✹										✹	5	8	2½	4		Blue-gray foliage, slow-growing, conical
C. leylandii 'Castlewellan'													10	20	3	6½		Dull bronzy yellow foliage; to 20m
C. leylandii 'Haggerston Gray'													13	26	5	8		Commonest form of Leyland cypress; to 80ft+
C. leylandii 'Robinson's Gold'													10	20	3	6½		Soft, golden yellow foliage; to 65ft
C. macrocarpa		✹	✹										10	20	3	6½		Green foliage, narrow crowned when young
C. macrocarpa 'Goldcrest'		✹	✹										10	20	3	6½		Golden green foliage, narrow habit; to 50ft
C. macrocarpa 'Golden Pillar'		✹	✹										10	20	3	6½		Golden green foliage, narrow habit; to 50ft
C. nootkatensis			✹										6½	11½	3	6½		Regular conical habit, pendent side branches
C. nootkatensis 'Pendula'			✹										6½	11½	3	6½		Narrow spreading branches and hanging foliage
C. sempervirens 'Stricta'	✹											✹	8	16	2	3		Very narrow habit; to 50ft

✹ *flowering*

Ginkgo

Maidenhair tree

This deciduous tree is assigned to a position between the ferns and the conifers in the evolutionary family tree. However, it is usually treated as an honorary conifer.

Ginkgo is remarkably tough and tolerant of all forms of pollution—two of the trees growing close to the center of the nuclear blast at Hiroshima survived, and fossils from coal deposits show recognizable Ginkgo dating back 200 million years.

The leaves are fan-shaped and have an oily texture; an extract of the leaves is used as a health tonic. The seeds are tasty, but come with a drawback—the female fruit is surrounded by a stinking oily layer! The habit is generally narrow in young trees, only really broadening at around 100 years, but by 250 years old, the crown is much broader.

soil	Any well-drained soil is fine, even less than satisfactory soils
site	This produces the best results if put in the sun or light shade
pruning	Does not have a strict pruning regime, but will regrow if cut back
general care	Very easy to cultivate and take care of. They are especially excellent in urban areas
pests & diseases	Relatively trouble-free. Does not have any particular problems with pests and diseases

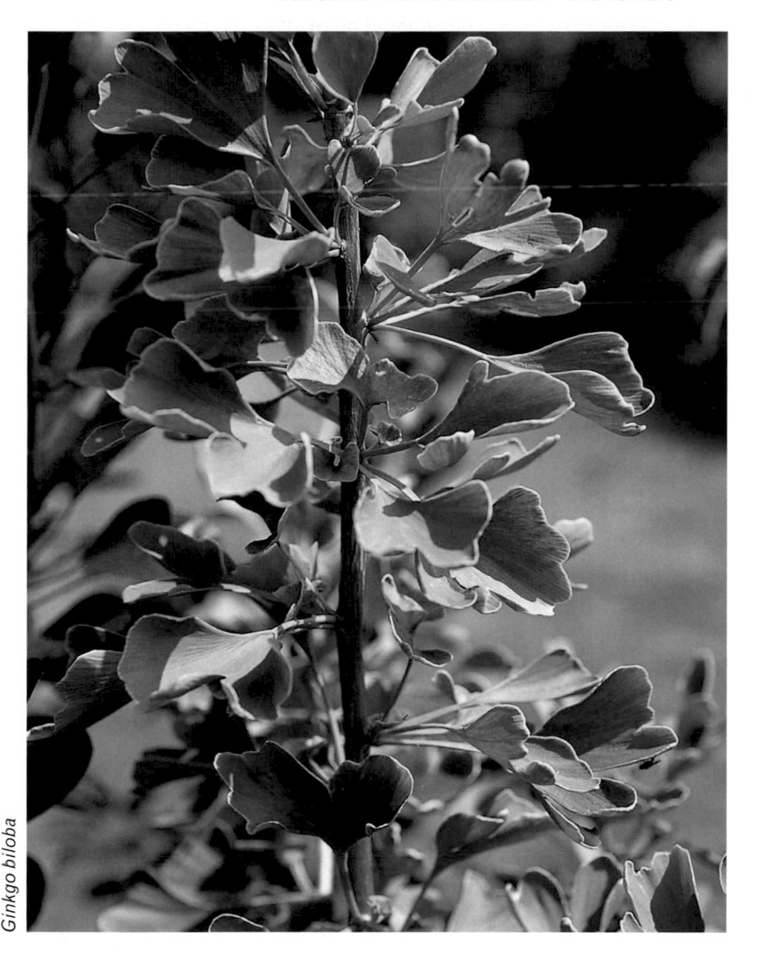

Ginkgo biloba

As a deciduous tree, Ginkgo will tolerate pruning. The chief reason for planting Ginkgo in the garden is the outstanding golden yellow autumnal color, which has a clarity lacking in other trees, except perhaps *Acer cappadocicum*. The leaves hang on the trees for several weeks in mid- to late fall. It also make an excellent specimen tree.

If growing Ginkgo for fruit, it is necessary to plant both sexes, or to graft a male branch onto a female tree. Ginkgo will grow in a wide range of soils, provided they are well drained. It can be propagated from seed and from semi-ripe cuttings in summer.

	SPRING	SUMMER	FALL	WINTER	height 5yrs (ft)	height 10yrs (ft)	spread 5yrs (ft)	spread 10yrs (ft)	color of blossom	
Ginkgo biloba	flowering				6½	13	3	6½		Seed-raised plants will be either male or female
G. biloba 'King of Dongting'	flowering		harvest		6½	13	3	5		Female form; to 50ft
G. biloba 'Saratoga'	flowering				6½	13	3	5		Narrow crowned male selection; to 50ft+

flowering  harvest

Juniperus

Juniper

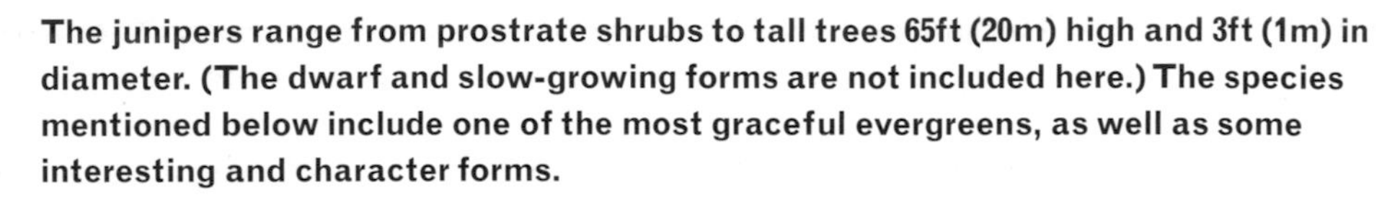

The junipers range from prostrate shrubs to tall trees 65ft (20m) high and 3ft (1m) in diameter. (The dwarf and slow-growing forms are not included here.) The species mentioned below include one of the most graceful evergreens, as well as some interesting and character forms.

Juniperus chinensis 'Kuriwao Gold'

The characteristic that separates the junipers from the various cypresses is their fruit. The woody cone of Cupressus has become the fleshy cone of Juniperus. However, in the maturing cone of *Juniperus chinensis* 'Kaizuka', the marks of the cone scales can be clearly seen.

Junipers need full sun, but will grow on a wide range of soils. This includes chalk soils, as well as less well-drained substrates. *Juniperus recurva* var. *coxii* has pendulous foliage, which is bright green to grayish-green and has a dry, rustling feel. It makes a small conical tree.

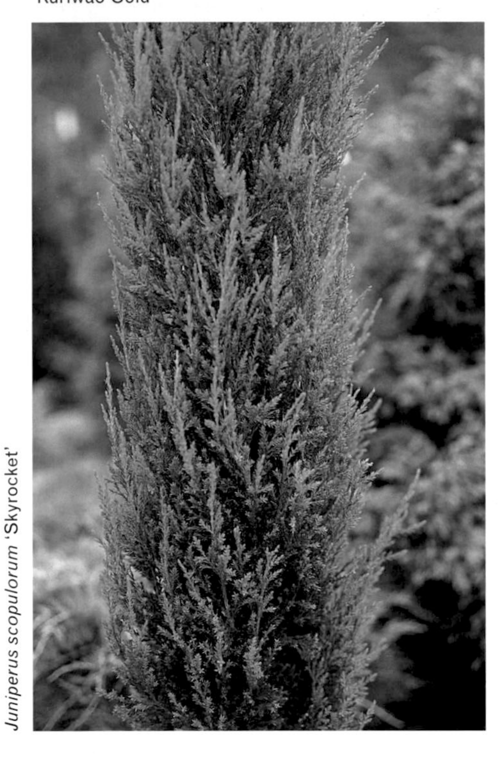

Juniperus scopulorum 'Skyrocket'

Juniperus communis 'Hibernica' is a narrow, pencil-shaped form of the widespread common juniper, whose foliage can be burned to smoke fish. *Juniperus scopulorum* 'Skyrocket' is an equally narrow crowned form, but growing a little larger, to about 26ft (8m) with blue-gray foliage. *Juniperus chinensis* 'Kaizuka' makes a large sprawling shrub, whereas 'Pyramidalis' is conical, as is 'Aurea' but with golden foliage.

Juniper berries are used as flavors in cooking and also to make gin. They take one to three years to ripen, depending upon the species.

They are even slower to germinate, taking up to five years, although most come up in the second spring. They can also be propagated from cuttings, taken at most times of the year.

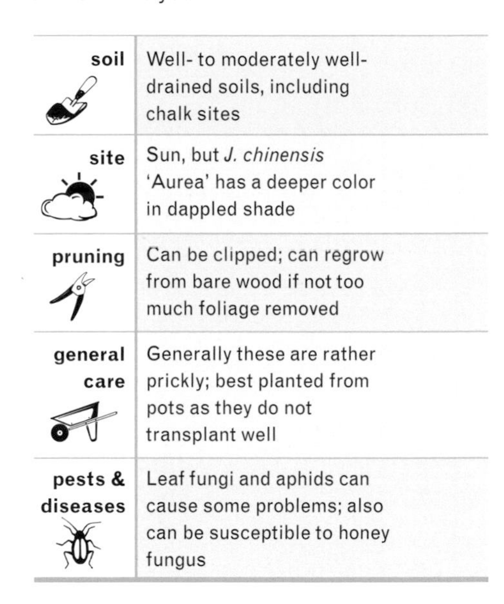

soil	Well- to moderately well-drained soils, including chalk sites
site	Sun, but *J. chinensis* 'Aurea' has a deeper color in dappled shade
pruning	Can be clipped; can regrow from bare wood if not too much foliage removed
general care	Generally these are rather prickly; best planted from pots as they do not transplant well
pests & diseases	Leaf fungi and aphids can cause some problems; also can be susceptible to honey fungus

	SPRING			SUMMER			FALL			WINTER			height 5yrs (ft)	height 10yrs (ft)	spread 5yrs (ft)	spread 10yrs (ft)	color of blossom	
Juniperus chinensis 'Aurea'		flowering											5	8	2½	4	gray	Golden foliage; male form; to 20–26ft
J. chinensis 'Kuriwao Gold'						harvest	harvest	harvest					5	8	4	8	white	Female form with bright green foliage; to 20ft
J. chinensis 'Pyramidalis'		flowering											4	6	1½	2½	gray	Conical form, prickly juvenile glaucous leaves
J. communis 'Hibernica'				flowering			harvest	harvest					4	6½	1½	2	gray	Narrow upright habit to 16–20ft
J. recurva var. *coxii*			flowering					harvest					5	8	2½	4	gray	Conical bush or small tree; to 33ft
J. scopulorum 'Skyrocket'													6	10	1½	2		Narrow upright habit, blue-gray foliage, to 26ft

flowering harvest

Larix

Larch

The larches are the largest genus of deciduous conifers. They have narrow columnar-conic crowns (except old trees, which become broader) and cast only a light shade.

Larix decidua

The new foliage is attractive green and flushes before most broad-leaved trees think of coming back into life. The flowers, especially the female cone flowers, are attractive bright red, pink, or, less often, greenish-yellow, and are carried from a young age. Then there is the fall color, bright yellow in *Larix decidua*, pale yellow or orange in *Larix kaempferi*. One-year twigs are brightly colored, yellow in *L. decidua*, reddish-purple in *L. kaempferi*. They thrive on a wide range of soils, with *L. decidua* liking well-drained ones and *L. kaempferi* tolerating heavier clays. In the garden they make attractive specimen trees, and are also good for shelter plantings or as supports for climbing plants, like Wisteria or species roses. They are best propagated from seed sown in spring.

soil	Both: well-drained. Larix: heavy, best on acidic/neutral. Metasequoia: shallow water
site	Larix: sun, no shade. Metasequoia: best only in the sun
pruning	Larix: none required, but can be lightly reshaped. Metasequoia: none needed
general care	Larix: quick-growing but plant as small plants. Metasequoia: on dry soils, will appreciate water in summer
pests & diseases	Both of these are generally fairly trouble-free from most pests and diseases

Metasequoia

Dawn redwood

***Metasequoia glyptostroboides* is one of the most graceful of conifers and makes a fast-growing deciduous tree, which turns from yellow-brown through pink to red-brown in the fall.**

The habit is conical, becoming more columnar in older trees. The bark is orange-brown or red-brown, smooth at first then fibrous and stringy on the ridges. It thrives on the widest range of soils, from acidic soils through to alkaline ones, as well as dry sands through to very damp soils. It will more or less flourish in whatever you try to grow it in, although the very best growth is on fertile, moist to damp soils. It will happily grow in 6in (15cm) of water, albeit more slowly.

In the garden it can be used as a specimen tree, being particularly effective around or in a (shallow) pond for its reflection. It can be propagated from semi-ripe cuttings in summer—but make sure you choose a shoot with buds since the fine shoots are deciduous—or from hardwood cuttings in winter. Fresh seed, if available, germinates readily on a damp starting mix.

Metasequota glyptostroboides

	SPRING	SUMMER	FALL	WINTER	height 5yrs (ft)	height 10yrs (ft)	spread 5yrs (ft)	spread 10yrs (ft)	color of blossom	
Larix decidua	flowering		harvest		10	20	5	8		Fast-growing light and narrow crowned tree
L. kaempferi	flowering		harvest		10	20	5	8		Purplish-red winter twigs with waxy bloom
L. kaempferi 'Pendula'	flowering		harvest		10	20	5	8		Twigs hang down from side branches; to 50ft
Metasequoia glyptostroboides					6½	13	3	5		Excellent habit with feathery foilage; to 50–80ft

flowering *harvest*

Picea

Spruce

The spruces are narrow-crowned, evergreen trees. They are strongly monopodal, i.e., with a single main stem and only light side branching. The width can be as much as 13ft (4m) radius with most species when mature. The exception is *Picea omorika*, which even as a 80ft (26m) tall tree is only up to 5ft (1.5m) in diameter. This is because it is adapted for areas with wet snow and the branches hang down close to the trunk, only arching out near the tips (making the tree almost impossible to climb!).

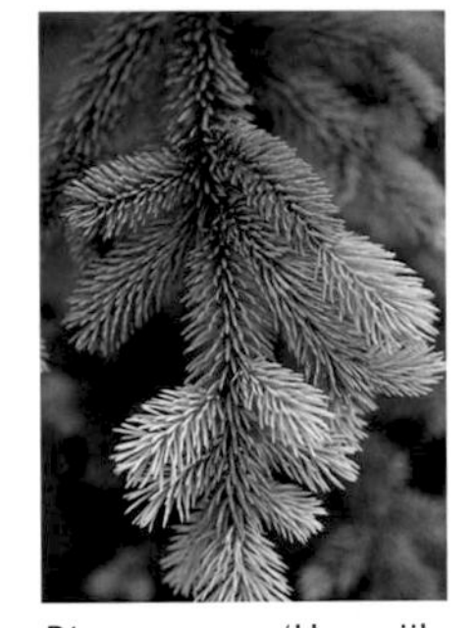
Picea pungens 'Hoopsii'

Picea orientalis is an attractive species for its short needles, its brick-red male cones in mid-spring and red female cone flowers, and its habit. The cultivar 'Aurea' has new foliage that is golden yellow before turning dark green and merging with the older leaves. *P. breweriana* is the most attractive of the common species. The leaves are dark, glossy green on the top side and silvery green on the underside. The habit is spectacular, with the side branches off the trunk festooned with long hanging and unbranched twigs up to 6½ft (2m) in length. *P. pungens* is represented by blue foliage selections. The best color is found on the one-year foliage and this contrasts with the dull green of older foliage.

P. abies is not a brilliant choice for a Christmas tree as it drops its needles (a better one to choose would be *Abies nordmanniana*).

Spruces can be propagated by seed sown in spring. The forms can be grafted onto seedling rootstocks either in late summer or late winter, keeping the rootstock slightly dry to stop it bleeding and drowning the scion.

Picea abies

Picea orientalis 'Aurea'

soil	Well-drained, acidic to slightly alkaline; *P. omorika* tolerates more alkaline soils
site	These trees perform at their best in a situation with full sun
pruning	None required; only lightly trim into existing foliage bearing shoots
general care	Easy to cultivate. Grafted plants may need staking to get them to form an erect leader
pests & diseases	Aphids can kill needles—*P. pungens* and *P. abies* look poor, but *P. omorika* and *P. breweriana* are resistant

	SPRING	SUMMER	FALL	WINTER	height 5yrs (ft)	height 10yrs (ft)	spread 5yrs (ft)	spread 10yrs (ft)	color of blossom	
Picea abies	flowering		harvest		8	15	3	6½		Common Christmas tree and forestry tree
P. breweriana	flowering		harvest		6	10	3	5		Very attractive weeping tree; to 50ft
P. omorika	flowering		harvest		8	15	3	5		Very tolerant of poor site conditions; to 50–65ft
P. orientalis 'Aurea'	flowering		harvest		8	15	3	6½		Attractive tree forming a columnar crown
P. pungens 'Hoopsii'	flowering		harvest		6½	11½	3	6½		New foliage vividly glaucous blue; to 33–50ft
P. pungens 'Koster'	flowering		harvest		6½	11½	3	6½		New foliage deep silvery-blue; to 33–50ft

flowering · harvest

Pinus

Pine

Pines are intriguing for their evergreen foliage. The leaves or needles are in small clusters of between two and five, which when fitted together form a perfect cylinder. Thus each leaf is either a hemisphere (two-needled pines) or triangular in section.

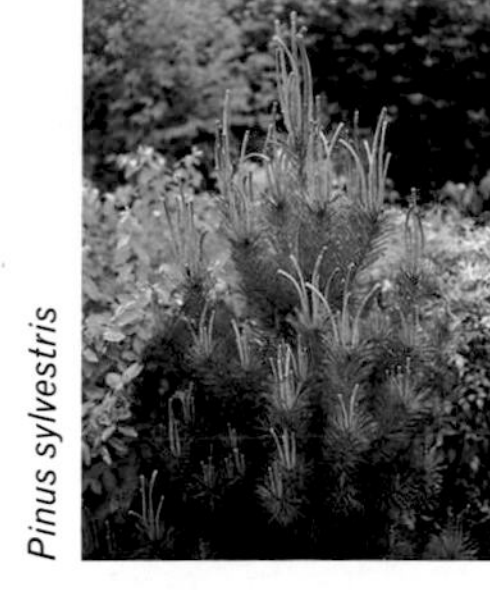

Pinus sylvestris

Each cluster, or fascicle, represents a short shoot and has, when new, a small dormant bud in the center, but these grow only if the tip of the shoot is damaged. The main shoots grow in a short period in early summer. Flowering trees have male cones at the base, foliage in the middle, and female cones at the tip of each "node" and only make side branches from the tip of the node. The female cones take two years to develop, except in *P. pinea* where they take three; the ripe cones may open over winter to release the seeds or remain attached to the tree awaiting a forest fire to open them.

In the garden, the larger-growing pines make specimen trees. They can also be used as shelter or to form a backdrop against which other features can be displayed. Often these functions go together, such as using the dark green foliage of *P. nigra* as a shelter and also to set off the bright yellow foliage of *Robinia pseudoacacia* 'Frisia'. *P. nigra* and *P. wallichiana* both grow well on soils over chalk or limestone. Pines can be propagated by seed sown in spring; they can also be grafted in late winter onto seedling rootstocks.

soil	Well-drained, especially acidic to neutral; *P. nigra* and *P. wallichiana* over chalk
site	Sun; not for shade except *P. wallichiana* that will tolerate light shade
pruning	No special pruning regime required, except to remove damaged branches
general care	Position is important as they need full side light to keep the lower branches healthy
pests & diseases	Young trees can be killed by honey fungus, but apart from this they are fairly trouble-free

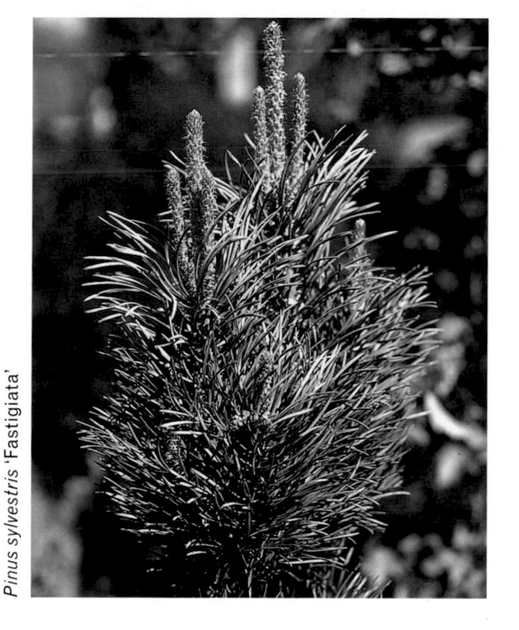

Pinus sylvestris 'Fastigiata'

	SPRING	SUMMER	FALL	WINTER	height 5yrs (ft)	height 10yrs (ft)	spread 5yrs (ft)	spread 10yrs (ft)	color of blossom	
Pinus aristata	✿		harvest		4	6½	3	5		Leaves retained for many years; to 33ft
P. bungeana	✿		harvest		5	8	3	5		Open crown; olive-green bark; attractive; to 33ft
P. nigra 'Black Prince'	✿		harvest		6½	13	4	6½		Dense, dark green foliage; good for chalk soils
P. pinaster	✿		harvest		6½	16	4	8		Fast-growing with open crown; large cones
P. pinea	✿		harvest		5	8	5	8		Cones ripen in three years, seeds large, edible
P. sylvestris	✿		harvest		6½	13	4	8		Blue foliage; bark in upper trunk orange
P. sylvestris 'Fastigiata'	✿		harvest		5	10	2½	3		Very narrow upright crown; to 26ft
P. wallichiana	✿		harvest		8	15	4	8		Soft blue-green needles pendent on branches

 *harvest*

Podocarpus

This genus contains a number of large trees from warm-temperate to tropical zones. Most are too tender for temperate conditions, and the hardier ones are small shrubs. *Podocarpus salignus* is hardy in cooler climates, provided it has some side shelter in cold gardens, and it can make a very attractive evergreen tree.

The foliage is somewhat yewlike, but much longer, to 4in (10cm). *Podocarpus totara* has shorter needles and makes a wider spreading tree with light, evergreen foliage.

Podocarpus salignus

They are attractive as a feature by themselves in the garden. They are particularly effective if planted as a small grove. The fruits are formed only where both male and female trees are present. They can be propagated by semi-ripe cuttings in late summer or by seed sown in spring.

soil	Podocarpus: well-drained. Pseudolarix: well-drained, preferably lime-free
site	Podocarpus: sun to moderate shade. Pseudolarix: prefers full sun
pruning	Podocarpus: can be trimmed. Pseudolarix: only to remove dead branches
general care	Podocarpus: best with side shelter. Pseudolarix: slow to get going, so keep weed-free when young
pests & diseases	Both of these are generally fairly trouble-free from most pests and diseases

Pseudolarix
Golden larch

This genus contains only one species, *Pseudolarix amabilis.* Amabilis translates as "lovely," and when in its fall glory, this is an understatement.

Pseudolarix amabilis

The leaves turn golden-orange before falling. The cones are spiky and fall apart to release the seeds, similar to Abies and Cedrus, rather than the persistent cones of Larix. Pseudolarix make a spreading tree, ultimately as broad as tall. It is slow to get established, often making little growth in the first two to five years, but then speeds up. It needs full light and a well-drained soil. Use it as a specimen tree. It can be raised from seed or from softwood cuttings in early summer.

	SPRING	SUMMER	FALL	WINTER	height 5yrs (ft)	height 10yrs (ft)	spread 5yrs (ft)	spread 10yrs (ft)	color of blossom	
Podocarpus salignus	flowering		harvest harvest		5	10	3	6½		Attractive, long-leaved tree, to 33–50ft
P. totara					5	8	3	6½		Wide spreading as a mature tree; to 33ft
Pseudolarix amabilis	flowering		harvest		4	8	3	6½		Golden orange color in fall; wide spreading

flowering harvest

Pseudotsuga
Douglas fir

***Pseudotsuga menziesii* makes a large and fast-growing evergreen tree. It has an excellent reddish timber and is widely used in forestry.**

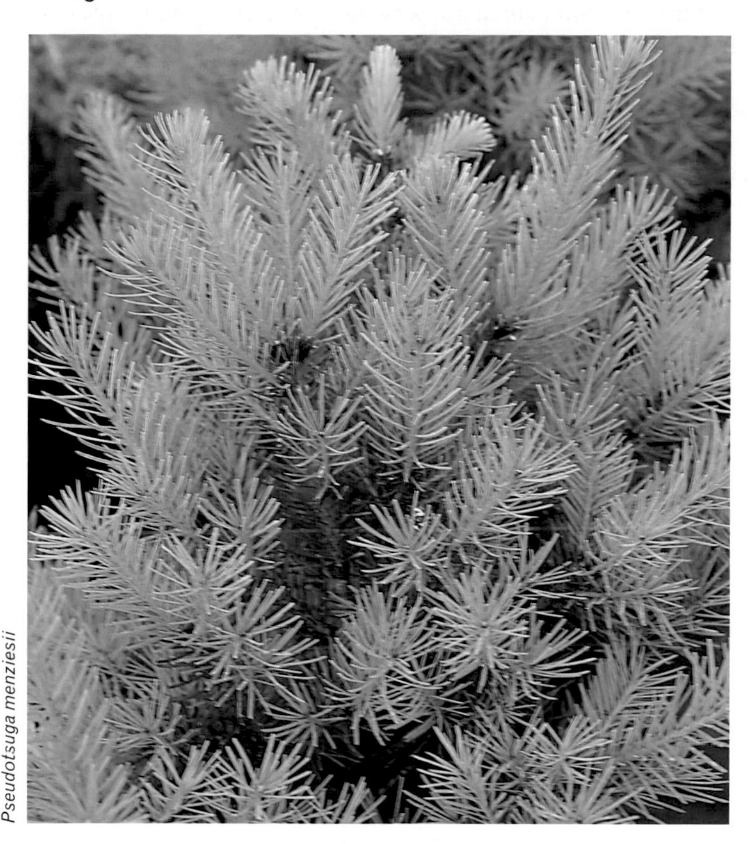

Pseudotsuga menziesii

The forms with blue foliage, *Pseudotsuga menziesii* ssp. *glauca*, are very attractive and make smaller trees. In the garden, Douglas fir makes a specimen tree or can be used as part of a shelter planting. It will withstand exposure but will thrive much better in a sheltered spot.

The trunk develops a thick, corky, deeply ridged bark in old trees. Douglas fir can be propagated from seed sown in spring, or cultivars can be grafted in late winter.

soil	Pseudotsuga: well-drained. Saxegothea: well-drained, acidic or lightly alkaline
site	Both sun lovers. Pseudotsuga will tolerate shade when young
pruning	Pseudotsuga: avoid if possible. Saxegothea: can be clipped
general care	Pseudotsuga: late spring frosts can cause damage. Saxegothea: in colder areas, give more shelter or shade
pests & diseases	Pseudotsuga: a needle-killing fungus can affect the leaves of blue forms. Saxegothea: generally fine

Saxegothea
Prince Albert's yew

***Saxegothea conspicua* is named after Queen Victoria's consort, Prince Albert. It is not a yew but a podocarp relative.**

Saxegothea conspicua

The foliage, though, is somewhat yewlike. It consists of a whorl of five or six side branches with a single extension shoot; this give a distinctive appearance to the foliage. It makes a tall tree with a narrow crown depending on climate—50ft (15m) or so after 50 years in warm areas, and no more than a shrub 10ft (3m) tall in more temperate climes. In the garden, use it as a large, evergreen specimen shrub or narrow crowned tree, depending on climate. It can also be used as part of a shrub bed, especially to set off golden or light green foliage. It is most easily raised from cuttings taken in late summer.

	SPRING	SUMMER	FALL	WINTER	height 5yrs (ft)	height 10yrs (ft)	spread 5yrs (ft)	spread 10yrs (ft)	color of blossom	
Pseudotsuga menziesii	flowering		harvest		10	20	5	8		Green/gray-green foliage; fast-growing; to 130ft
P. menziesii ssp. *glauca*	flowering		harvest		6½	13	3	6½		Blue foliage; slow-growing, medium tree; to 50ft
P. menziesii ssp. *glauca* 'Pendula'	flowering		harvest		6½	10	6½	10		Weeping branches and blue foliage
Saxegothea conspicua	flowering		harvest		6½	11½	3	6½		Evergreen shrub or narrow crowned tree

 *flowering*  *harvest*

Sequoia

Coast redwood

Sequoia is the tallest living tree in the world and is found naturally in the coastal regions of California and Oregon.

Driving down the northern California coast you can pass through groves of trees that are more than 300ft (90m) tall; in fact, the tallest redwoods are more than 370ft (113m).

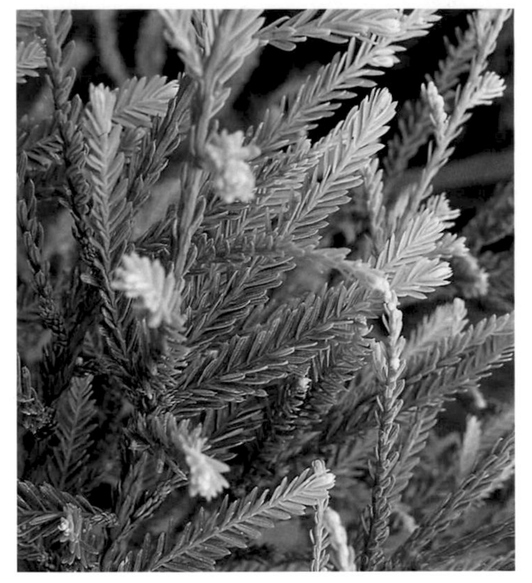

Sequoia sempervirens 'Adpressa'

But don't let this put you off. In the garden they won't grow nearly so tall, especially if your garden is mild with windier conditions, and not such a high rainfall or such frequent fogs, which enable them to grow so tall. A more realistic height is 50–65ft (15–20m). However, what the Sequoia does do is grow fast, even in slightly drier climates, making a tree 33–50ft (10–15m) in 20 years. They also are one of the few conifers that will reliably coppice if cut down to ground level.

Use the natural tree as an evergreen specimen or to form a grove. The cultivar 'Adpressa' is slower growing. Propagate 'Adpressa' from cuttings, best in late summer; and propagate the species from cuttings or seed sown in the spring.

soil	Both: moist to well-drained. Sequoia: can tolerate short-term flooding
site	Sequoia: sun to light shade. Sequoiadendron: enjoys the full sun
pruning	Sequoia: none but will coppice. Sequoiadendron: none; does not coppice
general care	Sequoia: can get burnt by cold, dry winds in winter but recovers. Sequoiadendron: fast-growing tree
pests & diseases	Sequoia: no particular problems. Sequoiadendron: honey fungus can kill this mighty giant

Sequoiadendron

Big tree

Sequoiadendron giganteum

Also known as the giant redwood, this is related to the sequoia and gives it name to the first National Park in the US—the Sequoia National Park. *Sequoiadendron giganteum* includes the largest living thing, a tree known as "General Sherman," which is a mere 272ft (83m) tall and is estimated to weigh 6,000 tons.

Sequoiadendron differs from Sequoia in having scalelike foliage, cones ripening in the second year, and in not being able to coppice. The bark is even thicker but not as soft. It is a hardier tree, not suffering winter cold damage. In the garden, it will make an evergreen specimen tree 65–100ft (20–30m) in height but with a stout trunk. The thick bark is often hollowed by tree creepers and other small birds in winter. It can be raised either from seed or by cuttings in late summer.

	SPRING	SUMMER	FALL	WINTER	height 5yrs (ft)	height 10yrs (ft)	spread 5yrs (ft)	spread 10yrs (ft)	flower color	
Sequoia sempervirens	flowering			flowering	13	23	6½	10		Expect 50–65ft in an urban setting
S. sempervirens 'Adpressa'	flowering			flowering	6½	13	3	6½		Short and broad leaves, flush creamy white
Sequoiadendron giganteum	flowering		harvest		10	20	3	8		Vigorous tree quickly making a stout bole; 65–100ft
S. giganteum 'Pendulum'	flowering		harvest		6½	11½	3	5		Side branches entirely pendulous, a bizarre tree

Taxodium

Swamp cypress

Taxodium is a deciduous tree that is superficially similar to Metasequoia. In the garden it makes a leafy specimen tree with fresh green summer foliage.

Taxodium distichum

Like Metasequoia, Taxodium will grow in shallow water and swampy sites, developing special structures, known as "knees," to get air to the roots. However, fastest growth is on well-drained but moist sites, and Taxodium is content to grow slowly on quite dry sites.

The leaves have the same combination of deciduous shoots and permanent bud-bearing shoots as Metasequoia, but only the leaves are deciduous. The leaves don't open much before early summer but it is usually late fall or early winter before they turn brick-red and drop.

Taxodium is particularly good near ponds or streams. It can be propagated from seed sown in damp seed starting mix in spring, from semi-ripe cuttings in summer, and from hardwood cuttings in winter.

soil	Taxodium: swampy to well-drained, very tolerant. Taxus: any well-drained soil
site	Taxodium: likes the sun. Taxus: good in both the sun to deep shade
pruning	Taxodium: none but will tolerate. Taxus: trim at any time; cut back to ground level
general care	Taxodium: growth in standing water is slow; branches brittle. Taxus: keep clippings away from animals
pests & diseases	Taxodium: no particular problems. Taxus: virtually immune but does not like waterlogging at the roots

Taxus

Yew

Yew makes the best hedges of any evergreen. It is generally viewed as slow growing, but will make a good hedge 6½ft (2m) high in five years—only a year slower than the Leyland cypress.

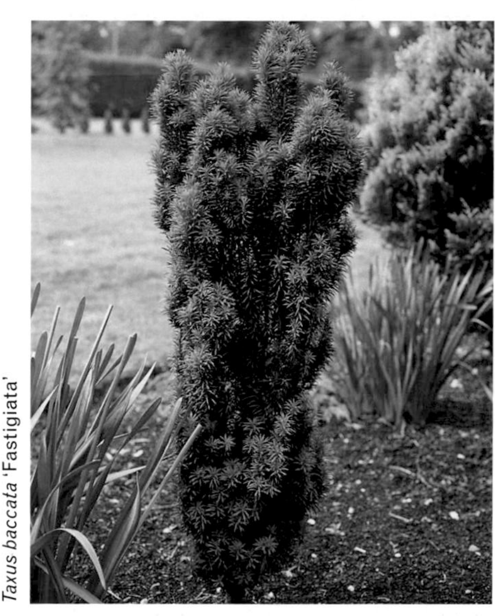

Taxus baccata 'Fastigiata'

Yew can be coppiced or reshaped at any age, quickly sprouting new growth from any branch exposed to the light or from the base. Another advantage is that it does not want to grow taller than 33ft (10m) or so, and, as a result, it does not romp out of control.

As an amenity tree, it has a beautiful habit, foliage, and bark. The foliage and bark are poisonous. This requires care where cattle, horses, or goats may graze. The fleshy red aril around the seeds on female trees is the one part not poisonous. The cancer drug Taxol is derived from yew.

Yew can be raised from seed, which will take a couple of years to germinate, or from cuttings, preferably taken in late summer.

	SPRING			SUMMER			FALL			WINTER			height 5yrs (ft)	height 10yrs (ft)	spread 5yrs (ft)	spread 10yrs (ft)	flower color	
Taxodium distichum	flowering	flowering					harvest	harvest			flowering	flowering	8	15	3	6½	■	Large-growing deciduous tree, very tolerant
T. distichum var. *imbricatum* 'Nutans'	flowering	flowering									flowering	flowering	6½	13	3	6½	■	Smaller with a narrow crown; to 50ft
Taxus baccata			flowering				harvest	harvest					6	10	3	6½	□	Evergreen, small tree, very shade tolerant
T. baccata 'Dovastonii Aurea'			flowering										4	6½	3	6½	□	Wide-spreading but low habit; male tree; to 16ft
T. baccata 'Fastigiata'							harvest	harvest					6	10	3	5		Upright habit, becomes broader with age
T. baccata 'Fastigiata Aurea'							harvest	harvest					5	8	3	5		As for 'Fastigiata' but deep yellow leaves
T. baccata 'Fastigiata Aureomarginata'			flowering										5	8	3	5	□	As for 'Fastigiata' but leaves with yellow margin

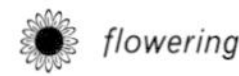 *flowering*  *harvest*

Thuja

Western red cedar

This genus has scalelike foliage, which is held in flat, spreading sprays. The foliage is delectably scented, often noticeable just by brushing up against the foliage, if not by crushing a small sprig.

The cones are small upright structures, not the globose "sputniks" of Chamaecyparis and Cupressus. It makes a vigorous tree, which has some live foliage within the crown. This means that it is much easier to reduce or reshape than the cypresses, which have their foliage mainly as a veneer at the edge of the crown (especially in closely trimmed hedges).

It makes an attractive specimen tree, generally wider at the base and conical above. Thuja is best on well-drained soils, but will tolerate poor drainage better than other cypresslike conifers—in the wild, *Thuja plicata* can grow in bogs, although very slowly! On good sites it can grow to 100ft (30m) or more, but in urban conditions 50–65ft (15–20m) is more likely.

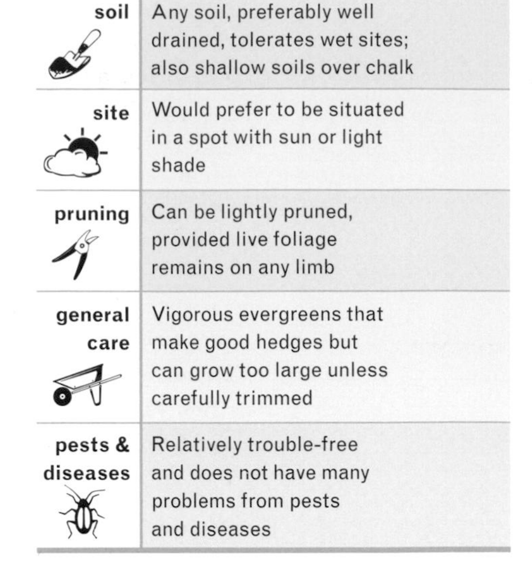

soil	Any soil, preferably well drained, tolerates wet sites; also shallow soils over chalk
site	Would prefer to be situated in a spot with sun or light shade
pruning	Can be lightly pruned, provided live foliage remains on any limb
general care	Vigorous evergreens that make good hedges but can grow too large unless carefully trimmed
pests & diseases	Relatively trouble-free and does not have many problems from pests and diseases

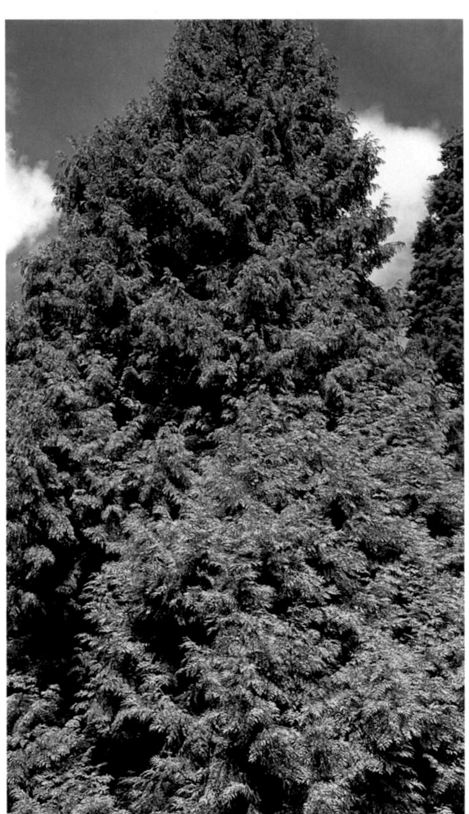

Thuja plicata 'Zebrina'

The range of tree cultivars is small, with many dwarf ones in *Thuja occidentalis*. The plant *Thuja orientalis*, which is sometimes referred to as *Platycladus orientalis*, has larger cones with prominent hooks on the scales, large rounded seeds without wings, and scentless foliage in erect, not flat, sprays. It grows on well-drained soils.

Thuja can be propagated from cuttings at almost any time of the year (though it is best in late summer/fall) or from sowing the small winged seeds onto the top of seed starting mix in spring.

	SPRING	SUMMER	FALL	WINTER	height 5yrs (ft)	height 10yrs (ft)	spread 5yrs (ft)	spread 10yrs (ft)	color of blossom	
Thuja plicata	flowering				6½	13	3	6½	■	Male cones small, black; foliage aromatic
T. plicata 'Atrovirens'	flowering				6½	13	3	6½	■	Dark glossy green foliage
T. plicata 'Zebrina'	flowering				6½	13	3	6½	■	Broad conical habit, wider than the species

flowering

Thujopsis

Hiba arborvitae

This tree is related to Thuja, having similar scale leaves in flattened sprays but without the scent that makes Thuja so endearing.

Thujopsis dolabrata

The individual scales are shaped like a hatchet, which is the meaning of the Latin name *dolabrata*, and are vividly silvered beneath. It is a slow-growing evergreen, although with time it can make over 50ft (15m). However, in garden settings it is more often a large multistemmed shrub and is useful as a small tree in a border. It thrives on a wide range of soils, requiring fair to good drainage. It can be raised from seed but is easier, and faster, from cuttings taken in late summer to early winter.

soil 	Thujopsis: well- to fairly well-drained. Tsuga: likewise, good on dry, acidic sands
site 	Both trees prefer to be situated where there is sun to moderate shade
pruning  	Thujopsis: tolerates pruning into green/live foliage. Tsuga: if there is sufficient live foliage
general care 	Thujopsis: slow-growing at first. Tsuga: in open sites it can get damaged by spring frosts when young
pests & diseases  	Both are relatively trouble-free and do not have many problems from pests and diseases

Tsuga

Hemlock

If you haven't selected a choice plant by now, with the final genus of the book comes *Tsuga heterophylla*, one of the most beautiful of all evergreen trees.

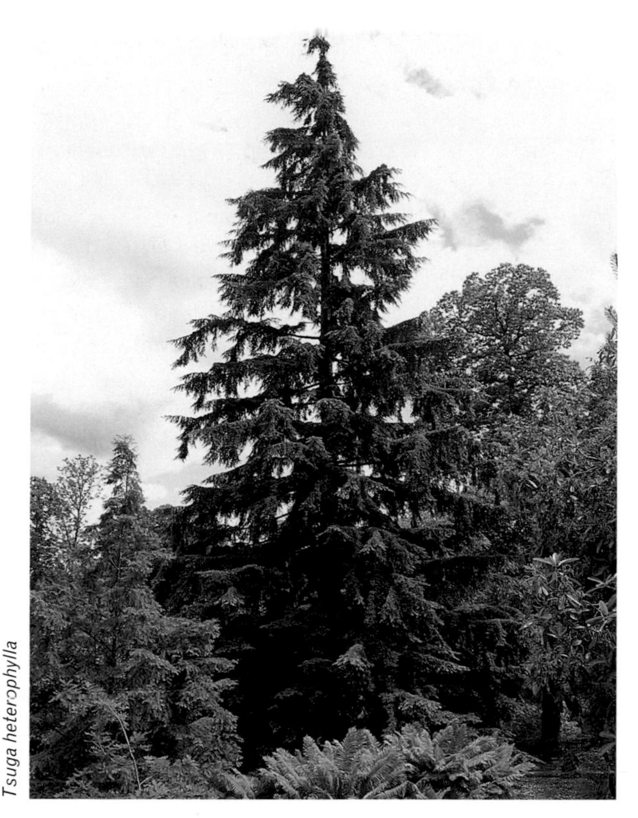
Tsuga heterophylla

Young trees are narrowly conical in shape with slightly pendent branches that carry the dense green foliage with silvery undersides. The leading shoot is nodding, giving a graceful aspect to the tree. Older trees are broader but where they have sufficient side light, retain the foliage down to ground level.

As a free-growing specimen tree, it is hard to beat. It is very shade tolerant and can be used in dark shady corners, where it is brighter than *Taxus baccata*.

Tsuga can also be used to make very attractive hedges. It grows on a wide range of soils, being especially suited to dry acidic sands. It can be raised from seed sown in spring or from cuttings in late summer.

	SPRING	SUMMER	FALL	WINTER	height 5yrs (ft)	height 10yrs (ft)	spread 5yrs (ft)	spread 10yrs (ft)	color of blossom	
Thujopsis dolabrata	flowering		harvest		3	13	1½	4	■	Slow-growing evergreen; to 26–33ft
Tsuga heterophylla	flowering		harvest		6½	6½	3	6½	■	Evergreen tree with attractive habit; to 50ft

 *flowering*  *harvest*

Troubleshooting

Growing a varied range of shrubs and trees attracts an equally varied selection of pests, diseases, and other problems. The following diagram is designed to help you diagnose problems with your shrubs or trees from the symptoms you can observe. Starting with the part of the shrub or tree that appears to be most affected—leaves or stems—by answering successive questions "yes" [✓] or "no" [✗] you will quickly arrive at a probable cause. Once you have identified the cause, turn to the relevant entry in the directory of pests and diseases for details of how to treat the problem.

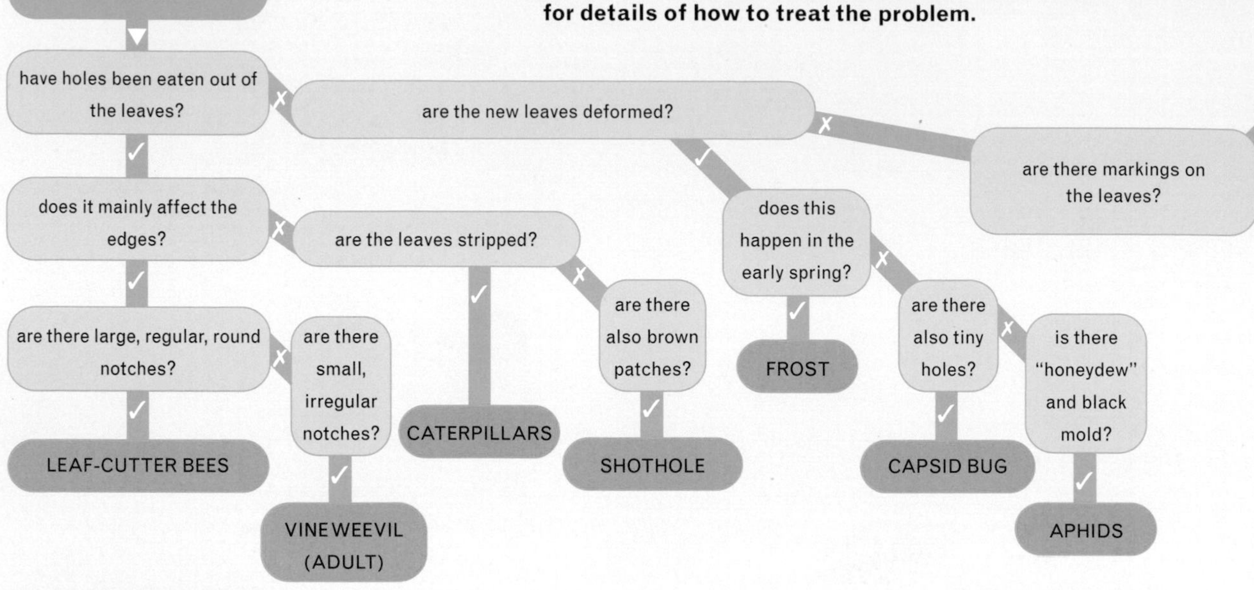

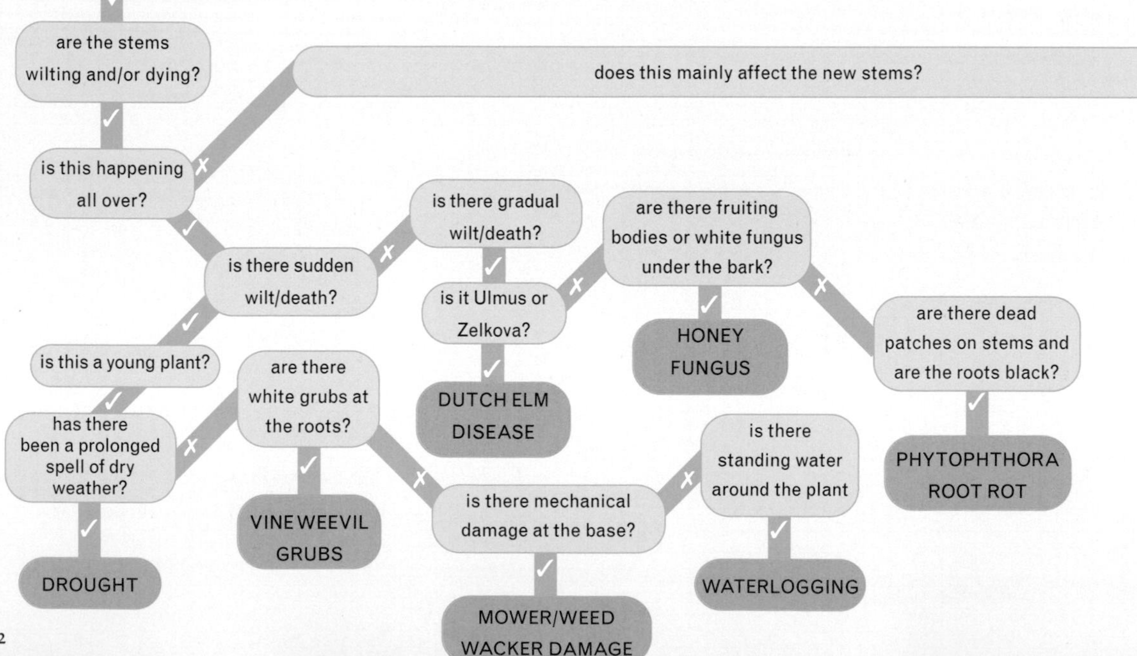

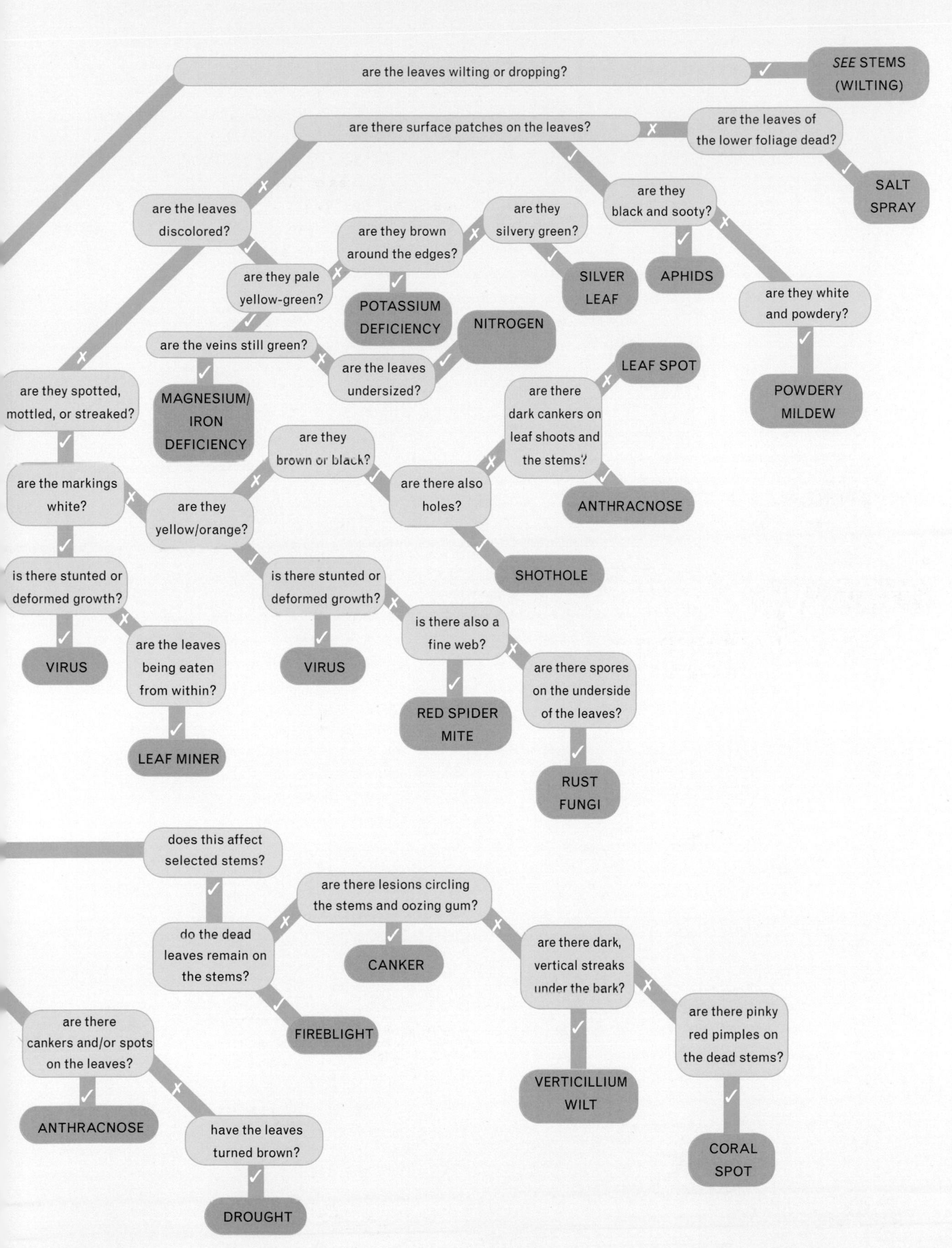

are the leaves wilting or dropping?
SEE STEMS (WILTING)
are there surface patches on the leaves?
are the leaves of the lower foliage dead?
SALT SPRAY
are the leaves discolored?
are they black and sooty?
APHIDS
are they silvery green?
SILVER LEAF
are they brown around the edges?
POTASSIUM DEFICIENCY
are they pale yellow-green?
are they white and powdery?
POWDERY MILDEW
NITROGEN
are the veins still green?
MAGNESIUM/ IRON DEFICIENCY
are the leaves undersized?
LEAF SPOT
are there dark cankers on leaf shoots and the stems?
ANTHRACNOSE
are they spotted, mottled, or streaked?
are they brown or black?
are there also holes?
SHOTHOLE
are the markings white?
are they yellow/orange?
is there stunted or deformed growth?
VIRUS
is there stunted or deformed growth?
VIRUS
is there also a fine web?
RED SPIDER MITE
are the leaves being eaten from within?
LEAF MINER
are there spores on the underside of the leaves?
RUST FUNGI
does this affect selected stems?
are there lesions circling the stems and oozing gum?
CANKER
do the dead leaves remain on the stems?
FIREBLIGHT
are there dark, vertical streaks under the bark?
VERTICILLIUM WILT
are there pinky red pimples on the dead stems?
CORAL SPOT
are there cankers and/or spots on the leaves?
ANTHRACNOSE
have the leaves turned brown?
DROUGHT

Pests & Diseases

Insect problems

Trees and shrubs are susceptible to a number of different pests and diseases, some of which can prove fatal. However, the majority of conditions can be treated successfully, as the following pages explain.

Vine weevil

Vine weevil can be a major problem on many trees and shrubs. The adult weevil is a black beetle nearly ½in (1cm) in length. It feeds on foliage after dark, making U-shaped notches in the leaves. However, the foliage damage is minor. The real damage is caused by vine weevil grubs—white maggot-like caterpillars, growing to ½in (1cm). The grubs eat the roots and bark below ground, up to just above ground level. This often kills the plant. Squash adults after dark and control the grubs by spraying the soil with either a solution of microscopic nematode worms (a biological control) or a chemical preparation.

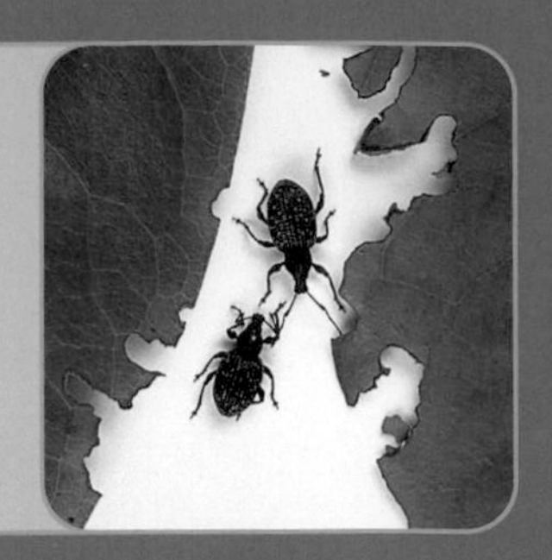

Aphids

Aphids are sap-sucking insects. They come in a large number of different species, ranging from green to black or white to a waxy wool. They quickly build up large colonies during the summer months. They can cause the death of shoot tips when present in large numbers, but are more of a problem for the honeydew they secrete. If control is necessary on a small scale, spray with a contact insecticide. Use one that only kills aphids, leaving their predators to mop up those missed by the spray. Killing both aphids and their predators is likely to lead to a new problem, as the aphids breed much faster than their predators.

Red spider mites

Red spider mites are also sap-sucking insects, which can cause weakening and death of leaves. They are scarcely visible to the naked eye because they are less than half a millimeter in length, but they spin a silky protective coat, which is more visible. There are several different species of red spider mite, which affect different groups of plants. They can be treated using a chemical spray such as derris or malathion, and this may need to be applied as often as twice a week. Alternatively, you could introduce natural insect predators—the best is *Phytoseilus persimilis*—which can be obtained by mail order through garden centers. Mites flourish in hot, dry conditions, so alter these wherever possible to protect your plants.

Scale insects

Scale insects are sap-sucking insects, which protect themselves with a protective scale and also by a waxy wool. Different species afflict different trees and shrubs, mainly sucking the sap from the trunks and branches of the plants, rather than from their leaves. These pests do not normally present a serious problem—although there is some evidence that they can reduce the growth rate of plants—but a heavy infestation can appear unsightly. Scale insects can be eradicated by washing the stems of the affected shrub with a soapy solution that removes the protective wax covering the insects.

Caspid bugs

Capsid bugs are green or brown insects, approximately ¼in (0.5cm) in length, which suck the sap from the buds and the young foliage of some trees and shrubs. These pests insert a toxic saliva into the plants they attack that causes areas of the expanding leaves to be killed. Capsid bugs can be controlled by spraying with a systemic insecticide (that is to say, one that is moved around within the plant), during the summer months.

Caterpillars

Caterpillars come in a vast range of shapes and sizes, readily eating the foliage of most shrubs, although the majority are found only on a restricted range of hosts. If unchecked, there would be no foliage left but fortunately most caterpillars are eaten by something else (whether a parasitic wasp or a bird) and the actual harm done is rarely of more than passing significance. Those that do survive turn into butterflies or moths.

Leaf-cutter bees

Leaf-cutter bees make neat semicircular holes in the margins of leaves. They are solitary nonstinging insects, which are useful for pollinating flowers and rarely cause any actual harm. The pieces of leaf are carried back to holes in the ground, usually on banks, where they are used to feed their grubs.

Leaf miners

Leaf miners eat the center of leaves, leaving dead or discolored patches, but cause little damage. They are particularly noticeable on evergreens, such as Ilex, purely because the leaves are retained for more than one year.

Fungal and viral problems

There are a vast number of fungi and bacteria in your garden. Most are very desirable, helping to break down organic matter or forming associations on the roots, which assist in the uptake of nutrients from the soil. However, a few are positively harmful.

Wilt

Wilt diseases cause the death of foliage and shoots by blocking the water conduction system. The most common examples are Dutch elm disease and Verticillium wilt. The disease often does not transfer from the current year's affected tissues into the new tissues laid down next year, so if the branch or shrub is not killed, they can recover. Control by removing affected branches, cutting back beyond signs of infection or damage. The disease will show as a staining of the outer ring of wood. Sterilize the blade between cuts to reduce infection.

Anthracnose

Anthracnose diseases are caused by fungi that kill new leaves and shoots. They are more prevalent in cold wet summers, but generally new growth is made, which is unaffected, and the tree or shrub quickly recovers. Anthracnose can also cause cankers on the stems of some trees and shrubs. If you need to control this condition, remove all affected parts of the plant and burn them. Then, spray the tree or shrub with benomyl or a copper-based fungicide.

Mildew

Mildew can cause serious harm to soft young foliage and in bad cases kills plants, such as powdery mildew on certain Rhododendron. The fungi form a white powdery covering and do not need damp conditions. Control is possible at an early stage by spraying with a fungicide.

Rust fungus

Each rust fungus has different stages of its life cycle on unrelated genera. However, the Buxus rust does not have an alternate host. Damage is produced only on the primary hosts, leaving purplish-brown, orange-, or yellow-colored masses of spores and causing loss of leaves. Fungal sprays can give control.

Cankers

Cankers are lesions that appear on the stem or bark, which are caused by a fungus or bacterium. If the stem of the plant becomes girdled by cankers, its distal portion may be starved and killed, which results in symptoms similar to those of wilt diseases. The best solution is to remove the affected branch.

Fireblight

Fireblight is a bacterial disease that kills shoots, and occasionally whole plants. It is restricted to Cotoneaster and other genera in the apple subfamily (Maloideae) of the rose family (Rosaceae). Infection is usually via the flowers or new leaves. It can be controlled by removing affected shoots at least 2ft (60cm) below any signs of the disease. Sterilize the blade of the pruners between each cut on a rag soaked in methylated spirits (rubbing alcohol).

Silver leaf

Silver leaf is a fungal disease that occurs in many woody plants, except in the conifers. It infects the wood, causing a brown discoloration of the current season's wood; often, but not always, the foliage on the affected branch takes on a leadened or silver sheen. The fungus usually enters the wood through pruning wounds. In mild cases, prune out the affected branches or see whether they recover naturally. In severe cases, remove the plant.

Coral spot

Coral spot disease is identified by the coral or pink rounded pustules on the bark. The fungus can kill healthy tissue but is normally associated with stressed, dying, or dead branches. It can be a problem on stressed trees, such as those recently moved or growing in waterlogged soils, but is rarely serious on healthy specimens. Remove affected shoots and attend to any stress by ensuring that newly planted shrubs are adequately watered, and attend to drainage if waterlogging is considered a problem.

Phytophtora

Phytophthora are a group of single-celled or yeastlike fungi, which are spread through water, and are most famous for the potato blight. Phytophthora root disease kills the roots of many trees and shrubs, including Chamaecyparis and Rhododendron, causing sudden death. The disease can occur after temporary flooding due to heavy rain. Because the disease does not produce fruit bodies, it is extremely difficult to confirm and can be mistaken for other conditions.

Honey fungus

Honey fungus is a group of fungi that vary in their severity. They can colonize dead and nearly dead tissue, but some can kill healthy trees. Some trees and shrubs, such as Chamaecyparis, Ligustrum, and Pinus, can be killed at any age. The fungus can be identified by the white mat of mycelium produced between the bark and the wood of an infected shrub. Resin may exude from the bark just above ground level. The best control is the removal of dead roots, but this is seldom practical. A phenol-based product is sold as a control measure.

Viral disease

Virus diseases can reduce growth rate or produce white variegations in foliage. Some cultivars with mottled white variegations are due to virus infection of the leaves, e.g. *Aucuba japonica* 'Variegata'. There is no effective control for this disease.

Nonbiological damage

Nonbiological agents can cause damage or deterioration of growth.

Nutrient deficincy

Nutrient deficiencies in trees and shrubs can cause discoloration of leaves, smaller leaves, and less growth. A shortage of nitrogen will show by the smaller shoots and pale or yellow-green leaves that become red, purple, orange, or yellow as they mature and fall early. Fertilizer can be given for immediate but short-term relief. The best solution is to increase the organic matter in the soil, allowing regulated release of nitrogen by soil bacteria. Phosphorus deficiency can give similar symptoms. Potash (potassium) deficiency shows as scorch of the leaf margin, with the margin becoming brown or gray-brown. This can be corrected by giving potassium as a feed. Both magnesium and iron can be deficient on alkaline soils.

Salt spray

Salt spray can kill the foliage of some flowering shrubs. It is especially common along roadsides as a result of deicing salt applied in winter; any parts of the plant splashed by passing cars will be killed, but foliage on the opposite side and higher up the plant will normally survive. Salt spray also occurs in coastal gardens, and occasionally storms can bring salt spray many miles inland.

Drought

Drought can cause immediate symptoms on the soft leaves of deciduous shrubs. At an early stage, the leaves will recover overnight, but as the drought becomes more severe leaves are lost and those remaining develop dead patches between the veins, and the twigs die back. The leaves of evergreens are much tougher and may not show immediate damage. However, they may be just as badly affected, so keep a close eye on them.

Frost

Frost damage occurs when the foliage or stems are frozen; this causes water to be withdrawn from the cell contents. Rapid thawing can exacerbate the damage, which is why walls that face the sun in the morning are not suitable for some trees and shrubs. Frost damage most often takes the form of killed foliage, especially emerging leaves, and shoots. However, it can distort new leaves if they are not killed.

Waterlogging

Waterlogging can cause death of roots, especially the fine roots that actually absorb water! If it occurs during the summer, the shrub can quickly die from lack of water, despite standing in water. Waterlogging over winter can be even more invidious. The tree or shrub starts to leaf out (flush) in the spring and may develop a full or nearly full crop of leaves. However, because it is drying the soil faster than it can extend new roots into the soil, the foliage suddenly dies. By that time, there is little that can be done. Try severely reducing the shrub, so that the few living roots are in balance with the quantity of foliage and water; if this fails, improve the drainage before planting the replacement. Less severe waterlogging is one cause of twigs dying back.

Lightning strikes

Lightning striking trees and tall buildings is an accepted fact of life. However, lightning can affect shrubs and hedges. They are not commonly struck directly but can be killed when the lightning runs along a hedge or as part of the force field around a "tall" target.

Mower damage

Weed wacker and mower damage are entirely avoidable sources of harm to plants. While the nylon line of a weed wacker may appear soft, it is, in fact, tougher than the bark of most shrubs. The net result is that the base is debarked, causing death if it is completely girdled. Mowers are not as efficient at killing shrubs, but are capable of knocking off large chunks of bark. The solution is to keep grass away from the base by mulching a minimum radius of 12in (30cm) around the base of the tree or shrub.

Index of Plants

This index lists the plants mentioned in this book by their common names where applicable and their Latin names in all other instances

General Index

Acknowledgments

Author's acknowledgments:
I wish to record my thanks to all the people, in many countries, who have helped me to learn more about trees, shrubs, and other plants. There are too many of you to list individually, but you will know who you are, and thank you. Also, to thank Heather for her support, understanding, and patience.—Keith Rushforth

The majority of photographs in this book were taken by Tim Sandall. A number of others were kindly contributed by the author, Keith Rushforth, and are credited in full below:

pp 40; 45(BL); 48(T); 59(x2); 60(B); 62(T); 65; 68(B); 71; 74(B); 77; 80; 81(T); 97(R); 102; 103(T); 106(x2); 110(T); 111; 121(T); 124(T); 125(L); 137(T)

Key: T = Top; B = Bottom; L = Left; R = Right

The publishers would like to thank Coolings Nurseries for their cooperation and assistance with the photography in this book, including the loan of tools and much specialist equipment. Special thanks go to: Sandra Gratwick; Garry Norris; Ian Hazon; and Brian Archibald. Coolings Nurseries Ltd., Rushmore Hill, Knockholt, Kent, TN14 7NN, England. Tel: 00 44 1959 532269; Email: coolings@coolings.co.uk; Website: www.coolings.co.uk

Thanks are also due to the Sir Harold Hillier Gardens and Arboretum and Hampshire County Council, England, for allowing photographs for this book to be taken on their premises.